A MONSTER IN FLEETING SILENC

Under vigil by a rigid sentry, a 10″ Columbiad in Fort Walker o
Head, South Carolina, surveys the now quiet waters of Port
Sound. In eloquent contrast, one of its Federal captors sits
the behemoth foot, some loved one's letter transporting him
tranquility of another place, and what to many seemed another time.

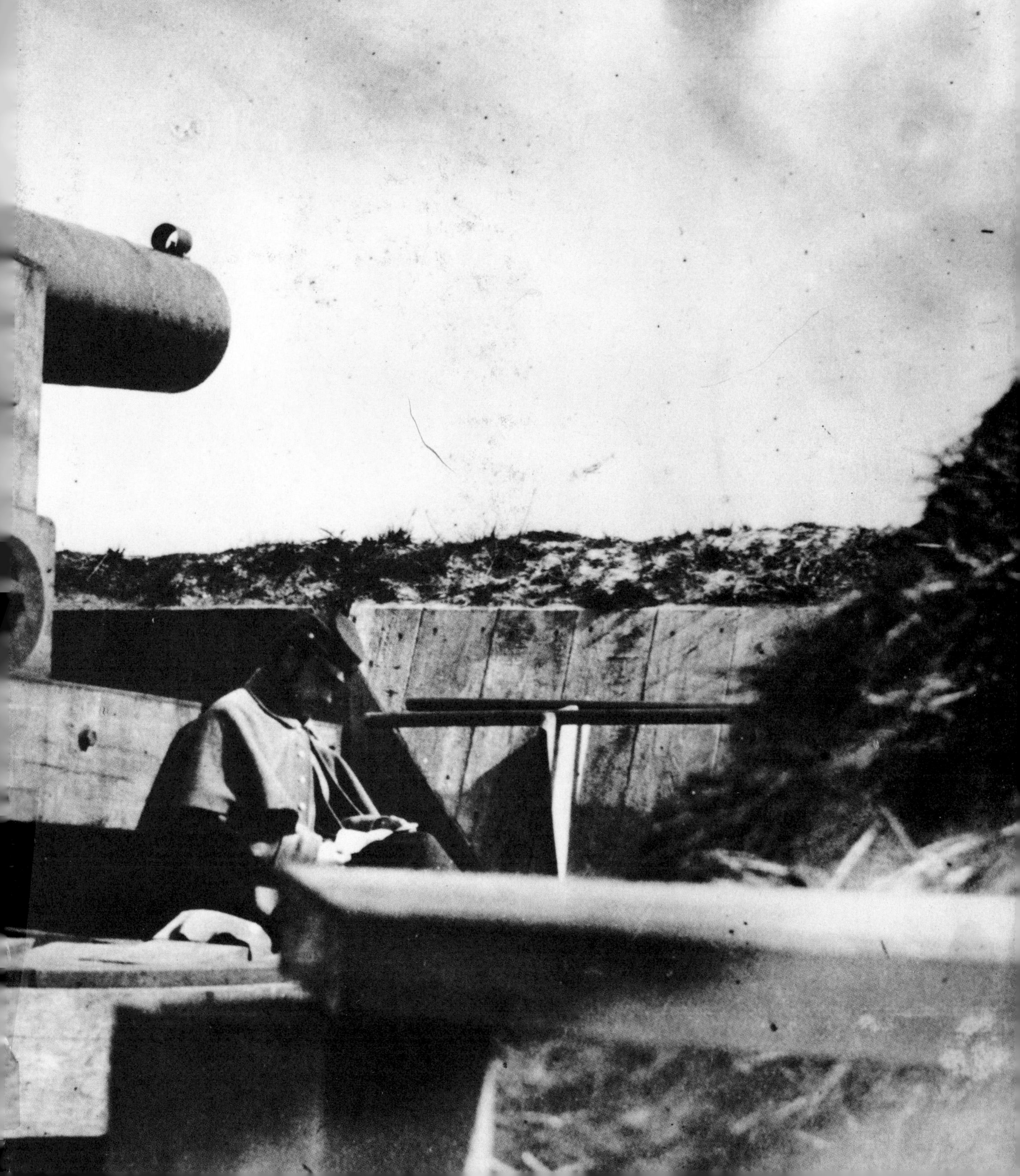

The Guns of '62

VOLUME TWO OF

The Image of War
1861–1865

EDITOR
William C. Davis

SENIOR CONSULTING EDITOR
Bell I. Wiley

PHOTOGRAPHIC CONSULTANTS
William A. Frassanito
Manuel Kean
Lloyd Ostendorf
Frederic Ray

EDITORIAL ASSISTANTS
Karen K. Kennedy
Denise Mummert
James Rietmulder

A Project of

The National Historical Society

Gettysburg, Pennsylvania

ROBERT H. FOWLER, Founder

EDITOR

WILLIAM C. DAVIS

SENIOR CONSULTING EDITOR

BELL I. WILEY

The Guns of '62

VOLUME TWO OF

The Image of War 1861-1865

DOUBLEDAY & COMPANY, INC.
GARDEN CITY, NEW YORK
1982

Overleaf: Part of the ruin of 1862. Rolling stock of the Orange & Alexandria Railroad, once used to supply a Union Army marching to Manassas, and now destroyed by it to deny it to the victorious Confederates. It, like so many other scenes this year, is indicative of the almost constant defeat suffered by the North. (U. S. Army Military History Institute, Carlisle Barracks, Pa.)

ISBN: 0-385-15467-4
LIBRARY OF CONGRESS CATALOG CARD NUMBER 81-43151

PRINTED IN THE UNITED STATES OF AMERICA
FIRST EDITION
DESIGNED BY PAUL RANDALL MIZE

Contents

YORKTOWN: THE FIRST SIEGE
A "NAPOLEON," A "PRINCE JOHN," AND OTHER DIGNITARIES DO BATTLE FOR RICHMOND
Warren W. Hassler, Jr.
11

THE NEW IRONCLADS
INVENTION WENT WILD IN THE RACE FOR NEWER AND MORE POWERFUL IRON BEHEMOTHS
William N. Still
49

MR. COOLEY OF BEAUFORT AND MR. MOORE OF CONCORD: A PORTFOLIO
TWO OF HUNDREDS OF UNSUNG ARTISTS, THESE PHOTOGRAPHERS CAPTURED SOUTH CAROLINA LONG BEFORE THE FEDERALS
86

THE PENINSULAR CAMPAIGN
THE FIRST CAMPAIGN GOING "ON TO RICHMOND," AND THE EMERGENCE OF A GENERAL CALLED "GRANNY" LEE
Emory M. Thomas
112

IN CAMP WITH THE COMMON SOLDIERS
THE REAL STORY OF THE LIFE OF THE CIVIL WAR SOLDIER; FOR EVERY DAY IN BATTLE, FIFTY IN CAMP
Bell I. Wiley
173

THE CONQUEST OF THE MISSISSIPPI
THE GREAT RIVER SPAWNED GREAT MEN TO CONTEST HER WATERS
Charles L. Dufour
255

JACKSON IN THE SHENANDOAH
A PECULIAR PROFESSOR AND A VALLEY WHOSE NAME MEANT "DAUGHTER OF THE STARS"
Robert G. Tanner
322

THE SECOND BULL RUN
TO MANASSAS ONCE AGAIN, ANOTHER BATTLE, ANOTHER DEFEAT
David Lindsey
348

THE WAR ON RAILS
SPIDERLIKE THE RAILS SPREAD OVER THE LAND, CARRYING THE WAR EVERYWHERE, AND FEEDING ITS VORACIOUS APPETITES
Robert C. Black, III
399

The Contributors
447

Abbreviations
449

Index
451

A NOTE ON THE SOURCES: A credit line accompanies each photograph in this volume. Each source is written out in full when first cited, but those that contributed many photographs are thereafter abbreviated. A list of abbreviations is included at the end of the book, and we would especially like to acknowledge the generosity of the sources on this list.

Introduction

1862 WAS A FIGHTER'S YEAR, a year of almost constant turmoil in embattled America. The guns of 1862 were seldom stilled. When the guns were silent, the soldiers of North and South marched from camp to camp, living the life of boredom and routine that had been the soldier's lot since warfare began.

And with them lived the makers of the image, the shadow-catchers, the photographers of America who captured these historic moments on glass and copper and paper. They followed the armies wherever they went in Virginia, down the Mississippi, along the railroads and byways that joined the now-divided sections, to the army besieging Charleston, and to the thousands of camps where the common men lived the real life of the soldier. There was the real Civil War, much of it a story as old as time.

The photographers' legacy has survived to the present, often forgotten, more often neglected, awaiting the resurrection of interest and appreciation, awaiting discovery. Here in *The Guns of '62* that resurrection, that rediscovery, takes place. After over a century, faces that have seen only darkness and dust look once more out toward posterity. The men and machines and places of America's most trying time live again.

This has been the goal of *The Guns of '62,* and the goal of the project of which it is a part, *The Image of War: 1861–1865,* since its inception. To bring back the lost, to discover the forgotten, to present in its six volumes the whole scope of the photographic record of the American Civil War as it has never been done before. Seven years of work and research, thousands of miles of travel, and countless dollars have been expended to build this portrait of America in crisis. This second volume of the series follows its predecessor, *Shadows of the Storm,* in combining authoritative narrative text by our foremost Civil War historians with the magnificent work of the Civil War photographers themselves.

The contributions of seemingly countless archives, public repositories, universities, public libraries, and private collectors have been invaluable. All are recognized in credits with their photos. Yet some special mention, in addition to that made in Volume One, is owed to several special benefactors. Manuel Kean of Philadelphia's Kean Archives, Charles Haberlein of the Naval Historical Center in Washington, D.C., Colonel Donald Shaw and Michael Winey of the United States Army Military History Institute in Carlisle Barracks, Pennsylvania, Russell Pritchard of the War

Library and Museum of the Military Order of the Loyal Legion of the United States in Philadelphia, and Edward Campbell and the staff of the Museum of the Confederacy in Richmond, Virginia, have all made special contributions via their collections and their expertise.

And mention is due most of all to the late Bell I. Wiley, who took such an interest in this undertaking and gave so much to it, yet did not live to see it completed. His own contribution to this volume in particular went far beyond his senior editorship. For here is his picture of the life of the common soldier of the Civil War in camp, the distillation of a lifetime of work and study and admiration. It is perhaps the final publication from his prolific pen, and a fitting one, for his respect remained ever-unbounded for the private soldiers who fought and felt *The Guns of '62*.

Yorktown: The First Siege

WARREN W. HASSLER, JR.

A "Napoleon," a "Prince John," and other dignitaries do battle for Richmond

YORKTOWN! Mere mention of the Virginia river port could conjure heroic images of great historical moment to both Northerners and Southerners at the start of the Civil War.

Both sides knew that it was at this quaint town on the south bank of the York River that Lord Cornwallis had surrendered his British Army to General George Washington's Continentals and their French allies, thereby virtually terminating the Revolutionary War with America triumphant. To Abraham Lincoln's Federals, it was well remembered that Washington had been a staunch nationalist, one who had gainsaid the particularism preached by the states' rights doctrinaires. To Jefferson Davis's Confederates—who naturally hoped to be able to retain control of the grass-covered redoubts still remaining at Yorktown—there was still fierce pride in the fact that Washington was a native son of the Old Dominion, a stalwart who had been the one indispensable man of the patriots' struggle to establish an independent nation.

And Virginia was destined to be a central battle arena of the Civil War. Even though they had occupied the great National naval base at Norfolk and had emerged victorious over the Union Army at the First Battle of Bull Run on July 21, 1861, the Southerners were well aware of Federal pressure on their seaward littoral. From the start of hostilities, blue-clad soldiers had maintained control of the most powerful Gibraltar in North America—Fort Monroe, located at Old Point Comfort at the tip of the historic Peninsula between the York and James rivers—a stronghold their forces would hold throughout the war.

Yorktown was a charming, staid village of tree-lined streets and neat, impressive houses. It was a prize the North coveted. Even though Confederate forces under John Bankhead "Prince John" Magruder and Daniel Harvey Hill had easily repulsed the inept and feeble attacks on June 10, 1861, of Benjamin Franklin Butler's troops at Big Bethel, a few miles from Old Point Comfort, by early 1862 the Union garrison at Fort Monroe under John E. Wool would be enlarged to some 12,500 soldiers. And the strategic offensive would remain with the Federals, now near Washington, D.C., being molded by the "Young Napoleon," George B. McClellan, into the truly superb Army of the Potomac.

"Little Mac," as the latter was called—a West Point graduate, a twice-brevetted hero of the War with Mexico, an official observer in the Crimean War, and a railroad president—argued long and hard with Lincoln and Secretary of War Edwin M. Stanton over what route the Army of the Potomac should take to move against the Confederate capital of Richmond. The administration favored the overland route through Manassas, but McClellan strongly recommended taking advantage of superior National sea power by moving his force down the Chesapeake Bay and landing it at Urbana on the lower Rappahannock River, or, as less desirable but nonetheless viable alternatives, disembarking it at Mobjack Bay or Fort Monroe. A quick move to West Point on the Pamunkey River—a tributary of the York—would bring the Federals to the point where they expected to employ the Richmond & York River Railroad to supply their short land march upon Richmond. After much disputation, McClellan was authorized to move with approximately 150,000 men on his amphibious operation. However, when the immense movement—one of the largest amphibious ones in warfare up to that time—actually unfolded in late March 1862, the Union commander's force was reduced—against his strenuous objections—to some 100,000 men.

The Confederate victor of Bull Run, Joseph E. Johnston, had gotten warning of the Federal plans and pulled his army back from Manassas to Fredericksburg on the Rappanhannock River. This rendered inoperative McClellan's scheme to debark at Urbana, so he determined to go ahead with the plan to land at Fort Monroe and advance up the Peninsula via Yorktown and Williamsburg toward Richmond. Further, and, McClellan would claim later, crippling to his strategy, was Lincoln's sudden insistence at the beginning of the operation on withholding Irvin McDowell's I Corps of some 38,000 men near Washington to assure the safety of the National Capital (although McClellan believed he had left Washington perfectly secure). The Union commander had earmarked McDowell's force as a flying column to move swiftly by water up the York to land on the Peninsula across from West Point so as to outflank and take in the rear the Confederate forces under Magruder on the lower Peninsula near Yorktown, where the Southern general had established his headquarters. Additionally, 10,000 of John E. Wool's troops which had been pledged to McClellan were now withdrawn from his use.

Also hampering the Union commander initially was the presence near Hampton Roads of the Confederate ironclad warship CSS *Virginia* (formerly the *Merrimack*), which was neutralized by the USS *Monitor* in the classic battle of March 9, 1862. The Federal naval authorities assured McClellan that he could now proceed with his Peninsular campaign, and they even promised naval assistance in reducing and running past the enemy artillery batteries and fortifications being

Major General John E. Wool, a hero of the Mexican War, turned seventy-seven just before the outbreak of war. Yet he showed no lack of energy in immediately ensuring the safety of Fort Monroe at Hampton Roads, Virginia, a vital base in Confederate territory, and in the course of the war a staging area for more than one major campaign. In the coming campaign for Yorktown . . . (U. S. ARMY MILITARY HISTORY INSTITUTE)

. . . Fort Monroe would play a significant part. The exterior of the officers' quarters. (USAMHI)

constructed by "Prince John" at Yorktown and across the river, which at that point narrows to less than a mile in width, at Gloucester Point. But Lincoln so lacked faith in McClellan that he not only withheld McDowell's corps but also demoted "Little Mac" from General-in-Chief of all the Union armies, a vote of no-confidence which left him in command of just the Army of the Potomac and not even of his base of supplies and communication. The President did not agree with McClellan's contention that the best defense of Washington was the heavy pressure McClellan was about to apply against Richmond. Lincoln was concerned about Rebel forces under "Stonewall" Jackson lurking in the Shenandoah.

Delays in assembling the vast shipping slowed the movement of the Union amphibious force to Fort Monroe, and once the troops began landing there—in the heaviest rains known to the region in twenty years—a shortage of supply wagons further impeded the advance. Only 42,000 men could be initially landed; several more weeks would be required for the rest of the army of about 100,000 to arrive and disembark. And McClellan was a most

The house at Fairfax Court House where McClellan made his headquarters. Here he planned his campaign for the Virginia Peninsula. A Timothy O'Sullivan image taken in June 1863. (USAMHI)

circumspect general, seldom one to take chances—especially since he was convinced time and preponderant resources were on the side of the North.

So colossal was the Federal undertaking that a foreign observer hailed it as "the stride of a giant." But Fort Monroe lacked sufficient wharf facilities for so gigantic a movement; therefore, a secondary landing place was brought into use at Ship Point, nearer Yorktown. Without the flying column of the I Corps sweeping up the York to West Point, McClellan—now informed by the navy that it would not be able to join in attacking the Confederate batteries at Gloucester Point and Yorktown, or to run past them—was obliged to slog through the seas of mud and lay siege to the latter stronghold.

Meantime, the Confederates had not been idle. The local commander, John Magruder—a native Virginian—was a tall, erect, dark-haired general of fifty-one who had won brevets in the Mexican War and who, as a master of bluff and legerdemain, could make his 15,000 defenders look much more numerous than they were. There were few more colorful Civil War figures than "Prince John." A dandy dresser, he was an artillerist who had gained a wide reputation in the old army as a bon vivant and bountiful host at a myriad of social functions. Magruder never wearied of penning entreaties to his superiors for more reinforcements of men and artillery. He would in due time be joined by Johnston's main army which would, with Magruder's own force, total some 56,000 troops. The limited wharf facilities in the old river port of Yorktown made it difficult to enlarge his force rapidly, as there was no railroad down the Peninsula from Richmond or Williamsburg, and the few roads, upon which the Southern troops had to march, were infamous in this unusually heavy rainy season.

For many months, Magruder had been working steadily on the fortifications to defend Yorktown and the lower Peninsula. The earthworks immediately around the town were fairly strong, and Magruder incorporated with his own new ones some of the old Revolutionary War British redoubts. The water batteries, down low near the York River, as well as the field entrenchments, were buttressed by cotton bales, used also as breastworks. Similarly, Gloucester Point, across from Yorktown, was fortified, though less strongly so.

Noting that the Warwick River ran across the Peninsula at right angles to McClellan's line of advance from Fort Monroe, Magruder determined to erect defenses behind this stream. To make the Federal advance and expected attacks more difficult, the Confederate commander built five

Major General George B. McClellan and his staff in the Yorktown operations. "Little Mac" was well named, standing a full head shorter than the rest. Immediately to his left is his chief of staff, Brigadier General Randolph B. Marcy, who also happened to be McClellan's father-in-law. To the left of Marcy stands Brigadier General Stewart Van Vliet, quartermaster. (CHICAGO HISTORICAL SOCIETY)

Secretary of War Simon Cameron, his administration tainted by charges of corruption, resigned his portfolio on January 11, 1862. This left McClellan working with a new war secretary, . . . (NATIONAL ARCHIVES)

dams which backed up water from the Warwick to such an extent that it inundated the countryside. This flooding allowed for only a few dry crossings at such points as Lee's Mill on the Confederate right and Wynn's Mill toward Yorktown, and where these roads passed, the Southerners erected batteries and rifle-pits.

Even to the experienced McClellan and other Union Army engineers, these enemy fortifications looked stronger than they actually were. Moreover, the Federal maps of the area were inaccurate, showing erroneously that the Warwick ran parallel to the York and James and therefore comprised no military obstacle. A probing attack on April 16 at Lee's Mill on the Federal left was repelled by the grayclads. So the Union commander set up his headquarters a little less than a mile west of the Farnholt House, on the Federal right, and began the slow process of a siege of the Yorktown-Warwick River defenses by regular approaches. This meant miners and sappers would dig parallels encompassing earthworks and wooden platforms for the cannon, with bombproofs for soldiers and ammunition.

The Federals were assisted by a large captive observation balloon, in the basket of which such high-ranking officers as Fitz John Porter ascended to examine the Confederate lines through their field glasses. Aloft almost daily, the Union air force suffered a near-catastrophe on one occasion when it slipped loose from its moorings "and sailed majestically over the enemy's works; but fortunately for its occupants it soon met a counter-current of air which returned it safely" to friendly lines.

. . . Edwin M. Stanton, a Democrat who opposed Lincoln's election, but who now became the President's strong right arm. (NA)

Like McDowell before him, McClellan built his army in and around Washington and northern Virginia while he formulated his plan of campaign. Several familiar faces from the Bull Run debacle are with him. General Samuel P. Heintzelman stands bearded in front of the pillar on the right, with his staff. Robert E. Lee's Arlington House was a favorite posing place. (USAMHI)

Owing to the dearth of experienced engineering officers, McClellan, who in the mid 1850s, had personally witnessed the siege of Sevastopol in the Crimean War, felt obliged to make many personal reconnaissances himself at the front lines of his besieging forces. He was often accompanied by his large and glittering staff, which included several volunteer aides from the French nobility, namely, the Orléans princes, including the Prince de Joinville and the Comte de Paris. On one of these occasions, while observing from a redoubt at the front, McClellan and his aides were spotted by Confederate gunners who opened fire upon them. As an eyewitness described it, when several enemy artillery projectiles struck close by, the startled prince "jumped and glanced nervously around, while McClellan quietly knocked the ashes from his cigar."

The strained relations between the Union commander and the administration in Washington continued during the one-month siege of Yorktown in April 1862. As a petulant McClellan related one such incident in a letter to his wife, "The President very coolly telegraphed me yesterday that he thought I had better break the enemy's lines at once! I was much tempted to reply that he had better come and do it himself." On the Confederate side, when Johnston arrived, his rapport with Davis was not at all good, but the Southern commander was at least blessed in having a general—

McDowell, too, was to cooperate with McClellan, but when a threat appeared in the Shenandoah Valley, Lincoln held him back to protect Washington. McDowell and staff at Arlington House. (MINNESOTA HISTORICAL SOCIETY)

the masterful Robert E. Lee—positioned in Richmond as a buffer between himself and the Confederate President. Lee could and did get along amicably with both Davis and Johnston, and he was responsible in a large degree for amassing the force on the Peninsula that Johnston and Magruder had deployed at the Yorktown-Warwick River line.

As April waned, both sides worked feverishly to strengthen their positions. McClellan—who excelled at this sort of thing—laboriously wheeled into position some 114 big guns, howitzers, and mortars. Some of these were impressive pieces of siege weaponry. For example, close to the Farnholt House near the York River, a Federal battery was established which comprised five 100-pounder Parrotts and one monster 200-pounder Parrott. Others included 10-inch and 13-inch siege mortars. The Confederates, on the other hand, while possessing some large, modern, rifled pieces, also had to make do with older and less effective 32-pounder naval smoothbores and columbiads. After completing a 4,000-yard-long first parallel, McClellan's troops then began a second parallel much closer to the main Confederate defenses. All these activities were slowed by continuing torrential rains, execrable roads, and shortages of supply wagons.

But Joe Johnston saw the writing on the wall. He knew his troops and defenses could not stand up to the greatly superior weight of metal that the mushrooming Union batteries would be able to throw when they were ready to open fire. "We are engaged in a species of warfare," Johnston acknowledged in a message to Davis and Lee on April 30, "at which we can never win. It is plain that General McClellan will adhere to the system adopted by him last summer, and depend for success upon artillery and engineering. We can compete with him in neither." Lee and the Confederate President concurred.

Finally, on May 4, just as the massed Federal artillery was about to open a mammoth bombardment of Yorktown, Johnston wisely withdrew his troops and as many of his guns as he could, blew up some of his powder magazines, and retreated precipitately toward Williamsburg and Richmond. "Yorktown is in our possession," McClellan telegraphed Washington triumphantly. So was Gloucester Point. Only then could the Union commander speed troops up the York River to Eltham's Landing, near Brick House Point, opposite West Point, to speed the Confederate retreat—a retreat that was made possible by a partially successful rearguard stand made by the graycoats on May 5 at Williamsburg.

As McClellan's Army of the Potomac moved into the evacuated Warwick River and Yorktown fortifications, they captured some seventy-seven heavy guns that Johnston had been unable to remove in his hasty retrograde movement—a loss the Confederates could ill afford. But the Federals also discovered, at the cost of some fatalities, a new engine of destruction in the form of primitive but effective land mines, then called "torpedoes." These were apparently innovated and ordered to be placed in positions around wells, springs, and elsewhere by Gabriel J. Rains. These land mines were regular 8-inch and 10-inch columbiad shells buried a few inches in the ground, and rigged with

The always ready-to-pose Brigadier General Louis Blenker, with hand in coat, at his brigade headquarters near Washington. After being left out of the fight at Bull Run, he, too, would be withheld from McClellan. On his left stands Brigadier General Julius Stahel; on his right Prussian nobleman Prince Felix Salm-Salm. (WESTERN RESERVE HISTORICAL SOCIETY)

the ordinary cannon friction primer, or fulminate of mercury, so that they detonated when moved or stepped upon. So angered was McClellan at these devices that he ordered Confederate prisoners to discover the torpedoes and remove them. Some Southerners also considered the use of the "torpedoes" unethical, and James Longstreet directed Rains to halt the practice. But later in the war both sides employed land mines efficaciously.

Following the capture of Yorktown, McClellan moved up the Peninsula via Yorktown to close in on Richmond. Yorktown was held by the Federals throughout the remainder of the war, its dockage facilities being used, along with those at Fort Monroe and later of City Point, in the final campaigns of the war against Richmond and Petersburg. Yorktown was the first major operation of the initial massive campaign of the Civil War in the eastern theater of operations, and it drew to the scene a number of photographers who were attracted there not only by the large military movements then unfolding, but also because of the historical associations of the place during the final and pivotal campaign of the revolution which had paved the way for the birth of the republic.

The skillful defense of the Yorktown-Warwick River line by first Magruder and then Johnston, combined with McClellan's caution, enabled Lee to take steps to better defend Richmond with fortifications and additional troops so as to hold the capital of the Confederacy through three more years of grim warfare before the final ennobling scene took place at Appomattox Court House.

On to the Peninsula. Shipping the siege train for the 1st Connecticut Heavy Artillery, at the lower wharf at Yorktown. A Brady & Company photo from May 1862. (SOPHIA SMITH COLLECTION, SMITH COLLEGE)

More of the wealth of ordnance and ammunition shipped to the Peninsula to help subdue Johnston and Magruder. A Brady & Company image taken after the fall of Yorktown. (USAMHI)

Flattered by the attention from European commanders, the Federal officers delighted in posing with them. Brigadier General William F. Barry with British officers and two French noblemen. (NATIONAL LIBRARY OF MEDICINE)

Several pose here on May 1, 1862, at headquarters in Camp Winfield Scott. Seated in the front row, left to right, are Captain L'Amy of the Royal Army and the Duc de Chartres. In the center row, seated, are Colonel Fletcher of the Royal Army, the Prince de Joinville, and Stewart Van Vliet. Standing from the left are Colonels Beaumont and Neville of the Royal Army, an unidentified man, the Comte de Paris, and another unidentified civilian. (USAMHI)

Louis Philippe Albert d'Orléans, Comte de Paris on the left, and Robert Philippe Louis d'Orléans, Duc de Chartres, on the right. Both wear the Union uniform in their capacity as aides to McClellan. (CHS)

James F. Gibson's May 3, 1862, image of, from the left, the Duc de Chartres, the Prince de Joinville, and the Comte de Paris on the day of Yorktown's fall. (WAR LIBRARY AND MUSEUM, MOLLUS-PENNSYLVANIA)

The Prince de Joinville, a familiar sight in McClellan's army. (USAMHI)

Colonel V. DeChanal, French military observer. (USAMHI)

Gibson's photo of several of the British observers. (LIBRARY OF CONGRESS)

Lieutenant George T. Munroe, Royal Canadian Rifles. (USAMHI)

The commander of Royal Army forces in Canada, Lieutenant General Sir John Michel, K.C.B. (USAMHI)

H. M. Hippisley of the Royal Navy. (USAMHI)

And best known of all, Colonel Arthur Fremantle of the Royal Army, who wrote of and published his experiences with both Union and Confederate armies. (THE NEW-YORK HISTORICAL SOCIETY)

But this campaign was for the Americans. McClellan's topographical engineers, photographed by Gibson on May 2, 1862. The use of the pistols to hold the corners of the map was a bit melodramatic of the engineers, but their services were invaluable in an area for which reliable maps were not available. (LC)

A special feature of McClellan's army was Colonel Hiram Berdan and his United States Sharpshooters, men selected and trained for their marksmanship and equipped with special rifles. (USAMHI)

McClellan's antagonist looked every inch a great general. The resplendent Major General John Bankhead Magruder—"Prince John." He managed to completely mislead McClellan about his strength in the works at Yorktown, thereby delaying the Federals for precious days while Richmond forwarded more Confederates to the front. (LOUISIANA STATE UNIVERSITY, DEPARTMENT OF ARCHIVES AND MANUSCRIPTS)

Isaac M. St. John was Magruder's chief engineer at Yorktown, responsible largely for the defenses that so intimidated McClellan. (USAMHI)

Brigadier General Samuel R. Anderson was nearly sixty but still exercised active command of one of Magruder's brigades. Ill health forced him to resign just one week after the evacuation of Yorktown. (USAMHI)

At Lee's Mill, soon after McClellan began his investment of Yorktown, Magruder stood off an engagement on April 16. Here is McClellan's uncharacteristically unpretentious headquarters during the battle. Brattleboro, Vermont, photographer G. W. Houghton, who accompanied Vermont troops to the Peninsula, made this image as part of his excellent series of unpublished photographs. (VERMONT HISTORICAL SOCIETY)

Houghton's portrait of Brigadier General William F. Smith, commanding a division that included the Vermonters. It was taken in April 1862, at the Gaines House. Seated at left is Captain Romeyn B. Ayers, later a noted general. (VHS)

Magruder made his headquarters in the large house on the left in this photo of Yorktown made by Brady's company within days of the evacuation. (USAMHI)

George N. Barnard's photograph of Magruder's headquarters in June 1862. "Prince John" not only dressed in style but lived that way as well. (USAMHI)

The sally port into the defenses around Yorktown, just after McClellan occupied the quiet town. (USAMHI)

The ravine behind the defenses where the Confederates placed their powder magazine. These huts were occupied by Magruder's command until a few weeks before Barnard caught this scene. (LC)

Both North and South drew inspiration from the American successes in the Revolution, and Yorktown was a storied place indeed. Here on the right the building that served as headquarters for Charles Lord Cornwallis during Washington's siege of Yorktown. Magruder used it as a hospital, as would Dorothea Dix shortly afterward. Brady & Company's May 1862 image. (KEAN ARCHIVES)

The front line of the works Magruder and St. John built to hold back McClellan. (USAMHI)

Making the best use of the materials at hand, St. John sometimes employed bales of cotton along with sandbags in building his earthworks. When hit, the bales really showed what they were made of. (USAMHI)

Barnard's June photo of a Confederate battery, with McClellan's Battery No. 1 in the distance. The Confederates liked to name their cannons for their generals. As seen by the remnant of an ammunition box in the foreground, this gun—now gone—was named after Major General D. H. Hill. (USAMHI)

A naval battery near the Nelson church in Yorktown, shown on George N. Barnard's July 1862 image. At left are arranged loads of canister—tin cans filled with lead or iron balls—and stands of grapeshot, clusters of a dozen or more larger iron projectiles fired like a scatter-load from the cannon. (LC)

Magruder also erected defenses at Gloucester Point, including this large Dahlgren smoothbore. (USAMHI)

The much-touted Water Battery, strongest of the Confederate works preventing McClellan's easy conquest of Yorktown that he expected. (USAMHI)

The Water Battery became a favorite place for the Federals to pose after Magruder evacuated. Barnard was happy to catch them as they lounged in the works . . . (USAMHI)

. . . and walked the parapet overlooking the York. (USAMHI)

Part of Magruder's defenses, with the York River in the background. (USAMHI)

These Rodman guns in the Water Battery bear Magruder's name on their carriages, probably put there when they were being shipped to him from elsewhere in the Confederacy. (LC)

Gloucester Point, with Yorktown in the distance, and more Dahlgren naval guns. (NLM)

Magruder took as many of his cannons with him as possible when he evacuated. Others had to be abandoned to the enemy, and this one, at least, he did not mind leaving. An exploded gun at one of the inland batteries. By Barnard. (USAMHI)

McClellan's Battery No. 1 below Yorktown, taken by Gibson in May 1862. McClellan's earthworks are masterpieces. (LC)

Gibson's photo of Battery No. 4, whose eight mortars lobbed shells into Yorktown constantly. The barge holds their powder and shells. Built into the earth itself are the gunners' quarters, a "bombproof" protecting them from enemy fire. (LC)

Another view of Battery No. 1. The works are made of gabions—wicker baskets filled with earth, piled around built-up soil, and topped with sandbags. (USAMHI)

The Farnholt House behind Battery No. 1, seen at left. Gunners used the roof to observe the effect of their shells. (USAMHI)

McClellan's headquarters, Camp Winfield Scott, taken by Gibson on the day Magruder evacuated. (USAMHI)

"Little Mac's" tent in the center, the day of his "victory" over Magruder. (LC)

Always the tourists, Federal soldiers visit "Cornwallis' Cave," the small cavern where the British general reputedly took refuge from Washington's artillery in 1781. (NLM)

Magruder used the cave as a powder magazine. Brady's assistants used it as a backdrop for images like this. (USAMHI)

And officers of the 1st Connecticut Artillery pulled enemy shells from within the cave for jaunty poses like this one, published by Brady & Company. (LC, FITZ JOHN PORTER PAPERS)

Magruder's evacuation was not a simple affair, even given the superb deception he had worked on McClellan. Brigadier General Lafayette McLaws was largely responsible for capably covering the retreat. It won him a promotion. (MUSEUM OF THE CONFEDERACY, RICHMOND)

Brigadier General Gabriel J. Rains also contributed his part. One of D. H. Hill's brigade commanders, he laced the roads out of Yorktown with hidden shells triggered to explode when stepped upon. "Infernal machines" they were called, or "torpedoes." He had just pioneered the antipersonnel mine. Even many Confederates thought it a barbarous concept. (USAMHI)

Major General Gustavus W. Smith attacked McClellan's pursuing Federals at Eltham's Landing on May 7 while he covered the withdrawal of Magruder's army. It was effectively the end of the Yorktown campaign. (TULANE UNIVERSITY)

The New Ironclads

WILLIAM N. STILL

Invention went wild in the race for newer and more powerful iron behemoths

ON MARCH 9, 1862, occurred what has rightly been called one of the most important naval engagements in American history. Two iron-armored warships, the USS *Monitor* and the CSS *Virginia,* met in mortal combat, the first such battle in history. Although not the first ironclad warships completed and battle-tested, they were the first completed in North America and the first that fought against each other. They were responsible for the decision by both Abraham Lincoln's and Jefferson Davis's governments to create a powerful naval force of armored vessels.

The Confederates took the first step. Perhaps this was inevitable considering the fact that the South lacked both a navy and the potential to keep pace with their opponents in building warships. On May 9, 1861, Confederate Secretary of the Navy Stephen R. Mallory wrote in an oft-quoted report, "I regard the possession of an iron-armored ship as a matter of the first necessity. . . . If we . . . follow their [the United States Navy's] . . . example and build wooden ships, we shall have to construct several at one time; for one or two ships would fall easy prey to her comparatively numerous steam frigates. But inequality of numbers may be compensated by invulnerability; and thus not only does economy but naval success dictate the wisdom and expediency of fighting with iron against wood." That same day the Confederate Congress appropriated $2,000,000 for the purchase or construction of ironclads in Europe. Although the Confederacy would contract for several powerful armored vessels in England and France, initial efforts were unsuccessful. Secretary Mallory then determined to construct ironclads within the Confederacy. In the middle of July the decision was made to convert the *Merrimack* into the *Virginia,* and six weeks later contracts were awarded for the construction of two ironclads later named the *Arkansas* and *Tennessee* to be built in Memphis; a fourth one, the *Mississippi,* was to be built in New Orleans. In September the *Louisiana* was also laid down in New Orleans. These five initial armorclads were designed to operate on the open sea as well as on inland waters. They were designed not only to break the blockade, but as Secretary Mallory wrote, to "traverse the entire coast of the United States . . . and encounter, with a fair prospect of success, their entire Navy." In other words, Mallory's initial ironclad strategy was offensive in nature.

The strategy was a failure. Only three of the vessels, the *Arkansas, Louisiana,* and *Virginia,* became operational; the other two were destroyed while

To his credit, Secretary of the Navy Gideon Welles, ridiculous wig and all, supported the ironclad idea from the first. Despite his lack of naval experience he saw what many could not, that wooden ships were things of the past. (NA)

still under construction. Of the three that were commissioned only the *Arkansas* was used for offensive purposes. During its brief career, it achieved some dramatic success, despite poor design and construction. It was 165 feet in length and carried a battery of ten guns. Its armor was made up of railroad T-rails, and it was powered by inadequate riverboat machinery. The casemate, unlike those found on the other Confederate ironclads, was perpendicular rather than slanted. On July 15, 1862, this awkward-looking warship ran through a large fleet of Union vessels anchored above Vicksburg and successfully resisted several planned attempts to destroy it. In August the *Arkansas* was to participate in a combined operation on Baton Rouge, Louisiana, but because of a breakdown in the machinery, the ironclad was blown up by its crew.

The *Louisiana*'s career was briefer and less successful. As envisioned by its builder, E. C. Murray, the armor-clad was to be 264 feet in length, 64 in beam, with a battery of twenty-two guns and propelled by two paddle wheels and two 4-foot propellers. The most unorthodox feature in his design was twin wheels along the centerline, one abaft the other in a well. The ship was still being fitted out when Admiral Farragut's squadron began its ascent of the Mississippi River. The large Confederate ironclad was towed down the river and moored near Fort Jackson. Here as a floating battery it engaged the Union vessels and was destroyed by its crew when the fort surrendered.

The *Virginia* achieved the most notable success of the initial ironclads. It was converted from the captured and partially destroyed sloop-of-war *Merrimack* at the Gosport Navy Yard in Norfolk. Frequently considered to be the prototype of all the Confederate ironclads, it was in fact an experimental vessel constructed only because the Confederacy needed to get a powerful ironclad operational as quickly as possible in that part of the South. The 262-foot vessel had a casemate 170 feet long, inclined on the sides with the ends horizontally rounded. The rounded ends along with the bow and stern of the hull being submerged were unique; no other Confederate ironclad incorporated these features. The armor, rolled at Tredegar Iron Works in Richmond from railroad iron into plates, was 4 inches thick attached in two layers. The ironclad carried a battery of ten guns, four to a side and a pivot rifle at each end. On March 8, 1862, it attacked units of the North Atlantic Blockading Squadron in Hampton Roads and destroyed the frigate *Congress* and the sloop-of-war *Cumberland*. The following day it fought the *Monitor* and for over a month successfully defended the entrance to the James River. Early in May, Norfolk was captured. With no base to return to and a draft too deep to allow it to ascend the James, the ship was destroyed by its crew to prevent its capture.

With the destruction of the *Arkansas, Louisiana,* and *Virginia,* the first Confederate ironclad program ended. Mallory's vision of a few powerful armored vessels to sweep Union warships from the seas was a failure. Unlike the Confederates', the Union Navy's initial ironclad program was tentative; professional opinion differed over the type of armored vessel to build. Early in August 1861, Congress appropriated $1,500,000 for the "construction or completion of iron or steelclad steamers or steam batteries," and authorized the creation of a board of naval officers to examine proposals and make recommendations. Then in

The Union Navy granted contracts for three radically different ironclad vessels at first. Here the USS New Ironsides, *powerful and effective, though largely conventional in design.* (SMITHSONIAN INSTITUTION)

September the board recommended that contracts be awarded for three vessels; a seagoing broadside type of vessel commissioned *New Ironsides,* a lightly armored wooden vessel, the *Galena,* and a revolving turret vessel, the *Monitor.* While the board of naval officers deliberated, the army had already contracted for seven ironclads for service on the Mississippi River and its tributaries.

These seven ironclads have been called "Pook turtles" after their designer, Samuel M. Pook, or the "city class," because they were named after western river ports. They were commissioned the *Cairo, Carondelet, Cincinnati, Louisville, Mound City, Pittsburg,* and *St. Louis* (later *Baron De Kalb*). Pook designed wooden, flat-bottomed light draft and low freeboard center-wheelers measuring 175 feet in length. Each gunboat was to be armed with ten 8-inch shell guns. With slanted casemates covered with 2½-inch armor, they were similar in appearance to Confederate ironclads. These ironclads had defects found on nearly all of the armored vessels of this type built by both sides during the war—they were underpowered, too heavy, and vulnerable to high, arched "plunging fire" directed at their roofs. Nevertheless, they saw more service than any other class of river ironclads, fighting in various engagements from Fort Henry to Vicksburg and beyond. Three of them (*Cairo, Cincinnati,* and the *Baron De Kalb*) would be sunk.

The army was also responsible for the conversion of four large river vessels into ironclads. A snag boat was converted into the casemated ironclad *Benton* while the *Essex,* also casemated, was a rebuilt center-wheel ferryboat. The *Benton* carried sixteen heavy guns while the *Essex* carried six. Two side-wheelers named the *Lafayette* and the *Choctaw* were purchased in St. Louis and converted under the supervision of navy Commander William "Dirty Bill" Porter. Although the *Lafayette* would have a sloping casemate, the *Choctaw* would have a stationary turret with inclined sides and a curved top—"a war dome, like the dome on the Court House in St. Louis"—and be pierced to hold four guns. Just forward and aft of the wheels

The USS Galena *was not a success, its thin iron sheathing proving easily vulnerable to Confederate shore batteries at Drewry's Bluff in May 1862. James Gibson's photo taken in July.* (USAMHI)

But very effective, and very revolutionary, was the design for the USS Monitor. *Much of the vessel was constructed here on Long Island.* (U. S. NAVAL HISTORICAL CENTER)

were two small casemates. On top of the forward casemate, which housed two howitzers to sweep the decks if the enemy should board, was located a conical pilothouse, covered with 2 inches of iron. Commander Porter designed the armor himself. The *Choctaw* had two 1-inch layers of iron and a 1-inch layer of vulcanized India rubber cushions, while the *Lafayette*'s sloping casemate was covered with 1-inch iron over 1-inch India rubber. The navy took over the eleven ironclads after they were completed, and they operated as units of the Mississippi Squadron throughout the war.

The navy also contracted for ironclads on the western rivers. Three of them, the *Chillicothe, Tuscumbia,* and *Indianola,* were built by Joseph Brown in Cincinnati. Each had a small casemate forward containing two 11-inch rifled guns and a casemate astern between two paddle wheels. All three were regarded as inefficient. The *Chillicothe*'s first commanding officer pronounced it a "cumbersome scow," and after the battle of Grand Gulf in April 1863, the *Tuscumbia*'s captain referred to his vessel as "a Disgrace."

These river ironclads were all laid down or converted during 1861 and early 1862, months before the engagement between the *Monitor* and the *Vir-*

And here it rests in Gibson's July 9, 1862, photograph, taken on the James River. The turret shows the indentations made by the Virginia*'s solid shot during their epic battle at Hampton Roads.* (USAMHI)

ginia. The *Galena* was also under construction at Mystic, Connecticut, during these months.

The *Galena* was, according to Commodore Joseph Smith, senior officer of the Ironclad Board, "a Lighter boat . . . intended to have more speed than other ironclads to work in part under canvas." It resembled the wooden steam warships of that day except that the upper part of its sides was rounded inward or "tumbled home" at an angle of about 45 degrees to deflect projectiles. A battery of six guns was mounted on a gun deck protected by armor not quite 4 inches in thickness. It had two 1-inch plates of armor on its sides separated by an air space in which there were iron bars. Although it was rigged as a schooner, all the masts, except the fore lower mast kept for a lookout position, were removed. It was built by C. S. Bushnell and Company and commissioned in April 1862. In May, the *Galena* was one of the vessels of the North Atlantic Blockading Squadron that ascended the James River and engaged the Confederate batteries at Drewry's Bluff. It was badly damaged; its thin armor penetrated thirteen times. Later the armor was removed, and the *Galena* completed the war as a wooden-hulled ship.

The *New Ironsides* was a traditional broadside type warship, but 170 feet of its 230-foot hull were covered with iron armor 4½ inches in thickness. The armor belt covered the sides and deck, generally amidship, with bow and stern unarmored. This citadel protected the main battery of sixteen 11-inch Dahlgren guns. Classified a frigate, this large (more than 4,000 tons displacement) and powerful ironclad was built by Merrick & Sons in Philadelphia. *New Ironsides* spent its entire Civil War career with either the South Atlantic or the North Atlantic blockading squadrons. In April 1863 the armored warship participated in Admiral Samuel F. Du Pont's attack on Confederate positions in Charleston harbor, and in this and subsequent attacks it was hit repeatedly by enemy fire without suffering any damage. In October it was slightly damaged by the Confederate torpedo boat *David,* but after repairs it participated in Admiral David D. Porter's attacks on Fort Fisher. *New Ironsides* was the most powerful ironclad completed by the Union during the war and undoubtedly the most effective in the combined operations along the Southern coastline. It was the only seagoing armored cruiser to be completed during the war. An improved armored cruiser, the *Dunderberg,* was laid down but not completed until after Appomattox. The board of naval officers who had recommended the three original armored vessels wrote that "ocean going [armored] cruisers are for the time being impracticable." This report may have had some effect on Union policy concerning armored vessels, but the major factors were the influence of Assistant Secretary of the Navy Gustavus Fox and the *Monitor's* designer, John Ericsson, and the impact of the battle between the *Monitor* and the *Virginia* on Northern public opinion.

As early as December 1861 the Navy Department had requested $12,000,000 to construct twenty additional turreted vessels. As designed, they were to mount a type of turret developed by Captain Cowper Coles of the British Royal Navy. Ericsson, however, persuaded the navy to substitute a turret designed by him for the Coles turret. The *Monitor's* success was primarily responsible for this decision.

The *Monitor* was a unique warship. Designed as a harbor defense vessel, instead of a standard ship hull it had a large armored "raft" 172 feet by 41 feet, 6 inches supported by a lower section of wood 122 feet long and 34 feet wide. The "raft" was designed to increase stability in a seaway and protect the hull from ramming. The vessel's power plant consisted of two boilers and two engines that were of Ericsson's design, as was the revolving turret, which was the armor-clad's most novel feature. The *Monitor* incorporated numerous technical advances for that time including forced ventilation of living spaces, a protected anchor which could be raised and lowered without it or the crew members being exposed to enemy fire, and a protected pilothouse. The turret carried two 11-inch Dahlgren smoothbores. The *Monitor* was completed in early February 1862, and a month later it left under tow to join the North Atlantic Blockading Squadron. Its fortuitous arrival at Hampton Roads in time to challenge the *Virginia* is well known. The *Monitor* won a tactical victory in preventing the destruction of Union vessels in the Roads, and in doing so it produced such an intense enthusiasm in the North that a "monitor fever" swept the Union. From then until the end of the war the Union would concentrate on building monitor-type vessels. It is ironic that the Union Navy which obviously had to

While monitors would become a mania in the East, on the western waters a different sort of ironclad came about. The first river ironclads were converted snag boats, like the Benton. *With sixteen guns mounted on its deck, it was the most powerful vessel on the Mississippi and flagship of Foote's fleet at Island No. 10 and Davis's fleet in the battle at Memphis.* (KA)

assume an offensive strategy in order to win the war, adopted as its principal ironclad a type of vessel that was basically defensive in nature.

On March 21, three weeks after the battle, Ericsson received contracts for six enlarged and improved versions of the *Monitor* while four additional ships of the same class were ordered from other builders. These were the ten *Passaics*—the *Passaic, Montauk, Catskill, Patapsco, Lehigh, Sangamon,* (later renamed *Jason*), *Camanche, Nahant, Nantucket,* and *Weehawken.* Like the original *Monitor,* each had a single turret, increased thickness of armor, a permanent stack, and a more powerful battery. These vessels as a class were to see more service than any others of the monitor fleet. They were the major ironclad units of both the South Atlantic and North Atlantic blockading squadrons. Monitors of this class participated in the combined operations against Charleston and Savannah, and in the James River.

In 1862 the Navy Department also initiated the construction of double-turreted monitors. The *Onondaga* was built at Continental Iron Works, Greenpoint, New York, under contract with George W. Quintard. Commissioned early in 1864, it was 226 feet long and carried a battery of two 15-inch Dahlgren smoothbores and two 150-pounder Parrott rifles. This vessel spent its entire war career in the James River and was decommissioned after the war. Four additional double-turreted monitors were built in navy yards—*Miantonomoh, Monadnock, Agamenticus* (later

Soon new ships were under construction, however, at places like the Carondelet Marine Railway at Carondelet, Missouri. Here two "city class" ironclads are being built. Their builder, James B. Eads, could construct one in forty-five days, start to finish. (NA, U. S. WAR DEPARTMENT GENERAL STAFF)

renamed *Terror*), and *Tonawanda* (later renamed *Amphitrite*). These vessels were twin-screw, wooden-hulled ironclads over 258 feet in length. Of these four, only the *Monadnock* was completed prior to the end of the war, but it saw no combat. This class, however, was considered the most efficient of the monitor type built during the war and these vessels remained in service for many years afterward.

In September 1862, orders were given to various builders for nine more Ericsson monitors. *Canonicus, Catawba, Oneonta, Mahopac, Manhattan, Tecumseh, Saugus, Manayunk* (later *Ajax*), and *Tippecanoe* (later *Wyandotte*) were similar to the *Passaics,* but with certain significant improvements —a defensive slope around the base of the turret to prevent jamming, a stronger hull, and a heavier battery of 15-inch guns. Five of this class were commissioned in time to see Civil War service, and the *Tecumseh* was sunk during the Battle of Mobile Bay.

The last of the coastal monitors contracted for in 1862 were the two giant single-turret monitors, *Puritan* and *Dictator*. Displacing more than 3,000 tons each and with large fuel capacities, these vessels were intended as oceangoing vessels. They were built in New York under contract with John Ericsson. Their 312-foot hulls were to be protected by 6-inch side armor. The single turrets would carry two 15-inch Dahlgren smoothbores each. The *Dictator,* after being commissioned in December 1864, joined the North Atlantic Blockading Squadron but saw no action. The *Puritan* was never completed.

The largest single class of monitor-type vessels was the *Casco* class. In the spring of 1863, contracts were signed for the construction of twenty of this type. However, during the war only eight were completed, and they were considered unseaworthy. Five of them were converted to torpedo boats, but none saw action.

Monitors were also constructed for operations on the western rivers. Shortly after the Hampton Roads engagement, James B. Eads received a contract to build three single-turreted monitors of his own design, although the Navy Department insisted that Ericsson's turret be used instead of one designed by Eads. The three river monitors, named *Osage, Neosho,* and *Ozark,* were unlike other monitors in that they were propelled by stern wheels. Unfortunately, the wheels (protected by armored casings) made it impossible for the turrets to turn a full 360 degrees. The *Ozark* was larger and carried additional armament of questionable value—four pivot guns located upon the open deck. They were unusual-looking vessels with virtually nothing

Here the finished products rest at anchor at Cairo, Illinois. These "Pook turtles" were the backbone of the Mississippi fleet. At left the USS Baron De Kalb, *in the center the USS* Cincinnati, *and on the right the USS* Mound City. *The* De Kalb *was formerly the USS* St. Louis, *the first of Eads's boats to launch.* (NYHS)

Another converted snag boat became the USS Essex, *an unfortunate vessel that would be much damaged and beset with difficulty throughout the war. A photograph by Dr. J. T. Field taken while the ship lay moored off Memphis in 1864. Mortar boats lie to its left bow.* (CIVIL WAR TIMES ILLUSTRATED COLLECTION)

showing above the waterline but the turret, the iron-plated house for the stern paddle wheel, and the tall, thin stacks.

Eads received a second contract for monitors. The four vessels built under this contract—*Chickasaw, Kickapoo, Milwaukee,* and *Winnebago*—were double-turreted ironclads, with one turret by Ericsson's design and one by Eads's design. The Eads turret was more sophisticated than Ericsson's. The guns in the turret were mounted on a steam-operated elevator which dropped them to a lower deck where they were loaded and then hoisted and run out through ports opened by automatic steam-operated shutters. These vessels carried four guns each—two per turret—and were the only monitors ever built with triple screws and rudders. They were principally employed with the West Gulf Blockading Squadron operating in Mobile Bay and its vicinity and were generally considered the most serviceable of the river monitors.

The monitor-type had the great advantage of achieving a maximum of impenetrability through two radical factors—low freeboard and the concentration of guns in the armored turret. The guns could be aimed without moving the ship. In confined and sheltered waters the monitors were excellent defensive ships, but they had serious defects that affected Union naval operations. A majority of them were essentially floating batteries that had to be towed from port to port; even in the rivers they could rarely stem the current. They were unseaworthy and had so little reserve buoyancy that a leak could be fatal. For these reasons they were unsuitable for blockade service, the primary mission of the Union Navy. In anything but a flat calm a monitor's deck was awash. The crew had to remain below with hatches battened down. As Admiral Du Pont wrote: "How can such vessels lay off ports . . . and protect the wooden vessels."

The western rivers were generally more suitable for the monitor type, but even here there were problems. The gunboats' maneuverability was poor, and they had little protection from plunging shot, a serious defect considering the many miles of bluffs along the waterways.

Even more important was their unsuitability for offensive operations. Loading their guns usually required from six to eight minutes. "This delay," as one authority has written, "violated the cardinal principal of naval gunnery, volume of fire." In the attack by the *New Ironsides, Keokuk,* and seven monitors on Fort Sumter in April 1863, only 139 rounds were fired by the combined batteries of the ironclads' guns. At the same time 76 guns in the Confederate forts rained some 2,206 shots on the Union vessels. As Admiral Du Pont wrote Secretary Welles, "I . . . remind the Department that ability to endure is not sufficient element wherewith to gain victories, that endurance must be accompanied with a corresponding power to inflict injury upon the enemy . . . that the weakness of the monitor class of vessels . . . is fatal to their attempts against fortifications."

The most unusual turreted vessel commissioned during the Civil War was the converted wooden sloop-of-war *Roanoke.* Like her sister ship, the *Merrimack,* converted by the Confederates into the *Virginia,* she was cut down, and three center-line turrets were installed. With a high freeboard, she was not a monitor-type vessel. Because of instability and a deep draft, she was considered unsuitable for active service and spent the war defending New York harbor from possible attack by Confederate cruisers.

While the Union ironclad building program after 1861 emphasized the monitor type of vessel, the Confederate program on the other hand would change from one which stressed offensive vessels in 1861 to one emphasizing defensive vessels. The apparent unseaworthiness of the *Virginia* and the ironclads built in New Orleans and Memphis, the lack of adequate facilities and qualified technical expertise, the belief that powerful armor-clads

William "Dirty Bill" Porter designed the conversion of the Essex *and commanded her, while also taking a hand in the fashioning of the ungainly* Lafayette *and* Choctaw. (LC)

could be obtained in Europe, and most important, the growing threat to the Confederacy from invasion and amphibious assault all contributed to this change in policy. From 1862 until the end of the war, the Confederate naval construction program would concentrate on small, shallow-draft harbor-defense armored vessels. Approximately forty of these vessels were laid down, and half of them were completed.

These small defense ironclads were designed by naval constructor John Porter. He developed a standard design which was sent to builders and contractors throughout the Confederacy. The original plan was for a 150-foot flat-bottomed vessel with hull to be partially armored and casemate to be completely covered with iron armor. The ironclad would carry a battery of six guns and be screw-

Then came the behemoth ironclads, designed by "Dirty Bill" Porter and built by Eads. The USS Lafayette *carried eight heavy guns and a shield of iron laid over rubber, intended to make shot bounce off the casemate. In practice, it did not.* (USAMHI)

propelled. Although this design was utilized by the shipbuilders, it is, nevertheless, almost impossible to generalize about the Confederate armor-clads. There were noticeable differences because of modifications in size, machinery, armor, and battery. In size they ranged from the *Albemarle* and the *Neuse* (139 feet) up to several under construction during the latter months of the war that were over 250 feet in length. The 310-foot *Nashville* was the largest of this class.

The thickness of armor measured from 2 to 8 inches, but all of it was 2-inch laminated iron plate. On several vessels such as the *Arkansas* and *Louisiana* railroad iron—T-rails—was substituted because rolled plates were not available. The marine engines and boilers varied from ship to ship. Some of them were manufactured in the South; more of them were salvaged from other vessels. The method of propulsion consisted of either wheel or screw or a combination of both, as in the *Louisiana,* which had two wheels and two screws. A majority of them were screw steamers with either one or two propellers, but several such as the *Nashville* and *Missouri* were paddle-wheelers because of the accessibility of that kind of machinery. The machinery and propulsion units were notoriously inadequate and inefficient.

The Confederacy had more success in arming its ironclads than in providing motive power for them. There was really never a shortage of heavy guns although some of the ships' initial batteries consisted of a variety of guns. Smoothbores were carried at one time or another by nearly all of the armorclads, but in contrast to the Union Navy, which advocated smoothbores during and after the war, the Confederate Navy concentrated on rifled guns. The standard rifled gun used on the Confederate ironclads was the Brooke gun, a cast-iron banded cannon developed by John Brooke, who headed the Confederate Navy's Bureau of Ordnance and Hydrography. The principal types used on the ironclads were 7-inch and 6.4-inch guns. The Confederate Navy also equipped its ironclads in 1863 with spar torpedoes, egg-shaped copper vessels containing from fifty to seventy pounds of powder, fitted to a long pole attached to the bow of the vessel. Although Union naval officers universally referred to the Confederate ironclads as "rams," only a few of them actually had rams built on.

The 150-foot *Richmond,* laid down at the navy yard in Norfolk and completed in Richmond, was the first of Porter's harbor defense vessels completed. Other 150-foot ironclads commenced included the *Chicora, Raleigh, Palmetto State, North Carolina, Huntsville, Tuscaloosa,* and *Savannah.* Larger vessels included the *Jackson* (renamed *Muscogee*), *Fredericksburg,* and *Milledgeville* (175 feet); the *Virginia II* and *Charleston* (180 feet); *Missouri* (183 feet); the *Columbia, Texas,* and *Tennessee* (216 feet); and the *Nashville* (310 feet). Porter also designed a smaller vessel of this class to be used in the North Carolina sounds. Only two of these 139-foot ironclads, the *Albemarle* and the *Neuse,* were completed.

Although the casemated ironclad remained the standard "home water" vessel constructed within the Confederacy, two double-ender ironclads with two octagonal casemates were laid down in Richmond and Wilmington. They were similar in appearance to the Union double-turreted monitors,

Equally formidable in appearance was the USS Choctaw, *it, too, carrying eight heavy cannons. Both ships were ready to ply the rivers by late 1862.* (KA)

but since the casemates were not moveable turrets, pivot guns were to be utilized. Neither vessel was completed because of the lack of iron armor. No monitor types were constructed in the Confederacy, although one to be built at Columbus, Georgia, was approved. The proposed vessel was apparently never laid down. Secretary of the Navy Mallory preferred the standard casemated ironclad. Less than two months before General Lee surrendered at Appomattox Court House, the secretary was writing, "for river, harbor, and coast defense, the sloping shield and general plan of armored vessels adopted by us . . . are the best that could be adopted in our situation. In ventilation, light, fighting space, and quarters it is believed that the sloping shield presents greater advantages than the *Monitor* turret."

The ironclads did contribute significantly to the Confederate war effort. They did not break or seriously challenge the Union blockade, but after the spring of 1862, this was not their primary objective. From then until the end of the war their real function was to defend the rivers, inlets, and ports. In this they had some success. Of the five seaports—Savannah, Charleston, Wilmington, Mobile, and Galveston—taken in the last six months of the war, two were taken by land forces from the rear, and two indirectly as a result of pressure from the rear. In all of the cities but one, Galveston, the Confederate Navy had ironclads as part of the harbor defense. Nevertheless, they suffered from serious defects in design and construction. The fundamental problems of weight, speed, seaworthiness, and mechanical inadequacies were never solved.

To a lesser degree the same was true of the Union armored vessels. Yet, they were superior in design and construction—not surprising, considering the available facilities and technological expertise in the North. This was particularly true of the monitors, which would remain the standard armored vessels in the United States Navy until the 1880s.

Like the Confederate ironclads the Union armored vessels played an important role in the Civil War. They were unsuitable for blockade duty, but in the amphibious operations along the coast and in the rivers and confined waters they proved their worth. Truly the Civil War was the ironclad era.

The USS Ozark *was unusual on the Mississippi. It carried a turret of Ericsson's design forward, and mounted four other cannons on the main deck.* (USAMHI)

A variety of less formidable ironclads and "tinclads" plied the Western rivers, boats like the USS General Grant, *shown here at Kingston, Georgia.* (NA)

David D. Porter had little good to say about any of the Mississippi ironclads. He was a devotee of the conventional Ericsson monitor design. (USAMHI)

And so, obviously, was John Ericsson himself. Arrogant, egotistical, and painfully difficult to work with, he was still a genius of sorts, and the Union turned to him through most of the war for its monitor designs. (NHC)

Admiral Hiram Paulding backed Ericsson's original Monitor *design and worked hard to expedite its building and adoption by the navy. He succeeded.* (NYHS)

Captain Francis H. Gregory, a hero of the era of iron men in wooden ships, superintended the construction of ironclads for Welles. (NYHS)

Chief Engineer Alban Stimers managed most of the construction of the original Monitor, *fought aboard her at Hampton Roads, and later lost his reputation with the unsuccessful* Casco *class of light-draft monitors.* (NHC)

Officers working under Gregory, like Chief Engineer James W. King, oversaw individual ironclads to completion. King supervised the Manayunk, Catawba, *and* Tippecanoe. *Later he built the* Ozark, Chickasaw, *and* Winnebago, *out west.* (LC)

The first turreted ironclads to follow the Monitor *were those of the* Passaic *class, and they were the workhorse ironclads of the Atlantic coast. Here the launch of the* Camanche *of that class. This launch took place in San Francisco, California, where the vessel was shipped in parts and reconstructed. An 1864 photograph by C. E. Watkins.* (CHARLES S. SCHWARTZ)

The USS Catskill, *photographed in Charleston harbor in 1863, one of the most powerful—and most damaged—*Passaics. (USAMHI)

The anchor well of the Catskill. *Note how the anchor could be raised and lowered from within, without exposing men to fire.* (NHC)

An officer's cabin aboard the Catskill. *A beam of light enters through the skylight scuttle overhead. A watertight bulkhead door is closed behind the desk and above it on the bulkhead is a print of the original* Monitor *at sea.* (NHC)

The Catskill's *turret machinery, the enormously heavy turret resting on and being turned by the massive vertical shaft at left.* (NHC)

The engine room of the Catskill, *showing part of the steam engine that powered not only the screw, but also the turret machinery.* (NHC)

A similar, unpublished view of the engine room of the Camanche *while it was being reassembled in San Francisco.* (CHARLES S. SCHWARTZ)

The USS Nahant *undergoing repairs at Hilton Head, South Carolina, after being heavily damaged in the April 7, 1863, attack on Charleston, carried out largely by* Passaic-*class monitors like the* Nahant. (USAMHI)

Rear Admiral Samuel F. I. Du Pont commanded the fleet that attacked Charleston. Seeing the relatively low firepower of the monitors and seeing the heavy damage inflicted on them by Confederate batteries, he formed a poor opinion of monitors as offensive vessels. His entire monitor fleet fired 139 shots in the same time that it received at least 346 hits. (USAMHI)

The next step in improving monitor firepower was two turrets. The Onondaga *was commissioned in March 1864 and proved thoroughly reliable, though it saw very little action. Here it is in the James River, scene of most of its war service.* (USAMHI)

Next came the Miantonomoh *class, ships like the* Tonawanda, *shown here. Only one of them was finished in time to serve in the war, but they were far more seaworthy than their predecessors.* (P-M)

The Miantonomoh *itself actually steamed to Europe, proving the deep-sea capabilities of the monitor type. It appears here at the Washington Navy Yard in 1865. On the left is the USS* Montauk *of the* Passaic *class. In the distance is the light-draft monitor* Chimo *and, just visible behind it, the tall masts of the Confederate ironclad ram* Stonewall. (NHC)

Ericsson, meanwhile, turned his mind to much larger seagoing monitors, his Dictator *class. Only two were built, and neither was very successful. Here the* Puritan *peeks out of the shiphouse at the Continental Iron Works at Green Point, New York.* (NHC)

The launch of the USS Dictator, *December 26, 1863, at the Delamater Iron Works.* (THE MARINERS MUSEUM, NEWPORT NEWS, VIRGINIA)

Ready to slide down the ways, the Dictator *looms above the speakers' platform, flag-draped for the dedication ceremonies.* (NYHS)

Stimers's light-draft monitor Casco *on the James River. The* Casco-*type monitors were found to be ill-designed and barely awash, so their turrets were left off and they were turned into torpedo boats instead.* (USAMHI)

The launch of the light-draft USS Modoc, *photographed by the New York artist J. H. Beal in 1864.* (NHC)

James Eads designed powerful light-draft river "monitors" Osage *and* Neosho *to operate in barely four feet of water. Ungainly, they still proved effective against most enemy fire. Here the* Osage, *probably in the Red River in 1864.* (LC)

Soon after the Osage *and* Neosho *were begun, Eads started work on another class of light-draft river monitor, the* Winnebagos. *These included turrets designed by Eads, which were far superior to Ericsson's. They did good service on the Mississippi and at Mobile Bay and proved to be the spiritual progenitor of warships for a century to come. Here the USS* Milwaukee, *commissioned at Mound City in August 1864. It struck a "torpedo" on March 28, 1865, and sank.* (USAMHI)

The only three-turreted monitor built during the war, the USS Roanoke. *Originally a steam frigate, sister ship of the* Merrimack, *which the Confederates converted to the CSS* Virginia, *the* Roanoke *also was a conversion. Nearly destroyed by the Confederate ironclad in the battle at Hampton Roads, it was taken to the Brooklyn Navy Yard and the work of making it an ironclad commenced barely two weeks after the battle. The result was not spectacular. The* Roanoke *served two years with the North Atlantic Blockading Squadron, but proved rather ineffective. This previously unpublished photograph shows it at Brooklyn in mid 1865, the old ship-of-the-line USS* Vermont *in the left background.* (NHC)

By the end of the war, sights like these two monitors lying off the Washington Navy Yard were commonplace. The war gave rise to a whole new generation of naval machines in the Union. An unpublished image by Kilburn Brothers of New Hampshire. (USAMHI)

The Confederates looked to a different sort of ironclad, one more compatible with their limited technology and industrial facilities. No photographs of the Virginia *seem to have survived, but all subsequent Confederate ironclads followed the same general pattern originated by John Porter and John Brooke. Here the CSS* Chicora *in Charleston Harbor. On January 31, 1863,* Chicora *and its sister ship* Palmetto State *became the only Confederate ironclads to put to open sea when they steamed out and engaged elements of the blockading fleet successfully, then returned to port.* (OLD COURT HOUSE MUSEUM, VICKSBURG)

Nearly as famous as the Virginia, *the CSS* Albemarle *was equally as unwieldy and slow, yet managed to threaten Albemarle Sound most effectively, sink one enemy warship, and aid materially in the capture of Plymouth, North Carolina. To counter this threat, Lieutenant William B. Cushing attacked it on the night of October 27, 1864, with a torpedo mounted on the end of a spar projecting from a steam launch. The* Albemarle *sank almost immediately and is here shown at the Norfolk Navy Yard in 1865 after being raised by the Federals.* (NHC)

In Georgia's waters, Confederates constructed this casemated ironclad, the CSS Jackson, *only to find themselves so short of iron that it was never completed. The builders destroyed the ship before the Federals could capture it. This image may be by A. J. Riddle, who photographed the Andersonville prison camp in 1864.* (TU, LOUISIANA HISTORICAL ASSOCIATION COLLECTION)

A remarkable unpublished view of the CSS Atlanta, *and perhaps the best illustration extant of the improvised nature of most Confederate ironclads. Taken after the war, this image probably shows the ship laid up at League Island, Pennsylvania, prior to its sale for salvage. It had been converted from the blockade runner* Fingal *in 1862, and the old* Fingal *hull shows clearly below the more streamlined additions that turned it into the* Atlanta. *This deep draft proved its undoing, for in its first engagement it ran aground and surrendered. The Federals later used it to patrol the James River.* (THE MARINERS MUSEUM)

The CSS Atlanta, *now the USS* Atlanta, *patrolling the James.* (USAMHI)

The CSS Tennessee *in Mobile Bay, after its surrender to Farragut. It was commanded in battle by Franklin Buchanan, who commanded the first Confederate ironclad, the* Virginia. (THE MARINERS MUSEUM)

The CSS Indianola, *formerly the USS* Indianola. *Captured from the Federals and towed to Vicksburg, the* Indianola *was undergoing refurbishment into a Confederate ironclad when its captors were forced to destroy it before the fall of Vicksburg.* (USAMHI)

A David *class Confederate torpedo boat. These light-draft, semisubmerged "ironclads" were well suited for harbor defense, stealing out in the night to attack blockade ships. They enjoyed little real success, but created considerable consternation among the Federals.* (NHC)

Mr. Cooley of Beaufort and Mr. Moore of Concord

A PORTFOLIO

Two of hundreds of unsung artists, these photographers captured South Carolina long before the Federals

THE WORK of two photographers, Samuel A. Cooley and Henry P. Moore, offers a remarkable view of South Carolina during this period.

Samuel A. Cooley represented that special class of quasi-official photographer, like George Barnard and Alexander Gardner, who sometimes did contract work for the government. Whenever possible, this group made private capital of their army contract work, implying that all of their work bore official sanction. Gardner called himself "Photographer to the Army of the Potomac." Cooley would use two titles—"Photographer Tenth Army Corps" and "U. S. Photographer, Department of the South." Perhaps it helped sales of their commercial views. Certainly Cooley could offer an unusual range of images, for he operated permanent establishments in three South Carolina locations, Folly Island, Hilton Head, and Beaufort, and in Jacksonville, Florida. Houses, hospitals, camps, vessels, forts, landscapes, and everything else came before his lenses, and he sold stereo views of all of them.

By contrast, little is known of Henry P. Moore, of Concord, New Hampshire. He operated at Hilton Head in 1862–63, and probably came chiefly to take marketable views of the 3rd New Hampshire for the folks at home. His remarkable images speak for themselves.

SAMUEL A. COOLEY

The entrepreneur photographer. (USAMHI)

"Cooley's" reads the sign in his Beaufort headquarters, and an unusual "gallery" it is. Clothing, flour, hams, books, butter, stationery, oranges, baskets, watches, and, of course, photographs, all could be bought over Cooley's counter. He stands in the white jacket leaning against his wagon. (USAMHI)

Another view of Cooley's Beaufort gallery, with a little less advertising visible. (USAMHI)

Cooley and assistants with his photographic wagon. Cooley himself stands second from the right, his hand resting on one of his cameras. (WRHS)

Cooley's favorite subject, Beaufort, South Carolina, seen from the river. The artist had a wonderful eye for the still-life possibilities of the camera. (USAMHI)

The Fuller House, one of Beaufort's showplaces, and now the headquarters of General Rufus Saxton. A sentry box stands outside the gates to the house. (SOUTH CAROLINA HISTORICAL SOCIETY, CHARLESTON)

John S. Fyler's store and, next to it, the post office, one example of Cooley's sometimes extraordinary talent for still scenes that have life and seeming movement. (USAMHI)

A commissary storehouse, shot in October 1864, one of the contract images of government buildings made by Cooley. Right next door stands a fishing tackle and general provisions store. (SOUTH CAROLINA HISTORICAL SOCIETY)

Bay Street in Beaufort, and J. W. Collins & Company's rather unusual clothing store. In addition to coats, vests, pants, and caps, Mr. Collins also sold oats and bran and, as advertised on the sign in his doorway, "cold soda." It certainly seems to attract more customers than the dress shop next door. (WRHS)

The Beaufort Hotel and, on its right, the office of the Adams Express Company, one of the early private mail and package carriers in the country. (SOUTH CAROLINA HISTORICAL SOCIETY)

Another Beaufort post office, right next to the Adams Express. Since large sums of money often traveled in the post to and from the soldiers, the ground floor windows are barred with iron mesh to prevent burglary. (USAMHI)

Bay Street in 1862, another view of a typical Southern town. (SOUTH CAROLINA HISTORICAL SOCIETY)

The west side of Bay Street. (USAMHI)

The Beaufort Hotel again and, to its left, the commissary storehouse and fishing tackle shop. The dandies in front of the hotel may be Southern gentlemen who demurred on soldiering, or they may be Yankee traders who followed the army to sell to the soldiers. (USAMHI)

A quiet street scene in Beaufort. (USAMHI)

A house used as a hospital for "contrabands," the slaves who gathered around the Union armies wherever they went, seeking freedom and protection. (SOUTH CAROLINA HISTORICAL SOCIETY)

The one-time home of Dr. John A. Johnson, and now a hospital, with linen and blankets airing on the balcony. (USAMHI)

The Beaufort Arsenal on Craven Street. (SOUTH CAROLINA HISTORICAL SOCIETY)

The United States Marine headquarters on Bay Point, rather a small headquarters, but then it was rather a small Marine Corps. (USAMHI)

The machine shops at Bay Point and, in the foreground, bits and pieces of the machinery they worked on here, mostly for maintenance on the ships of the South Atlantic Blockading Squadron. (USAMHI)

At right the saltwater condenser for purifying water, and in the background several vessels docked awaiting coal. (USAMHI)

A parade, the generals on their white chargers, the men and boys watching from the sideline. Cooley missed no opportunity to shoot a scene with a mass of men. The more subjects in an image, the more who might want to buy a print . . . and perhaps an orange or two from his gallery. (CWTI)

Hundreds of heavy guns passed through Hilton Head on their way to fight rebellion. They and their accoutrements lie here in some disarray. In the lower left corner, against the sand, can be seen the shadow of Cooley's camera. (USAMHI)

The headquarters of Major General David Hunter, now recovered from his Bull Run wound. Cooley did a much more brisk business at Hilton Head than at Beaufort. (USAMHI)

HENRY P. MOORE

Henry P. Moore, too, went to Hilton Head, where there was more bustle and activity than in sleepy Beaufort. The wharf looked over a bay jammed with warships, transports, tugs, and lighter craft. (USAMHI)

Here immense quantities of supplies for the army besieging Charleston were received. (USAMHI)

The Hilton Head signal station and, on the ground, several carriages for siege guns. (USAMHI)

Moore took his camera atop the signal station to photograph the hospital in the far distance and an ordnance storeyard in the foreground. Cannons and carriages lay awaiting shipment to the front. (USAMHI)

Another, larger, signal station was needed in 1863 on St. Helena Island. The engineers who built it based their tower on four existing trees still growing. (USAMHI)

And on Otter Island they built another, which Moore captured in the act of signaling to a ship out on the horizon. (USAMHI)

But at Hilton Head, Moore's best work was his portraits of the men in their camps, and particularly those of the 3rd New Hampshire. Here Lieutenant Colonel J. H. Jackson stands at left, his son Captain T. M. Jackson second from the right, and his servant Cyrus at right. (USAMHI)

Signal corpsmen, March 1, 1862. (USAMHI)

The 3rd New Hampshire's surgeon, A. A. Moulton, and his somewhat gothic-looking wife. (USAMHI)

Cook's galley of Company H. In the hut in back stand tin plates and cups for the mess. In the center foreground stands the cook, G. N. Wheeler, at his camp stove. The man seated on the small barrel is W. Blake, about to grind coffee beans in the grinder at his feet. In the right background an unknown New Hampshire officer peers from his tent to see what Moore is doing. (USAMHI)

The meal prepared, another cook looks on as the bandsmen of the 3rd New Hampshire dine, their drums and fifes set casually about the area. (USAMHI)

A nonchalant group of the New Hamphire boys pose for the artist, their table reflecting their leisure doings. It lies cluttered with books, a cigar, letters from home, cased ambrotypes of female loved ones, dominoes, and an ink bottle from which one man is writing his letter. The man seated on the other side of the table reads a page of crude cartoons from an issue of Harper's Weekly. (USAMHI)

The bandmaster's tent, with bandmaster G. W. Ingalls at left studying his music while his servant polishes his boots. Sam Brown reads a New Hampshire newspaper at the center of the table, while musician D. A. Brown on the right does the same. Their horns lie on the table (USAMHI)

These New Hampshiremen added considerable decoration to their Hilton Head quarters. Seashells, palmettos, cactus, driftwood, all contributed to a scene quite out of the ordinary for Civil War camps. These musicians can enjoy their meal in the most pleasant surroundings. (USAMHI)

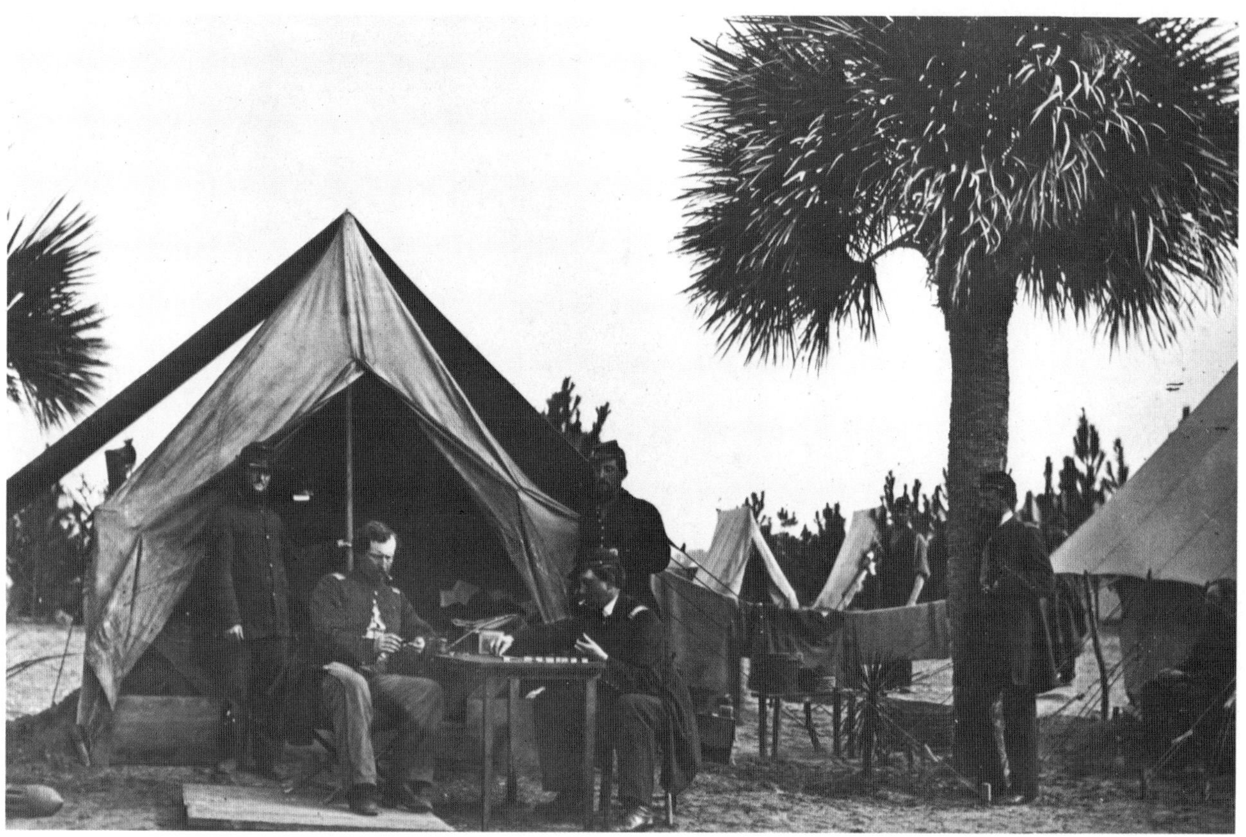

And the officers loved their dominoes. (USAMHI)

The splendid plantation residence of John E. Seabrook on Edisto Island, in 1862. At far left is his library—at right, his wine cellar. Lying like a white carpet on the lawn in front of the house is cotton captured aboard the blockade runner Empire *and spread out to dry in the sun.* (USAMHI)

A closer view of the Seabrook mansion, now headquarters of Colonel E. Q. Fellows and staff. The post adjutant, Martin James, stands under the square marked on the image, his office indicated by the √, and his sleeping quarters by the #. Made by Moore on April 7, 1862. (KA)

Seabrook's fishpond, with his house in the distance at left. Bandmaster Ingalls steers the boat. (USAMHI)

H. P. Moore's images of the Seabrook plantation touched upon art. Here Seabrook's extensive garden as seen from the mansion house. One of Seabrook's slaves, a little boy, stands atop the sundial at right center. Standing with folded arms in the foreground is Colonel E. Q. Fellows, commanding the 3rd New Hampshire. It is early spring, April 7, 1862, and already the garden is verdant. Half a continent away, the second day's fighting at Shiloh is raging. (KA)

More cotton drying on Seabrook's grounds, being tended by freedmen who were once his slaves. In the distance at center stands the USS Pocahontas. (USAMHI)

Seabrook's library. (USAMHI)

Men who died before Moore could catch them in life pose silent and still in death. Almost all are of the 3rd New Hampshire—almost all died of disease. Hilton Head could kill despite its tropical beauty. (USAMHI)

And however easy it might have been to forget the war, they could not, and neither did Moore. Deceptive in its peacefulness, this scene could turn warlike at any time, and the soldier reading his letter beside the gun carriage in Fort Wells is certainly not far from his weapon. The sights atop the Rodman gun could fill with enemy vessels or blockade runners, and the tranquility of this image would vanish. Moore, for all his commercial instincts, knew as well that he was capturing a special part of the war for posterity. Thanks to him, these scenes will remain captive for all of time. (USAMHI)

The Peninsular Campaign

EMORY M. THOMAS

The first campaign going "on to Richmond," and the emergence of a general called "Granny" Lee

THE ARMY OF THE POTOMAC was awesome. In the spring of 1862 it was the largest, best equipped armed force ever assembled in the Western Hemisphere. From the masses of volunteers who had descended upon Washington, George B. McClellan had fashioned a mammoth war machine—150,000 men, plus the material to support and sustain this host. With such force McClellan confidently intended to deliver the *coup de grace* to the would-be Confederacy.

McClellan had taken command in the aftermath of the Union debacle at Bull Run in July 1861. He began at once to mold his army and endured pleas and pressure to commit to battle prematurely. Termed "Young Napoleon" by the press, McClellan believed he understood the complexity of "modern war." He first had to spar with ranking United States General Winfield Scott until the aged Scott finally retired from the service in November 1861; then McClellan suffered the "help" of his Commander-in-Chief Abraham Lincoln and other martial amateurs in the administration and Congress.

Having built so splendid an army and waited so long to employ it, McClellan could not afford to err; when he marched, he would have to win. As the campaigning season of 1862 loomed imminent, Lincoln felt the need to rebuild his faith in "Young Napoleon." In frustration, the President issued his own General War Order Number One, which prescribed a "general forward movement" to begin on all fronts on February 22. Beyond this action, he and others in Washington could only chafe at McClellan's caution. Lincoln realized his administration had invested too much in McClellan to cut its losses now. Whatever "Young Napoleon" did or did not do would have to be Union strategy and policy.

Beyond the Potomac waited Confederate armies, the chief of which, commanded by Joseph E. Johnston, occupied the ground around Manassas near the battlefield of Bull Run. Johnston, who ironically held much the same low opinion of his President, Jefferson Davis, as McClellan did of Lincoln, had only some 40,000 troops. But he had 10,000 reinforcements nearby, and he had had all fall and winter to improve a position which had proven impenetrable the previous summer.

For the Army of the Potomac to emulate the tactics of First Bull Run and smash headlong into these waiting defenders seemed to McClellan artless and wasteful. Accordingly he determined to strike the Southerners elsewhere. He wanted to transport his army by water to the tiny port town

After Johnston and Magruder abandoned Yorktown, the Confederates found Norfolk untenable and evacuated on May 9. Before leaving they did their best to destroy the navy yard. Timothy O'Sullivan's December 1864 photograph shows how thoroughly they did their task. (P-M)

of Urbana on the Rappahannock and interpose the Army of the Potomac between Johnston's Confederates and Richmond. Johnston, however, foiled the Urbana approach by evacuating Manassas and moving to Culpeper Court House where he might counter attacks from the east and north with equal facility.

However sound was Johnston's movement, he acted in haste without fully apprising his President of his intentions. And he had had to destroy at Manassas enormous quantities of supplies his government had labored so diligently to collect. Davis, then, had doubts about Johnston nearly equal to Lincoln's about McClellan.

His Urbana landing scrapped, McClellan shifted to a strategic plan which was even more ambitious.

Now McClellan could pursue his original intention of campaigning up the Virginia Peninsula toward Richmond. Here he poses for a Brady camera with members of his staff including, standing at right, Van Vliet. (KA)

He proposed to transport the Army of the Potomac by water to Fort Monroe on the tip of the Virginia Peninsula between the York and James rivers. Union troops had maintained possession of the fort throughout the war, and McClellan planned to use this friendly perimeter as a staging area for an assault upon Richmond from the east. The combined army-navy operation and the eastern invasion route may have seemed complicated logistically, but it offered several advantages over a more direct assault. The Peninsular approach would not compel the Federals to cross the many streams and rivers which crossed the direct route to Richmond. The advance would take place on the relatively flat, tidewater coastal plain. The James, York, and Pamunkey rivers would permit the Union Navy to support McClellan's army with both supplies and gunfire during the advance to Richmond. If Johnston or any other commander dared confront the Army of the Potomac on the Peninsula, he would risk the prospect of having a portion of the blue army landed behind him and thus encirclement and destruction. On the other hand, if the Confederates chose to give battle nearer Richmond, McClellan had the siege artillery with which to blast his way into the city and destroy the opposing army at the same time. Withholding McDowell's corps, Lincoln assented to the plan, and McClellan promptly moved his army to the Peninsula and began his month-long siege of Yorktown.

On April 14 in Richmond the Confederate high command met for fourteen hours to plan some response to McClellan's Peninsular approach. Johnston favored a concentration near Richmond because he thought the Federals too strong on the Peninsula. Robert E. Lee, the President's chief military advisor, and Secretary of War George W. Randolph contended that the Southern army would have to confront the threat somewhere and that the Peninsula was as good a place as any. President Davis feared losing his army and capital if the campaign produced siege operations in front of Richmond. Accordingly Davis instructed Johnston to move his entire force to the Peninsula. Johnston complied without enthusiasm and in the days which followed occupied the Yorktown line with 56,000 troops. He was all too aware that McClellan had nearly twice as many men on the other side of the thin curtain of earth. Thus Johnston, on the eve of the grand assault which would be the climax of McClellan's siege operations, determined to withdraw. On the night of May 3 the Confederates abandoned the Yorktown line and began retracing their steps up the Peninsula toward Richmond. Actually they stepped into seemingly bottomless mud—the result of an extraordinary amount of rain during April.

As Southern columns clogged the spongy roads westward, McClellan's Federals on May 4 rushed empty earthworks. To Washington McClellan announced a great victory at small cost. Then he set about directing the pursuit of his elusive enemy. Five Union divisions plunged into the Peninsular mud, by now well-churned by the retreating Confederates; four more divisions stood ready to move by water up the York to cut off the Southern withdrawal.

Johnston's rear guard (James Longstreet's division) first felt the pressure of the Federal pursuit near Williamsburg. Just east of the old colonial capital on May 5 a sharp fight ensued. The Southerners first stopped the Union advance, then counterattacked, and finally withdrew into the darkness. The Battle of Williamsburg was bloody, but inconclusive. Johnston gained the time he needed to make good his escape, but the Confederate counterattack was a costly failure.

McClellan, meanwhile, was trying to hasten Johnston's envelopment by water. William B. Franklin's division made a landing on the Peninsula opposite West Point, but encountered Gustavus W. Smith's Confederates soon after. The wily Johnston anticipated McClellan's move, and the engagement between Smith's and Franklin's troops on May 7 at Barhamsville (Eltham's Landing) convinced McClellan that his trap had failed. Thereafter he contented himself with a methodical pursuit of his quarry up the Peninsula.

The rival commanders each expressed satisfaction at the developments thus far. Johnston was pleased to have made good his escape, and McClellan took pride in his conquest of the Yorktown line and his pursuit of a fleeing foe. Both generals consumed themselves in cautious movement: Johnston to the vicinity of Richmond and McClellan to the vicinity of Johnston.

In the process both ignored their navies and a succession of military "dominoes" involved in the movement up the Peninsula. When Johnston evacuated the Yorktown line, he left the port city of Norfolk exposed and untenable. When Norfolk fell—the Confederates evacuated the city on May 9—the *Virginia* became a ship without a port. When the *Virginia*'s crew failed in their attempt to lighten the heavy-draft vessel sufficiently to steam up the James, they had to destroy the ironclad. This in turn opened the James all the way to Richmond to Union gunboats and troop transports.

Curiously, neither field commander appreciated this circumstance. Lee was the first Confederate to react; he hastened the work on gun emplacements, river obstructions, and "torpedoes" at Drewry's Bluff. McClellan was seemingly too preoccupied even to comprehend the city's vulnerability. Indeed, it was President Lincoln himself, while visiting Fort Monroe, who gave the instructions which led to Norfolk's capture. The Federal Navy then pressed the issue, and on May 15 two ironclads, the *Monitor* and *Galena,* led three wooden gunboats up the James toward Richmond. The small

Lieutenant General Winfield Scott on June 10, 1862, by Charles D. Fredericks. Taken at West Point after his retirement, it shows a man now bitter at his treatment by the younger McClellan. Two weeks from now, however, "Little Mac" will begin to feel his comeuppance on the Peninsula. (USAMHI)

fleet encountered little difficulty until it reached Drewry's Bluff, which was only about seven miles from the Confederate capital. There Southern batteries and channel obstructions halted the Union advance. Had McClellan provided the expedition with a supporting army column of any size, the fight at Drewry's Bluff might have turned out quite differently. As it happened though, this repulse ended the Federal threat to Richmond by water.

Indeed water, in the form of rain, seemed to plague instead of assist McClellan's campaign as the Army of the Potomac advanced nearer Richmond. The Federal route lay up the northern half of the Peninsula to take advantage of supply lines from the York and Pamunkey rivers. At Cumberland Landing and White House the navy deposited massive amounts of supplies for transport overland via road and the Richmond & York River rail line to the troops. Throughout May unseasonal amounts of rain hampered the movements of men and supplies. Yet even though the Army of the Potomac seemed to ooze instead of march, it moved nonetheless ever closer to Richmond.

As he neared the city McClellan recognized the necessity to broaden his front and position his army on the south as well as the north side of the Chickahominy River, which bisects the Peninsula near Richmond. Two Federal corps had crossed the Chickahominy on May 30 when one of the most violent rainstorms in memory descended upon the area. The fresh rain turned the normally sluggish Chickahominy into a torrent which washed away bridges and left Erasmus Keyes's Union corps isolated from the rest of the army. Joe Johnston recognized his opportunity and determined to strike the exposed Federals with four Confederate divisions.

The Confederate attack appeared simple as long as it consisted only of lines drawn on a map. The lines, representing Southern troops moving along roads, converged at the village of Seven Pines, and there Johnston planned to attack a fraction of the blue army with masses of his own men. On the morning of May 31, however, Johnston's plan came unraveled. James Longstreet seemed most at fault; he took the wrong road and in so doing clogged the Confederate advance. As a result the supposedly coordinated attack degenerated into a series of single blows and an aborted Confederate opportunity. In the aftermath of the day's fighting Johnston fell wounded from his horse, leaving the Southerners not only confused, but also leaderless.

One of McClellan's commanders, Brigadier General Edwin V. Sumner, the oldest corps leader of the war. Born in 1797, he was called "bull head" because a musket ball supposedly bounced from his head in Mexico. During the coming campaign, however, he was wounded twice. (USAMHI)

On June 1, after an unsuccessful attempt to salvage victory from the Battle of Seven Pines (or Fair Oaks), Robert E. Lee arrived to assume command and lead the march back toward Richmond. To this juncture, Lee had disappointed himself and others in the Southern cause. Possessed of splendid credentials at the outset of the war, he had directed a doomed campaign in the Kanawha Valley of western Virginia, presided over a retreat from the coast in South Carolina and Georgia, and served in the President's shadow as Davis's military advisor. In this last capacity, Lee had ameliorated somewhat the relations between Davis and Johnston; but of this, no one but Lee was aware. Thus, he took command of Johnston's army in the wake of a bungled battle in the midst of a desperate campaign with little reputation beyond those who knew him. And the first direction he gave to his troops was to dig holes in the ground—to shore up the defensive works in front of Richmond.

Those who crowned Lee with the sobriquet "Granny Lee" or "King of Spades," however, missed his intention. Lee threw up breastworks so that he might defend Richmond with as few troops as possible; with the bulk of his army he determined to attack.

If the new Confederate commander needed time to make Johnston's army his own following the battle, McClellan seemed to be in a cooperative mood. He moved, slowly and cautiously, to consolidate his position before Richmond. Completing his shift of troop units south of the Chickahominy, McClellan stationed four corps (Franklin's, E. V. Sumner's, Samuel P. Heintzelman's and Keyes's) directly east of Seven Pines about six miles from its limits and about one mile from the Confederate works. North of the Chickahominy were the 30,000 troops of Fitz John Porter's corps. McClellan was careful for good reason; his intelligence operatives and spies informed him that the Confederate Army numbered 200,000 men. The estimate, largely the product of Allan Pinkerton's civilian agents, was much exaggerated; Lee had perhaps 65,000 to 70,000 troops with which to confront McClellan's 90,000 to 100,000 at this point. Nev-

Some of McClellan's generals, on May 14, 1862. Seated from the right they are Brigadier General John Newton, Brigadier General William F. Barry, VI Corps commander Brigadier General William B. Franklin, and Brigadier General Henry W. Slocum. (NLM)

ertheless McClellan believed the Army of the Potomac was outnumbered, and he renewed his pleas for reinforcements.

While waiting for his government to appreciate his situation and support him as he believed necessary, McClellan brought up his big guns, 101 pieces of siege artillery. These weapons, he believed, would compensate for his numerical inferiority and enable the Federals to blast their way into Richmond. To his wife, McClellan explained that he planned to "make the first battle mainly an artillery combat." The artillery would "push them in upon Richmond and behind their works." Then he would "bring up my heavy guns, shell the city, and carry it by assault."

With uncanny insight into the mind of his foe, Lee wrote to Davis on June 5, "McClellan will make this a battle of posts. He will take position from position, under cover of his heavy guns, and we cannot get at him without storming his works, which . . . is extremely hazardous." To counter the Union tactics, Lee proposed "to bring McClellan out," to make the Federals fight in the open, away from prepared fortifications and big guns. First he assured himself that his defensive works before Richmond were as strong as he could make them. Then he dispatched almost four brigades to the Shenandoah Valley to provide "Stonewall" Jackson with the strength to conclude his brilliant campaign there. Lee had need of the hard-hitting Valley Army at Richmond. Finally, he sent J.E.B. Stuart and 1,200 cavalry troopers to scout the Federal right flank.

Stuart left Richmond on the morning of June 12

and rode north twenty-two miles before making camp for the night. Next day the column turned east. The Confederates encountered slight resistance as they moved, and Stuart realized that the Union right flank was unsecured. Nevertheless, he pressed on—completely around McClellan's army and back into Richmond from the south on June 15. Stuart's "ride around McClellan" made him a hero and did wonders for Confederate morale; it also seemed to confirm McClellan's fears about Confederate strength. But most importantly the venture provided Lee with valuable information regarding the Federal flank.

During the latter half of June McClellan hesitated. He considered opening an additional supply route from Harrison's Landing on the James to supplement or supplant his bases on the Pamunkey. He contemplated an all-out assault on Richmond. Eventually he decided upon a limited advance to test Confederate defenses east of the city.

Meanwhile Lee was dreaming larger dreams. On June 23 he convened a meeting attended by Longstreet, D. H. Hill, A. P. Hill, and Jackson, and announced his plans. He would station 25,000 men commanded by Magruder and Benjamin Huger in the works to the east of Richmond; these troops would have to fend off the entire Union Army if Lee's plan miscarried. The divisions of Longstreet and the two Hills would mass on the Confederate left and strike the Union right at the village of Mechanicsville. And Jackson's Valley Army by rapid and secret marches would join Lee's force and strike the Federals in the rear of their right flank. If all went well, approximately 66,000 Confederates would assault Porter's 30,000 Federals from the flank and the rear. This would "bring McClellan out" of his works and, perhaps, destroy him. If, on the other hand, McClellan realized in time the weakness of the Confederate force covering Richmond, he was capable of blasting his way into the city. The stakes of Lee's gamble were high—victory or disaster.

Lee's campaign, known as the Seven Days Battles, began on June 25 when McClellan launched his limited attack upon the Confederate lines east of Richmond. Two Federal divisions advanced upon the Southern works, tested their strength, and then threw up field fortifications of their own. McClellan believed what Lee wanted him to believe—that the 25,000 Confederates were

Stewart Van Vliet, McClellan's chief quartermaster in the Peninsular campaign. (KA)

50,000. The same day McClellan also learned that Jackson's army was on the way down from the Valley. Immediately he sent a message to Washington announcing Jackson's presence and emphasizing his peril. "I am in no way responsible . . ." McClellan insisted, "I have not failed to represent repeatedly the necessity for reinforcements . . . if the result . . . is a disaster, the responsibility cannot be thrown on my shoulders; it must rest where it belongs." Then having prepared his government for the worst and exonerated himself, McClellan hastened to Porter's headquarters.

On June 26 Lee's three divisions formed for the attack on Mechanicsville. The commands of A. P. Hill, D. H. Hill, and Longstreet formed and waited. Nothing was supposed to occur until Jackson arrived, and Jackson was uncharacteristically late. Finally, at three in the afternoon, A. P. Hill could restrain himself no longer. Acting upon the assumption that Jackson must be nearby and poised for attack, Hill began the battle. The Confederates swept across the Chickahominy and through Mechanicsville. Then they crashed headlong into Porter's lines behind Beaver Dam Creek.

The Army of the Potomac at Cumberland Landing in May 1862, preparing for the push that will take it "on to Richmond." A Wood & Gibson photograph for Alexander Gardner. (LC)

Neither frontal assault nor flank attack could dislodge the Federals. The Confederates sustained 1,484 casualties against 361 Union losses and did precisely what Lee had not wanted to do—attacked the Unionists in their prepared works.

Darkness ended the day's fighting in the Battle of Mechanicsville, and still Jackson's troops had not arrived. Actually the Valley Army reached the vicinity at five o'clock in the afternoon; then Jackson, after being unaccountably late, became incredibly cautious. He made camp within the sound of the battle. The most rational explanation of Jackson's behavior focuses upon an irrational response to stress and exhaustion. He had ridden, fought, and marched too long with too little rest. And now a "fog of war" settled over him and clouded his otherwise clear mind. On the morning of June 27, Jackson finally found the battle. But the fact that the first shells fired by the artillery of the Valley Army landed among some of A. P. Hill's troops portended more confusion on Jackson's part.

Lee resolved to continue his attack on June 27;

he had little choice. During the previous night McClellan had removed Porter's troops to a new position near Gaines's Mill on Boatswain's Swamp. The Southerners attacked in the early afternoon, and again Porter's men withstood the assault. Jackson was supposed to send his troops crashing down upon the Federal flank, but once more he was late. At last, at seven o'clock in the evening, Lee was able to assemble his army for a concerted drive. In the face of this new attack, Porter's troops, who had been repelling piecemeal assaults for five hours, broke. Confederate infantry tore through the center of the Federal lines. In desperation Union General Phillip St. George Cooke, J.E.B. Stuart's father-in-law, ordered his cavalry to charge the oncoming Southerners. The charge only added to the general confusion, however, when it degenerated into a stampede to the rear in the face of Confederate rifle fire. At Gaines's Mill, at a cost of 8,750 Confederate casualties to 6,837 Union losses, Lee won his first clear victory. Yet during the night Porter was able to cross the Chickahominy and unite his battered men with the rest of the Army of the Potomac. McClellan's army was much alive and still a potent force.

McClellan himself was unnerved, however. Fearing for his supply lines to the Pamunkey and for the safety of his army, he determined to retreat to the James and open a new base of supply at Harrison's Landing. Some of his subordinates, notably Joseph Hooker and Phil Kearny, perceived that the Confederate forces directly before Richmond were as weak as they actually were. But McClellan rejected their counsel. He gave the order for his retreat and then vented his frustration upon his superiors in Washington. He dispatched a

One of Brady's assistants captures a scene at Cumberland Landing. Over 100,000 men await the order to advance against an enemy barely half their numbers. (LC)

A panorama showing the army at camp near Cumberland Landing. (CHS)

lengthy telegram in which he explained the situation as he understood it. In conclusion he placed the blame for this circumstance where he thought blame belonged. "If I save this army now, I tell you plainly that I owe no thanks to you or to any other persons in Washington. You have done your best to sacrifice this army." Fortunately for McClellan, the telegraph supervisor in Washington did not transmit these two final sentences to the President.

Satisfied that he had absolved himself of the responsibility for his "change of base," on June 28 McClellan set about saving his army. Confederates could see the smoke from burning supplies and wagons moving to the southeast. Nevertheless Lee had to act on less than confirmed intelligence when he committed his army to an all-out pursuit. Elements of the opposing armies fought on June 28, but the major effort to cut off and destroy the Army of the Potomac began the following day.

On June 29 Magruder was finally to have the chance for offensive, instead of defensive, action. Moving east, near the old battlefield at Fair Oaks, Magruder was in a good position to strike the retreating Federals. Jackson, too, had the opportunity to fall upon the Union rear. As it happened, though, both Confederate generals failed to move fast enough or decisively enough. Jackson never really got his command into action, and Magruder advanced timidly until his troops encountered the Federals near Savage Station. There, late in the day, the Confederates attacked to no significant effect. Understandably Lee was concerned that he would lose the chance to reap the benefits of his hard-won victories thus far. Accordingly on June 30 he again exhorted his subordinates to press the pursuit. He planned to bring the troops of Longstreet, A. P. Hill, Magruder, Huger, and Jackson together for a climactic battle. Once more, however, Magruder and Jackson were slow, and Huger, too, was late. As a result, Hill's and Longstreet's divisions struck the center of the Federal Army in a battle variously named White Oak Swamp, Frayser's Farm, or Glendale. The combat raged in all three of these places, and more, and the Union line held firm amid fierce fighting.

On the morning of July 1 McClellan seemed to have made good his escape. Porter's corps and the huge wagon train of army supplies were safely at Harrison's Landing. The remaining four corps of the Army of the Potomac were drawn up on the slopes of Malvern Hill, the last position they would

have to occupy before they reached Harrison's Landing and sanctuary. The Federal position seemed impregnable. Still, Lee hoped for total victory, and so he sent Longstreet to investigate "the feasibility of aggressive battle."

Longstreet believed he had discovered locations from which Confederate artillery might catch the Federals in a devastating cross fire. Lee gave the order to mass the guns where Longstreet indicated and instructed the infantry to charge in the wake of the artillery barrage. However, the Southern artillery never got completely into place or action. Hence Confederate infantry remained in place, and it seemed that there would be no battle.

Then in the middle of the afternoon the Federals began to move; they seemed to be withdrawing. Lee ordered an immediate attack. Southern troops charged up Malvern Hill to find the Army of the Potomac very much in place. The assault was slaughter. Union artillery raked the advancing ranks, and Federal infantry blazed away at the survivors. Yet the series of charges continued until dark. And in the night 8,000 casualties littered the field, 5,000 Confederate, 3,000 Union.

Lee had seized a last chance to destroy his foe and lost. Perhaps he sensed a moment of truth which might not come again. Regardless of the reason the result was disaster.

Although no one knew it for sure at the time, the Battle of Malvern Hill was the last of the Seven Days Battles and the conclusion of the Peninsular campaign. The Army of the Potomac withdrew to Harrison's Landing to recuperate. The Confederates remained nearby for a time; then Lee left a token force and took the bulk of his army to Richmond. The campaign established Lee as savior of the Confederacy. When he took command, the Army of the Potomac was in the suburbs of Richmond; a month later the same army cowered inert under the protection of naval guns twenty-three miles away. Lee was lavish in his praise of his own army, the Army of Northern Virginia. Later in his official report, however, he admitted, "Under ordinary circumstances the Federal Army should have been destroyed."

Although out-generaled, the Army of the Potomac had fought well. The men who had stood firm against the furious Confederate assaults at Gaines's Mill, Malvern Hill, and elsewhere would be back. But McClellan, the "Young Napoleon" who molded this splendid army, had proven himself unable to command it.

Two images by James F. Gibson almost form a panoramic view of troops at Cumberland Landing on the Pamunkey River. The landing appears at right. (*left,* LC; *right,* USAMHI)

Another Gibson panorama of the camps on the Pamunkey. (USAMHI)

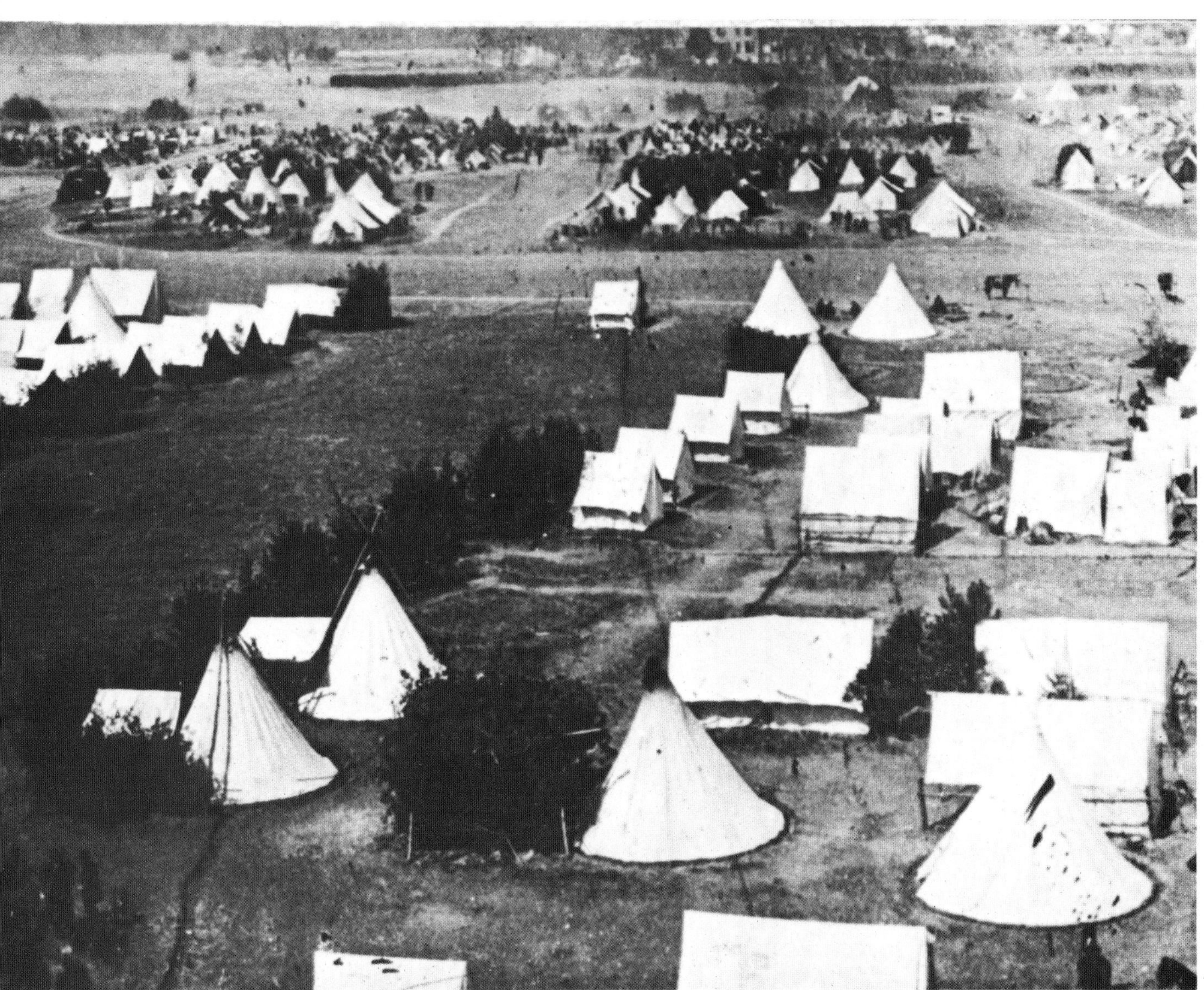

Probably Gibson's finest panorama. The enormity of an army on campaign is evident and overwhelming. (USAMHI)

In mid-May McClellan moved his base to White House on the Pamunkey, formerly the home of one of Robert E. Lee's sons. James Gibson photographed the house on May 17, 1862. (USAMHI)

And G. W. Houghton, the Brattleboro, Vermont photographer, caught this scene of the camps of the army at White House Landing. (VERMONT HISTORICAL SOCIETY)

Gibson's May 17 image of the destroyed bridge of the Richmond & York River Railroad over the Pamunkey. McClellan's people started the work of repair at once and . . . (NLM)

. . . soon it was rebuilt, though the steam engine here is on a barge. Tracks have not yet been laid on the bridge. And within a month, McClellan himself will have to destroy it once again when he retreats. (USAMHI)

George Washington was married in St. Peter's Church near White House. Now it is favored by touring Federals, including white-bearded General Sumner and his staff. (USAMHI)

Another view of St. Peter's, taken by a Brady assistant. (LC)

Contraband blacks flocked to the army's camps to become laborers and servants at White House Landing. (USAMHI)

And another sort of man gathered around the army, the romantic secret service men, the operatives and spies whose "intelligence" McClellan believed unquestioningly. The trouble was, their information proved consistently erroneous. Seated in the background, pipe in mouth, is the most unreliable of them all, Allan Pinkerton. Yet McClellan preferred to believe him since his reports of overwhelming enemy numbers confirmed "Little Mac's" own exaggerated fears. (NLM)

On the march again. David Woodbury caught men of the 5th New Hampshire and 64th New York at work on this military bridge over the Chickahominy in the last days of May, as the Federals are on their way to Seven Pines. (USAMHI)

On the battle line at Seven Pines, or Fair Oaks. Gibson's early June photo of Fort Richardson, near the Quarles House. (NLM)

Battery C of the 1st Pennsylvania Light Artillery, the extreme front line at Fair Oaks. (NLM)

Gibson's photo taken on the field at Fair Oaks, showing a fresh Union grave at left. (USAMHI)

Major General Gustavus W. Smith, center, and his staff. After the wounding of Johnston at Fair Oaks, Smith temporarily commanded the Army of Northern Virginia. (CHS)

Two old frame houses, an orchard, and a well, near Fair Oaks, where over 400 dead Federals were buried after the battle. (NLM)

Union Fort Sumner near Fair Oaks, looking toward the Confederate lines, taken by Gibson a few days after the battle. (USAMHI)

Another view of the twin frame houses beside the orchard. A central main house was meant to connect the two wings, but it was never built. (USAMHI)

Battery A, 2nd United States Artillery, by Gibson, men who fought at Fair Oaks. (LC)

While the armies fought at Fair Oaks, Professor T. S. Lowe gained a true bird's-eye view of the fight from his balloon Intrepid. *Here it is being inflated on Gaines's Hill, June 1, 1862. Lowe stands at right with his hand resting against the balloon.* (KA)

Lowe replenishing the gas in his balloon Intrepid *from the* Constitution. *Brady's assistant made a series of images of Lowe and his apparatus.* (USAMHI)

"Your message received announcing the success of Balloon and Telegraph combined—the most wonderful feat of the age." So said Thomas T. Eckert of the Union's Military Telegraph. On June 1, 1862, during the Battle of Fair Oaks, a photographer working for Brady captured the scene that made Eckert so ecstatic. Professor Thaddeus Lowe's observation balloon, probably the Intrepid, *is grounded after an ascent. From his observations, telegrapher Parker Spring is sending a dispatch over the portable field key attached to the roll of wire. Lowe may be the man in the white hat seated below him. A third man sits with his back to the camera, sketching the scene on a pad. It was a blending of two new means of rapid communications, a historic moment. "Give my compliments to Prof Lowe and Spring," said Eckert after receiving the first telegram; "if they feel as proud over the enterprise as I do, they have been well repaid and will long be remembered."* (KA)

On his way to the heavens, an officer ascends in Lowe's craft to observe the fighting at Fair Oaks. His climb is controlled by the soldiers anchoring the balloon. (LC)

Brady's assistant captures Lowe's balloon during an ascent at Fair Oaks. (BRUCE GIMELSON)

Brigadier General David B. Birney, son of the abolitionist leader James G. Birney, commanded a brigade at Fair Oaks. He was charged with disobeying an order from his superior, . . . (USAMHI)

. . . Samuel P. Heintzelman, during the battle. Birney was acquitted. (CWTI)

Brigadier General Willis A. Gorman, former territorial governor of Minnesota, shown here with his wife, commanded a brigade in Sumner's corps and won acclaim from several superiors. (NA)

And General Oliver O. Howard, who fought at Bull Run, commanded a brigade at Fair Oaks. A bullet there cost him his right arm. He still had both arms in this Brady studio portrait. (USAMHI)

And Brigadier General John J. Abercrombie, born in 1798, was still active enough to lead a brigade at Fair Oaks at the age of sixty-four. Here he was wounded, and he left active service for the duration of the war. (USAMHI)

A house used by the Federals as a hospital after the battle. Image by Gibson in June 1862. (USAMHI)

Another view of the hospital, used by wounded from General Joseph Hooker's division. Even it did not escape the battle, as evidenced in the collapsed chimney and damaged wall. (LC)

The Quarles House near Fair Oaks. Many Federal dead were interred here after the fight. (USAMHI)

Gibson's photo of the house used as a hospital by General Philip Kearny's brigade. The nondescript looking lot of men here may well be walking wounded. (NLM)

For most of the men in McClellan's army, Fair Oaks was their first real fight. One of these was McClellan's chief of cavalry, Brigadier General George Stoneman, shown here in camp after the battle. He and his cavalry took little part, in fact. (USAMHI)

Stoneman, seated at right, and Brigadier General Henry M. Naglee. The dog is nearly as photogenic as the generals. (USAMHI)

On March 18, 1862, with the threat of McClellan coming up the Peninsula, President Jefferson Davis appointed a new Secretary of War, George Wythe Randolph of Virginia. He appears here in an unpublished portrait. One of the few war secretaries to attempt to exercise real control of the War Department, he only lasted in office until November. But he worked well with the man that he and Davis chose to replace the wounded Johnston at the head of the Army of Northern Virginia, . . . (UNIVERSITY OF VIRGINIA, EDGEHILL RANDOLPH PAPERS)

. . . General Robert Edward Lee. Until now, Lee's war service had been less than glorious. Some called him "Granny Lee," and some, like South Carolina Governor Francis Pickens, doubted that his heart was in the cause. The next month on the Peninsula would answer their fears. (SOUTHERN HISTORICAL COLLECTION, THE UNIVERSITY OF NORTH CAROLINA AT CHAPEL HILL)

Ironically, Lee's opposite number in the Confederate Navy on the Peninsula was his own brother Captain Sidney Smith Lee. "There will be no interference with the naval forces under your command by the land forces serving in conjunction with you," the general wrote to the captain, expressing the hope that "the two services will harmonize perfectly." Even among brothers the age-old rivalry between army and navy had to be resisted. (WILLIAM A. ALBAUGH)

The pace of the campaign quickened when, on June 12, Lee sent Brigadier General James Ewell Brown "Jeb" Stuart on a four-day reconnaissance around McClellan's army. Lee gained valuable information, but at the price of alerting McClellan that something was in the wind. (VALENTINE MUSEUM, COOK COLLECTION)

One of the cavalrymen with Stuart, the scout who led him on his ride around McClellan, Lieutenant John Singleton Mosby. Previously unknown, he established his reputation in this war. He appears in this unpublished portrait in the uniform of a colonel. (USAMHI)

Major General Fitz John Porter and his corps were dangerously isolated north of the Chickahominy River, and late in June Lee determined to attack. (USAMHI)

A group of staff officers on the eve of the fighting on the Virginia Peninsula. The man lying at right with the dog is a twenty-two year old captain, George Armstrong Custer. He too, like Mosby, made a name for himself in this war. (LC)

Mechanicsville, Virginia, photographed in April 1865 by Gardner's assistant James Reekie. Here on June 26, 1862, was fought the second of the Seven Days Battles, when Lee attempted to strike Porter's exposed position north of the Chickahominy. (USAMHI)

Reekie's 1865 image of Ellison's Mill on the battlefield at Mechanicsville. The hottest of the fighting raged around and past this little structure as Porter successfully defended himself before withdrawing. (NA)

Confederate casualties at Mechanicsville ran high. Colonel Mumford S. Stokes of the 1st North Carolina Infantry took a mortal wound. (WRHS)

Brigadier General George Morell was instrumental in defending Porter's corps from Lee's attempted encirclement. (USAMHI)

Colonel Edward L. Thomas of the 35th Georgia took a bad wound at Mechanicsville. He recovered to become a fine brigade commander and, as pictured here, a brigadier general. (VM)

Faced with heavy numbers against him, Porter withdrew across the Chickahominy on bridges like this one on the Mechanicsville road. (LC)

Porter took a new position near Gaines's Mill, and here on June 27, 1862, Lee attacked again. Reekie's photo shows the destroyed mill in April 1865. (USAMHI)

The Gaines House. Less than two months before, Federal generals were posing for Houghton and others on this porch. Now it is Lee's headquarters. (MUSEUM OF THE CONFEDERACY, RICHMOND)

Brigadier General Andrew A. Humphreys served as McClellan's chief topographical engineer. Poor and inadequate maps plagued both sides on the Peninsula, where local traditions twist names and pronunciations. One road pronounced "Darby" was in fact spelled "Enroughty." (USAMHI)

Brigadier General Arnold Elzey—whose real name was Jones—was a hero at Bull Run. At Gaines's Mill he received a terrible wound which left him unfit for field command for most of the rest of the war. (DUKE UNIVERSITY, BRADLEY T. JOHNSON PAPERS).

Colonel James S. Connor, a veteran of Bull Run and the Hampton Legion, took command of the 22nd North Carolina shortly before Gaines's Mill. In this battle a rifle ball broke his leg. (LC)

Major General Ambrose Powell Hill performed the greatest share of the fighting for Lee at Mechanicsville and Gaines's Mill. He became one of Lee's premier commanders. (FRANK DEMENTI)

James J. Archer, appointed a brigadier just before the fighting on the Peninsula began, commanded the Texas brigade at Gaines's Mill with distinction. (P-M)

William Dorsey Pender won promotion to brigadier for his service at Fair Oaks, and now led a brigade for A. P. Hill. One of the army's most brilliant young commanders, he died as a result of a wound at Gettysburg a year later. (USAMHI)

Vermont photographer G. W. Houghton found this tent wrecked after a Confederate shell fired during the Gaines's Mill fighting struck it. (VHS)

Part of the cost of Gaines's Mill. Federal soldiers buried hurriedly in shallow graves by their retreating comrades were exposed by later rains. Reekie found them like this in April 1865. (WRHS)

On June 29 the fighting moved to Savage Station on the Richmond & York River Railroad. It is shown here the day before the battle, photographed by James Gibson. (VM)

"Prince John" Magruder had been fighting holding actions south of the Chickahominy while Lee attacked Porter. Now Lee ordered him to attack McClellan's rear. He pushed the Federal advance back to Savage Station. (USAMHI)

In the subsequent fighting, over 1,500 Federals became casualties. Here some wounded from Gaines's Mill and earlier fights await transportation to the rear at Savage Station. (USAMHI)

Vermont soldiers particularly distinguished themselves at Savage Station. Here the Green Mountain Boys of the 6th Vermont's Company I at drill. (LC)

Sick and wounded of the 16th New York being tended at Savage Station, photographed by Gibson on June 28. (MHS)

McClellan retreated to White Oak Swamp where the forces joined battle again on June 30. There in furious fighting Brigadier General George G. Meade was wounded twice in almost the same moment. (USAMHI)

Brigadier General James L. Kemper, once speaker of the house in the Virginia capital, now led a brigade in the nightmarish morass of White Oak Swamp. (USAMHI)

John Sedgwick, now a brigadier, was once major of the 1st United States Cavalry, whose colonel was Robert E. Lee. Now he led a division in Sumner's corps, but a bullet at White Oak Swamp put him out of the war for several weeks. (NA)

Major General Erasmus D. Keyes, veteran of Bull Run, commanded McClellan's IV Corps without particular distinction at White Oak Swamp. One of his brigade commanders, . . . (USAMHI)

. . . Colonel Philippe Régis Denis de Keredern de Trobriand, was the son of a French nobleman. He became one of the Union's finest brigadiers. (USAMHI)

George M. Sauerbier's image of the "Westchester Chasseurs," the 17th New York on parade. They are among many regiments mauled in the Seven Days fighting and at White Oak Swamp. (NA, BRADY COLLECTION)

The final battle came at Malvern Hill, where the retreating Federals made their stand. On July 1, 1862, Lee attacked repeatedly and with heavy losses. Regiments like the 4th Georgia, shown here in April 1861, could not move the enemy. (GEORGIA DEPARTMENT OF ARCHIVES AND HISTORY)

The 19th Georgia took part in repeated attacks. It was largely a family regiment. Standing at right is Lieutenant Colonel Thomas C. Johnson, and seated at right is Lieutenant William H. Johnson. The sergeant standing at back is R. A. Johnson, and the father of all three is seated second from the left. (EMORY UNIVERSITY, PHOTOGRAPHIC SERVICES, ATLANTA)

Despite heavy support from his artillery, commanded by Brigadier General William N. Pendleton, Lee could not break McClellan's line. Pendleton, an Episcopal clergyman, was often mistaken for Lee. When not fighting, he preached in the camps. This photo was probably taken in 1864 after the death of his son, thus the mourning band on his arm. (TONY MARION)

A remarkable J. D. Edwards image of Gaston Coppens's Louisiana Zouaves on parade in front of the general staff quarters at the navy yard at Pensacola, April 1861. Here was a real trouble regiment. "They are generally small," said a Richmond newspaper, "but wiry, muscular, active as cats, and brown as a side of sole leather." Mutinous, thieving, they never gave their superiors peace. One day's morning report a year from now would show only one man present for duty, the others being absent without leave or under arrest. But they fought like devils at Malvern Hill. The campaign almost destroyed the unit.

(SOUTHERN HISTORICAL COLLECTION, THE UNIVERSITY OF NORTH CAROLINA AT CHAPEL HILL)

What stopped Lee at Malvern Hill was the massed guns of McClellan's artillery chief, Colonel Henry J. Hunt. He gathered a hundred cannons to repel enemy assaults. (P-M)

There were no birds perched on the rammers of the 1st Massachusetts Artillery when it took part in Hunt's massive barrage at Malvern Hill. (USAMHI)

The 15th New York Engineers assisted in emplacing the guns that Hunt brought together. (KA)

Captain August V. Kautz led a company of the 6th United States Cavalry at Malvern Hill, but there was little for the mounted arm to do in this largely infantry campaign. He later became a feared Federal cavalry raider. (AMERICANA IMAGE GALLERY, CUSTODIAN OF THE RINHART COLLECTION)

Lieutenant Colonel Louis Thourot had command of the 55th New York at Malvern Hill when his colonel, . . . (WRHS)

. . . Régis de Trobriand, took over a brigade. He stands at right holding a rammer, while members of the 55th New York look on. (AMERICANA IMAGE GALLERY)

Brigadier General John H. Martindale, seated here in 1864 with his staff, reportedly declared that he would sooner surrender than leave behind his wounded at Malvern Hill. A court of inquiry acquitted him of the charge. (LC)

Defeated in his purpose to take Richmond and unable to withstand Lee's attacks, McClellan finally withdrew to Harrison's Landing on the James River, thus ending the campaign. His troops occupied "Westover," once the plantation estate of William Byrd, a remarkable Virginia gentleman of a century before. For now the war must move elsewhere. (USAMHI)

In Camp with the Common Soldiers

BELL I. WILEY

The real story of the life of the Civil War soldier; for every day in battle, fifty in camp

WHAT MOST YANKS AND REBS had in mind when they enlisted was to meet their foes in battle, and the sooner the better. Instead they learned after a while that fighting was to occupy only a small part of their army service. The long lulls between battles saw them occupied instead with drills, parades, inspections, and routine activities. However good or bad in the fight they might be, all Yanks and Rebs came to excell in "camp life."

Both in camp and on the march the first concern was food. At the beginning of the war the ration officially prescribed for both sides provided a daily allowance for each soldier of twelve ounces of pork or bacon, or twenty ounces of beef, fresh or salted; twenty-two ounces of soft bread or flour, or sixteen ounces of hard bread, or twenty ounces of corn meal; and to every one hundred rations: fifteen pounds of peas or beans and ten pounds of rice or hominy; ten pounds of green coffee, or eight pounds of roasted coffee, or twenty-four ounces of tea; fifteen pounds of sugar; four quarts of vinegar; three pounds and twelve ounces of salt; four ounces of pepper; thirty pounds of potatoes, when practicable; and one quart of molasses. This allowance exceeded that authorized in any European army. Even so, the Union government increased the allowance in August 1861 and the augmentation remained in effect until June 1864, when it was reduced to that provided at the beginning of the war. Experience had shown that the enlarged issue exceeded the needs of the soldiers and promoted wastefulness.

On the Confederate side authorities ordered a general reduction of the ration in April 1862, and later particular items were curtailed. In the autumn of 1863 Commissary-General Lucius B. Northrop reduced the bacon issue to one third of a pound, and the next year the flour or meal ration was cut to sixteen ounces. More often than not, owing to hoarding, bad management, and the breakdown of transportation facilities in the South, Johnny Rebs got considerably less food than that authorized by Northrop and his associates in Richmond.

In both armies the rations specified in regulations and the fare actually served in camp differed considerably. As a rule, Northerners enjoyed greater abundance and variety of food than did Southerners. Billy Yanks were never reduced to the low level of subsistence experienced by Rebs at Port Hudson and Vicksburg in the summer of 1863, but some of them experienced times of great hunger. Those who marched from Chattanooga to Knoxville and back late in 1863 had to subsist for

Where most of Civil War soldiering took place, the camp. Here the winter tents of the 40th Massachusetts Infantry at Miner's Hill, Virginia, in 1863. (USAMHI)

several days on corn gathered from the places where the horses fed and parched over the coals of their campfires. They experienced similar deprivation in Chattanooga before U. S. Grant and William "Baldy" Smith opened up the "cracker line" in October 1863. A Hoosier soldier wrote from Chattanooga on October 22, 1863, that for the past month he and his comrades had lived on "two meals per day and one cracker for each meal."

Mainstays of rations issued to both Rebs and Yanks were meat, bread (or the flour or meal with which to make it), and coffee. Meat was pork or beef, sometimes fresh from recently slaughtered animals, but more often salt-cured or pickled. Salt pork, widely known as sowbelly or sow bosom by the soldiers, was fried in skillets, boiled in pots, or broiled on the ends of sticks held above hot coals. It was also used as seasoning for vegetables cooked in containers suspended above campfires. Fresh beef was usually boiled. Pickled beef, commonly called "salt horse," was sometimes putrid and so briny as to make it unpalatable. An Ohio soldier wrote from camp in Maryland in 1862 that "we drew meat last night that was so damd full of skippers that it could move alone; some of them is stout enuf to cary a musket." A Mississippi Reb stated that the beef issued to his company was so rotten that "the buzzards would not eat it." An Illinois Yank wrote, "Sometimes we draw sow belly and sometimes old bull. The old bull is very good . . . but the sow belly, phew!"

The bread most often served to Johnny Rebs was cornbread, though sometimes they drew loaves of flour bread and occasionally they had hardtack. When left to their own resources they often converted the flour into hoecakes or biscuits, which they baked on slanting boards placed near their campfires. Some Rebs preferred to wrap bits of dough around a stick or ramrod and convert them into rolls by rotating them above hot coals. Many

Southerners were surfeited on cornbread. A Louisianian wrote near the end of the conflict, "If any person offers me cornbread after this war comes to a close I shall *probably* tell him to—go to hell."

Yanks rarely ate cornbread. They much preferred flour loaves baked in field ovens or prepared by comrades or black servants who cooked for companies or messes. During seasons of active campaigning and sometimes during periods of inactivity the only bread issued to them was hardtack.

Hardtack were crackers 2½ inches wide, 2⅞ inches high, and ⅜ inch thick. They weighed about 1½ ounces and were so hard that soldiers referred to them as "teeth dullers," and said they were more suitable for the building of breastworks than for human consumption. They came packed in boxes or barrels stamped "B.C.," probably for Brigade Commissary, but some soldiers insisted that the abbreviation represented the crackers' date of manufacture. Consumers often increased the edibility of hardtack by pulverizing them with rocks or musket butts, or soaking them in water. Hardtack crumbs were sometimes fried in bacon grease or mixed with soup or coffee.

Coffee, boiled in large kettles for quantity distribution or prepared individually in small cans or tin cups which most soldiers slung to their belts while on the march, was one of the most highly cherished items of camp fare. Soldiers of both armies consumed it in vast quantities. When the genuine "Rio" became scarce in the South owing to the blockade, Rebs resorted to "Confederate coffee" brewed from parched particles of corn, sweet potatoes, peanuts, or rye. Lacking sugar, they added molasses for "long sweetening." Some Rebs professed a fondness for their coffee improvisations, but their tributes reflect more of patriotism than actuality.

White "army beans" and brown Boston beans were often issued to Billy Yanks. Southern counterparts were field peas, sometimes of the black-eyed variety but more often the speckled whippoorwills.

An unpublished photograph showing the camp of the New Orleans Confederate Guards, probably in 1861, a scene that would be unusual for its neatness and well-equipped appearance by 1863. (TU, LOUISIANA HISTORICAL ASSOCIATION COLLECTION)

The 5th Vermont in camp in 1861, a G. W. Houghton photograph. (LC)

Peas and white beans were usually mixed with chunks of pork and boiled in iron pots. New Englanders liked to bake their brown beans in submerged pans surrounded by smoldering coals.

Sweet potatoes, Irish potatoes, and dried fruit were consumed in large quantities in both Union and Confederate camps. Potatoes were often baked in their skins and dried fruit was sometimes stewed and used as filler for fried pies.

Soldier life was conducive to the development of hearty appetites. Private Daniel Peck of New York wrote his sister in December 1862, "I am well and tough and as hearty as ever. I can finish twelve tack a day, three quarts of coffee, one half pound pork or beef, some dried apples & beans. But the beans punish me so I don't eat them. The foretaste is better than the after-taste."

Yanks and Rebs supplemented commissary issues with boxes of edibles of all sorts sent to them by solicitous relatives and friends at home. Delays in transit often caused spoilage of perishables, and poor packing or rough handling frequently resulted in breakage. But enough of the foodstuff reached its destination in usable condition to keep recipients asking for more.

Foraging, an army euphemism for stealing, was another frequently used source of enrichment of soldier rations. Yanks, partly because they spent most of their time in "enemy" country, were the greater offenders, but Rebs when subjected to hunger, as they frequently were, foraged freely on fellow Southerners. Pigpens, poultry houses, orchards, watermelon patches, cornfields, vegetable gardens, smokehouses, and turkey roosts were rarely immune to soldier incursions in any locality occupied by either Yanks or Rebs.

Another source of ration supplementation was the sutler who set up shop in army camps. Yanks saw more of sutlers than did Rebs because of the dearth of money among Southerners. Sutlers stocked candy, pies, cakes, pickles, canned oysters, sardines, and other edibles, along with stationery, writing pens, books, beverages, and other articles sought by their clientele. Soldiers usually regarded the sutler's prices as exorbitant, and one of their favorite diversions was to raid the merchant's tent and clean out his stock. Civilians too, black and white, residing in areas near army camps often peddled provisions to military personnel. Favorite articles of sale were pies and cakes, which purchasers sometimes referred to as "pizen cakes."

Early in the war soldiers on both sides complained frequently about the quality of their fare. But as the struggle continued and provisions became scarcer, protests centered more on quantity. This was especially true of Confederates. During the Chattanooga campaign a famished Texan of Bragg's army declared that if he ever got home he was going "to take a hundred biscuit and two large hams, call it three days rations, then go down on Goat Island and eat it all at *one meal.*"

The culinary abilities of Yanks and Rebs improved as they adjusted to soldiering and many of them boasted to civilian friends and kin that the food they prepared in camp compared favorably with that served at home. They also bragged about the proficiency acquired in laundering their clothes. On the march they had to wash their garments in streams, lakes, and ponds, as opportunity afforded, and hang them on tree limbs while they lounged naked on the banks waiting for the apparel to dry. But when settled in camp for considerable periods of time, as they usually were in winter, Rebs and Yanks often observed weekly washdays. These resembled the same occasions known at home, except that the washing was done by males with whatever facilities were at hand. Water was usually heated in pots, and clothes were soaped and scrubbed in tubs fashioned from barrels. Sometimes the scrubbing was done on corrugated metal boards, such as those used by the homefolk, but in most instances the dirt was removed by repeated dousing and twisting. Ironing was dispensed with, owing to lack of equipment and the view that wrinkles were an acceptable part of camp life.

Of all the places remembered in afteryears, it is the camp tent with all its associations that soldiers will most clearly call to mind. Lieutenant J. B. Neill of the 153rd New York sits peacefully in his tent, pictures of his wife on the table with his books, his camp cot in the shadows. Arrayed on the shelf above him are the few simple items that he carries from one field to another in this war. (USAMHI)

Colonel Henry Hoffman of the 23oth New York at his camp table, cigar in hand, clay pipe on the table. And . . . (NA)

. . . his tentmate Major W. M. Gregg at the same table. The occupant of the bed is too tired—or shy—to sit for the camera. (WRHS)

Still, practices known at home were considered ideal and in their housing arrangements soldiers were inclined to approximate them to the fullest possible extent. The shelter tents, or pup tents, used during periods of active campaigning were too small to permit much "fixing up." But larger tents, whether the bell-shaped Sibleys, the A tents, or the wall tents, which provided protection from sun and rain during relatively mild seasons when troops were not on the move, gave Rebs and Yanks an opportunity to apply their homemaking instincts. Guns were neatly stacked in the center or near en-

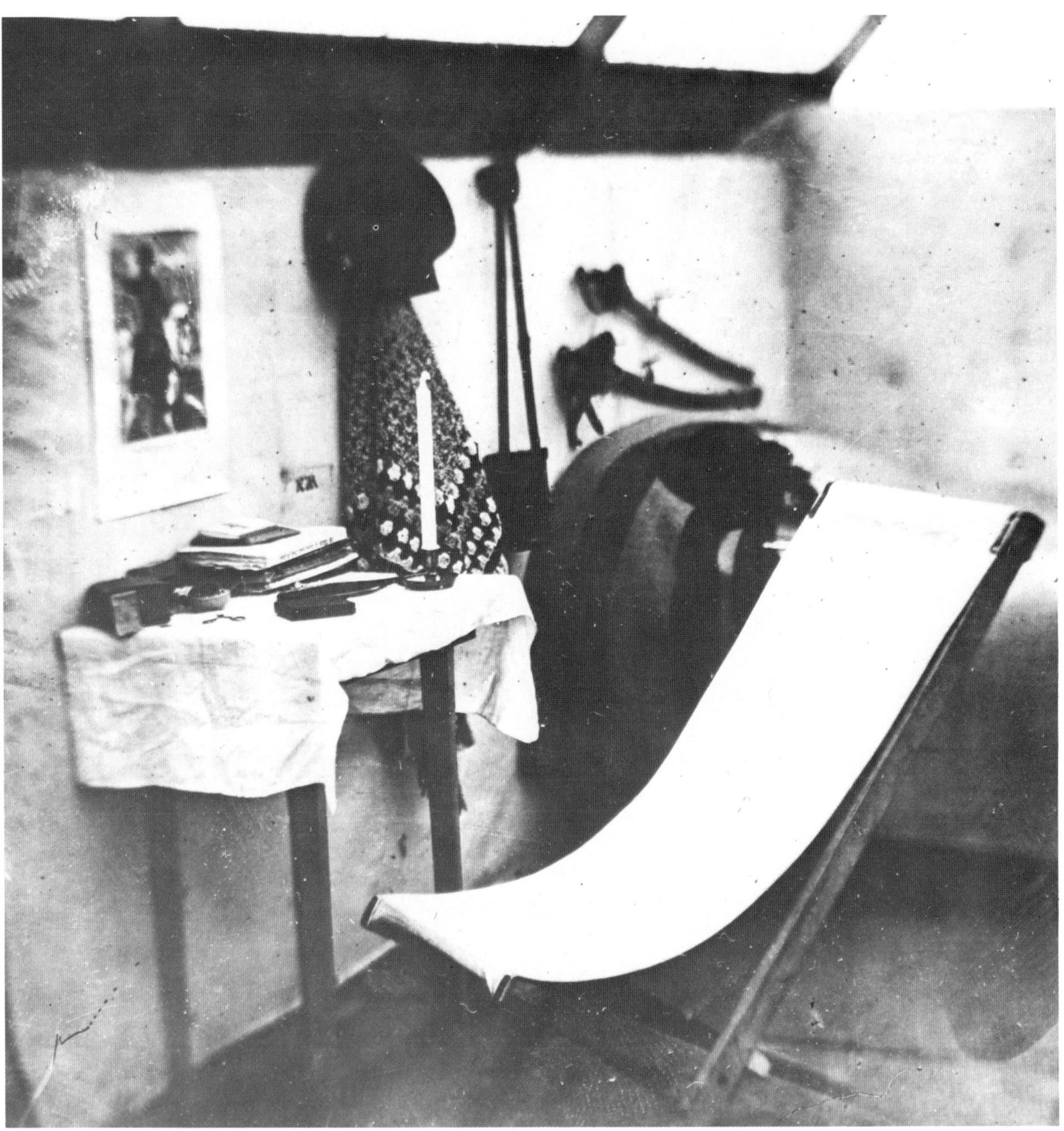

A typical officer's tent interior. Sabers, binoculars, a home-knitted shawl, a kepi, and a print adorn the canvas wall. On the table, a closed cased ambrotype, comb, candlestick, a few books, scissors, and a small sewing kit. (NA)

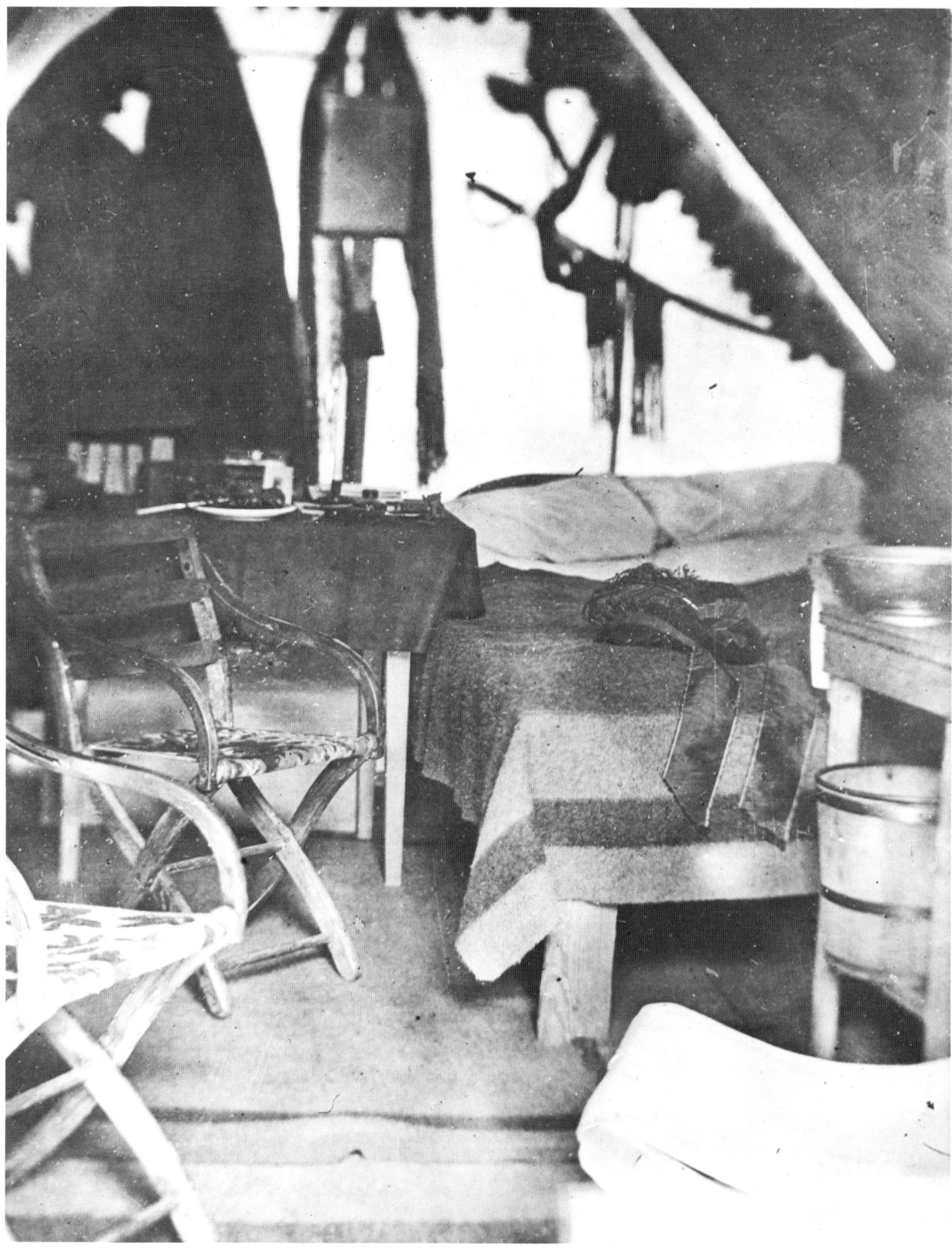

Some officers enjoyed a bit more space and luxury. The same personal and military items hang on the wall. A plumed hat rests on the bed, and the table is set for a meal. There is almost a look of permanence here. (NA)

When winter came, permanence was necessary. The 1st Connecticut Heavy Artillery builds its winter quarters in 1864. (USAMHI)

trances of canvas abodes. Bunks fashioned of boards and filled with leaves, straw, or other soft materials and covered with blankets were placed around the interior to suit the taste and convenience of the occupants. When not used for reclining, bunks served as seats. Additional seating was improvised from kegs, barrels, and cracker boxes. Tables and writing desks were made of boards "liberated" from abandoned buildings or obtained from crates discarded by commissary or quartermaster. Canteens, cooking utensils, haversacks, knapsacks and other items of equipment were suspended from tent poles or stacked on the ground. Light came from candles stuck in bayonet sockets.

Homemaking proclivities were indulged to the fullest extent in cold weather when soldiers settled in winter quarters. Winter residences were frequently rectangular cabins made of logs cut from nearby trees, dragged to the building site, notched, and put in place by the soldiers. Slanting roofs were made of boards or split logs covered with pine straw; spaces between the logs were filled with mud. A variation of the log hut was a hybrid structure part wood and part fabric, made by superimposing rectangular tents on log bases. These "winterized" or "stockaded" tents, like the log huts, were usually designed for four men. Sometimes the occupants increased roominess and warmth by excavating interiors to a depth of several feet. In some cases winter dwellings were warmed by stoves, which also were used for cooking, but more commonly heat for comfort and cooking was provided by fireplaces located usually at one end of the room. These were made of small logs chinked with mud and capped by chimneys made of the same materials. Draft was increased by topping chimneys with barrels, but these sometimes caught fire, routing soldiers from their bunks and threatening their abodes with destruction.

Some soldiers were content with floors of earth or

And moves in when they are completed. (USAMHI)

straw. Others, at considerable labor, covered the soil with split logs or with boards.

The average winter dwelling contained two bunks, one above the other, extending across the side or rear. The occupants made mattresses by filling cloth containers with pine needles, leaves, or straw. Ordinarily they placed knapsacks at the head of the bunks and suspended other equipment and extra clothing from nails or pegs driven into the walls. Seats, desks, and tables were made of logs, boxes, kegs, and barrels. Almost every company had a few fastidious members who insisted on providing their winter quarters with wallpaper and adding adornments in the form of mantelpieces, pictures, and fancy pieces of furniture.

When family or friends visited camp, as they sometimes did in the winter season, soldiers took great pride in showing off their homemaking prowess. Many described their comforts in letters to the folk at home. A Georgia private wrote his wife from camp near Fredericksburg in early March, 1863, "You would be surprised to know how comfortable a place I have to live in, a white [from snow] hous and a good fire place and a box, chunk, or the ground wich are all used for seats hear. We all take our seats, some reading, som writing, some laughing, some talking, som set up sleeping and some thinking of home. . . . Finely [finally] Mr. A. begines to tell whare he herd his first bum and how bad it sceard him and Mr. B. not to be out don tells what dangers he has pased through. Mr. C. he tells his tale. . . . Mr. E. . . . says that he thinks that he is the man that ought to have the next furlow. . . . [After a lively argument over who had the best claim to a furlough] H. commenses singing home sweet hom, all the crowd joines in and the hole wood resounds with the music."

In both winter and summer officers generally lived better than their men, and the higher the rank, with some notable exceptions, the greater their comfort. In winter they had more commodious huts, made usually by the soldiers whom they commanded, and when they lived in tents,

Whole cities of log huts dot the Southern landscape every war winter. (USAMHI)

They are Confederate as well as Union. Here Confederate winter quarters of J. E. Johnston's army at Manassas in 1862. (USAMHI)

they normally had relatively spacious wall tents. Sometimes an officer had a dwelling all to himself, save perhaps for a black servant who performed menial duties. His furniture, clothing, and food usually were superior to that of the rank and file. Normally he had no difficulty in obtaining liquor, a commodity often denied to ordinary soldiers. However, most thirsty privates were able to circumvent the prohibitions when they had funds, but the stuff that they obtained on the sly was often the rotgut variety the imbibing of which was apt to result in sobering sojourns in the guardhouse.

Camp life at its best was apt to be monotonous and lonely. Daily drills, Sunday reviews, and periodic parades increased in onerousness with the passing of time. Marches in rain and mud or in heat and dust were irksome and exhausting, and when accompanied by poor rations and polluted water, as they frequently were, they became almost intolerable. Exposure, overexertion, undernourishment, and the ravages of insects and germs produced floods of sickness, and hostile missiles added countless others to the list of the disabled. In the American Civil War the sick and wounded suffered most. Medicines and medical facilities fell far short of needs, especially on the Confederate side.

Both the ailing and the well sought diversion to combat their hardship and boredom. Music was a favorite pastime in both armies. Regimental and brigade bands often gave evening concerts at which they played sentimental, patriotic, and sometimes classical pieces. Occasionally bands would serenade officers, a practice which afforded pleasure to entire camps. General Lee, after listening to an informal band concert in 1864, stated, "I don't believe we can have an army without music." A Rebel private was prompted to remark at the conclusion of a stirring band concert in a Virginia camp, "I felt at the time that I could whip a whole brigade of the enemy." As a rule Billy Yanks, owing to the relatively greater number of musicians and instruments available in Northern units, enjoyed more and better band music than did Rebs. Some of the best music was provided by the Germans, about 200,000 of whom donned the Union blue.

In both armies the instrumental music heard

Built mostly from scavenged parts and ingenuity, these Confederate huts were good enough that Federals later used them. Manassas, 1862. (WRHS)

Union soldiers occupying once-Confederate winter houses at Centreville, Virginia. Winter, rain, and mud erased any care about who built them. "Corduroy" roads and walkways made of logs cross the mud. (LC)

most frequently was provided by individuals and small groups who brought violins, banjos, guitars, and flutes to camp with them and played informally for the entertainment of themselves and their comrades. A Mississippian wrote to a friend early in the war that he and his associates were experiencing lively times in camp. "Every night," he stated, "fiddlers are plentiful. . . . I wish you would happen in sometime while Will Mason is playing the violin & see some of his capers."

Many regiments had glee clubs who entertained fellow soldiers with a variety of songs. But, as in the case of instrumental programs, the most frequent, and probably the most appreciated vocal performances, were those given by informal groups brought together by the sheer love of music combined with a desire to entertain their comrades. A New York artillery captain wrote to a friend in 1863, "We have pretty lively times in the evenings, the Germans of my company get together and sing very sweetly and I try to join in with them."

Reading was another favorite diversion of Rebs and Yanks. What they enjoyed most was reading the letters of their homefolk. "Mail call" from company headquarters always brought throngs of eager soldiers rushing to claim missives from wives, children, parents, and friends. Arrival of mail was about the only incident that would cause men to interrupt their meals. Those whose names were called proceeded happily to some quiet spot to read and reread the latest word from home; those for whom no letters came slipped away in disappointment and envy to resume the drab routine of camp life. "Boys who will lie on their backs with hardly energy enough to turn over," wrote an Alabamian in 1862, "will jump up and hurry to

Winter quarters for some were far more luxurious. The 22nd Michigan at Camp Ella in Bishop, Kentucky, had regular barracks to withstand the cold. (GORDON WHITNEY COLLECTION)

the captain's tent to get it [mail]." A Texan wrote his wife in 1863, "I feel mightily down when the mail comes in and the other boys get letters and I don't." About the same time another Reb wrote his spouse that he "was almost down in histericks to hear from home." Yanks were less frequently disappointed than Rebs by nonreceipt of mail, because mail service in the North, owing to more and better rail and other communications facilities, was much better than in the South. Sometimes letters from rural areas of the South were not delivered in camp for several months. Slowness of Confederate postal service led correspondents to rely increasingly on personal delivery of letters by friends and relatives. Despite uncertainties and delays a large volume of mail reached its destination in both South and North. Unfortunately for the historian, only a small portion of correspondence received in camp was preserved, owing to the inconvenience of keeping it and fear on the part of recipients that it might fall into the hands of foes and become the subject of derisive comment.

Most soldiers enjoyed answering letters. A likely scene during any respite from camp duties was a Reb or Yank off to himself, with paper resting on stump, box, or knee "dropping a few lines" to the folk at home. Health was a favorite subject of comment and many a soldier complained to the homefolk of recurrent bouts with the "the sh-ts," a malady also known as "the Tennessee quick step." Correspondents almost always requested early responses and stressed a desire for information about the doings of children, the progress of crops, the condition of pets and livestock, and details of life in home and community. In the 165 extant letters that Robert M. Gill wrote to his wife Bettie in Mississippi before he was killed at Jonesboro, Georgia, August 31, 1864, one of his most frequent inquiries was about his little daughter, Callie. "Does she remember me?" he asked in one letter. "You must not whip her," he added, "I have a perfect horror of whipping children." The advice that innumerable Rebs and Yanks sent to their offspring was "mind your mother, say your prayers and don't neglect your books."

Next to letters, newspapers provided the most pleasure for soldier readers. Rebs had considerably less access to journalistic literature than did the men in blue because Southern papers did not approach those of the North in numbers, circulation, or coverage of events. Owing to scarcity of newsprint, deterioration of equipment, and inadequacy of financial resources most Southern newspapers declined in size and quality during the conflict, and some became casualties of war. The Memphis *Appeal* had to flee invading Federals so often that it came to be known as "the moving *Appeal.*" Both this paper and the Chattanooga *Daily Rebel* devoted considerable attention to military affairs and were eagerly read by soldiers of the Western armies. The same could be said of the Richmond dailies and Rebs serving in the Army of Northern Virginia. These journals were not driven to use wallpaper for newsprint as were the Vicksburg *Citizen* and the Opelousas, Louisiana, *Courier,* but all of them had their troubles. Circulation in Southern camps suffered from various circumstances including scarcity of money among Johnny Rebs and their families. Papers that found their way to news-hungry Confederates were literally worn out as they passed from hand to hand.

The war created a great boom for Northern journalism, and as circulation increased, both at home and in the army, reporters, photographers, and artists frequented camps to gather news and illustrations, and news vendors regularly made the rounds of military units and hospitals hawking the New York *Tribune, Herald,* and *Times,* the Boston *Journal,* the Philadelphia *Inquirer,* the Cincinnati *Gazette,* the Chicago *Times,* and other metropolitan dailies. Both Yanks and Rebs gave a high rating to the illustrated weeklies that thrived during the war years, including *Leslie's* and *Harper's* and the Richmond-based *Southern Illustrated News.* County and town newspapers were not often sold in camps but soldiers, and especially Billy Yanks, frequently received issues of local journals sent through the mail by publishers or homefolk.

Sometimes regiments and other units issued their own papers, and in rare instances informal groups wrote out news sheets by hand. Both printed and manuscript newspapers contained military information, poetry, gossip, and jokes. After being read in camp they were usually sent to the folk at home.

Their officers' quarters even boasted a little bit of gingerbread trim. (GORDON WHITNEY COLLECTION)

Wherever and whatever their accommodations, however, the soldiers enjoyed winter. There was little or no fighting and, with some protection from the cold, it was a peaceful time. (USAMHI)

Magazines such as the *Atlantic* and *Southern Field and Fireside* had some circulation in camp. Books of fiction, literature, and history never lacked readers in either Northern or Southern camps, but Yanks, owing to better education, more money, and superior distribution facilities had considerably better opportunity to read them than did Rebs. On both sides, but far more often in Northern than in Southern camps, soldiers had access to cheap paperback novels and joke books. Religious organizations flooded camps with tracts, most of them warning readers against the evils of profanity, liquor, and gambling. Among Rebels especially, owing to a dearth of other materials, these tracts always found readers. The most widely read book among both Yanks and Rebs was the Bible.

Religious services provided diversion for many soldiers. Yanks and Rebs often spoke disparagingly of chaplains, and there is considerable evidence to indicate that the better ministers, owing to the poor pay and the great hardships endured by chaplains, preferred service on the home front to that in camp. But "Holy Joes of the Sixties" were often sincere, dedicated individuals whose ministrations were much appreciated by the rank and file. In addition to attending Sabbath services, which usually featured the chaplains' sermons, religiously inclined soldiers often met on their own for prayer meetings led by one of their comrades. In the spring, when the season of active campaigning approached, revivals sometimes swept over the camps, but these occurred more frequently and on larger scale among Confederates than among Federals. This was due in part to the greater strength among Southerners of evangelistic denominations and to the greater religiousness of their officers, including such high-ranking leaders as Lee, Jackson, and Jeb Stuart. Interestingly, the largest and most fervent revivals experienced by Confederates came after 1862, when owing to the worsening of the military situation and the increasing prospect of exposure to death in combat, Southerners felt a greater need to seek spiritual guidance and comfort.

The religious activity that Yanks and Rebs probably enjoyed most of all was the singing of hymns. Favorites included "Sweet Hour of Prayer," "My

Faith Looks Up to Thee," "Rock of Ages," "All Hail the Power of Jesus' Name," "Amazing Grace," "On Jordan's Stormy Banks I Stand," and "There Is a Fountain Filled with Blood." Religious organizations encouraged singing by distributing pocket-size hymn books prepared especially for army use.

When opposing armies were stationed near each other much fraternization occurred. On these occasions Northern newspapers were swapped for those published in the South, and coffee was exchanged for tobacco. Sometimes trade was carried on by means of small boats equipped with sails set in such a manner as to take the vessels across river, lake, or bay separating opposing forces. Throughout fighting areas, Yanks and Rebs swam together, drank together, and even gambled together. Friendly intercourse was sometimes interspersed with communication that was not so cordial. During the siege of Vicksburg, for example, Yanks would call out to Confederates, "Say, Rebs, how do you like your new general?" Southerners would respond, "What do you mean by new general? We've still got old Pemberton." The Federals would retort, "Oh, yes you have, General Starvation." Rebs would come back with the inquiry,

These Confederates of the 1st Texas at Camp Quantico, near Dumfries, Virginia, perform their camp chores with a casual air of contentment. They are the "Beauregard Mess," and this winter of 1861–62 they will be warm. (ROBERT MCDONALD)

Some even used civilian skills to build chimneys and fireplaces. They read books and newspapers and letters from home, and they trained mascots like dogs and birds. (LLOYD OSTENDORF COLLECTION)

"Say, Yanks, have you got yourselves any nigger wives yet? Do you suppose they will improve the Yankee breed any?" The Federal taunt, "Say Reb, haint you got any better clothes than them," once provoked the response, "Who do you think we are, a set of damn fools to put on our good clothes to go out and kill damn dogs in." Then the shooting would resume.

Clowning among themselves, horseplay, teasing, and joking made soldiering more tolerable for many. A person appearing in camp in any unusual garb was almost certain to become the target of much disparagement and ridicule, such as "Come up outer them boots; I know you're in thar; I see your arms sticking out." Or, "Look out, that parrot shell that you're wearing on your head is going to explode." Unpopular officers were sometimes subjected to groans or catcalls as they walked company streets or reclined in their bunks. Some Georgia soldiers once rode their colonel on a rail, letting him dismount only when he promised better behavior.

A Federal officer stationed at Murfreesboro wrote that in March 1863, when General Rosecrans and his staff rode through a camp of Yanks living in pup tents they "were greeted with a tremendous bow-wow. The boys were on their hands and knees, stretching their heads out of the ends of the tents, barking furiously at the passing cavalcade." The general, he added, instead of becoming angry, laughed heartily and promised the barkers better living accommodations.

Impromptu diversion was afforded by the appearance of a rabbit in camp or along the route of

Music occupied the time of many, as did cards. Here in the quarters of Dr. David McKay of the Army of the James, unusual luxury is evident. Ample space in an old occupied house, a fireplace, instruments galore, all combine to make the "5 Drons" and their "Fun & Fury" quarters more than habitable. (USAMHI)

march. Sometimes the excited animal was pressed so long and so hard by yelling soldiers as to be caught. Then an argument was apt to ensue as to what individual or mess was to have the pleasure of eating the captured hare. Hunting, with or without guns, and fishing, with hooks or seines, was always a welcome diversion, not only for the fun that it provided, but also for the enrichment that it gave to issues of hardtack and sowbelly.

Sports and games flourished during periods of leisure. Football was mentioned occasionally in the letters of both Yanks and Rebs but baseball, of the four-base or two-base "town-ball" variety, was a more popular exercise. The ball was often soft and in one version of the game the mode of putting out the runner was to hit him with the ball. Bats were frequently sticks or boards. Scores sometimes were very high. In a game at Yorktown, Virginia, in

The average soldier and officer settled for much less, like the quarters of these officers of the 1st Rhode Island Light Artillery, Battery E. But still they have their books, their maps decorating the wall, and a well-stocked table. (USAMHI)

1863, the 9th New York Regiment beat the 51st New York by a score of 58–19.

Holidays such as the Fourth of July and, in Irish regiments, St. Patrick's Day, were celebrated by horse races, boxing, wrestling matches, foot races, leap frog, cricket, broad jumping, and free-for-all scuffles. These festivities were often accompanied by swigging of whiskey or beer on the part of participants and spectators, and at the end of the day guardhouses might overflow with soldiers suffering from black eyes, bruised limbs, and even broken bones.

In winter, when the weather became cold enough to coat lakes and ponds with ice, Yanks found pleasure in skating. Rebs rarely had skates or the skill of using them, but if soles were thick enough they scooted awkwardly over the ice in their shoes. Sleds, often improvised from boards or tubs, carried soldiers down snow-covered hills and merriment was enhanced by occasional spills. Snowball battles were frequent occurrences. Sometimes participants would fight in regiments or brigades, commanded by the same officers who led them in battle. Prisoners were taken and paroled, and the wounded were attended by doctors or nurses. Since contestants occasionally loaded their snow pellets with cores of rock or metal, wounds were sometimes more than superficial. Early in

Life in camp was not all relaxation. There were tasks aplenty to keep the men busy and fit. Chopping wood, sweeping, polishing boots, mending socks, and clowning all filled the idle hours. The denizens of "Pine Cottage" did their chores first, then dressed for the camera. (USAMHI)

The "Wigfall Mess" of the 1st Texas Infantry, chop their wood and carry water and wash their dishes. (THE MUSEUM OF THE CONFEDERACY, RICHMOND)

1863, near Fredericksburg, the 26th New Jersey Regiment and a Vermont unit formed a line of battle and pitched into each other with such fury that "the air was filled with white missles and stentorian cheers went up as one or the other party gained an advantage." After a series of charges and countercharges, each resulting in the taking of prisoners, "victory rested with the Vermonters and the Jersey boys surrendered the field." A Georgia Reb stationed near Fredericksburg wrote his wife in February 1863, "Some times the hole brigade formes and it looks like the sky and the hole elements was made of snow. . . . General Longstreet and his agitant took regs the other day and had a fight with snow balls but the Gen. charged him and took them prisners." A heavy fall of snow in March 1864, at Dalton, Georgia, led to a series of vigorous encounters among Rebs of the Army of Tennessee. A participant in one of them wrote on March 24, "We had a Great Battle yesterday between the 63rd and 54th Va. Regt. It lasted some 2 or 3 hours. . . . [When] the 54th was like to drive us all out of camp . . . I . . . made a charge & drove them out, kept them out until we quit. The officers of the 54th invited me over after the fight . . . to drink with them, complimenting me for Bravery." He added, "I enjoyed the sport fine but it made horse [hoarse] on account of our great charges and cheering." Another Confederate wrote that in a snow fight involving members of New Orleans' Washington Artillery, "every man in our camp, both black and white," participated and that during the fracas, "Capt. C. H. Slocomb lost two front teeth, Lieut. Challeron [got a] black eye," and five privates came out with bloody noses. Among the captured property, he added, "is the flag of the Ga. Regiment, 8 or 10 caps and Hats, 1 frying pan and 4 or 5 pones of corn bread."

Less boisterous than snowball fights but equally enjoyable were the sham courts-martial, the minstrels, and the plays staged by Yanks and Rebs. In the simulated trials, enlisted men derived special pleasure from assigning officer roles to the rank and file and finding them guilty of such offenses as neglect of duty, drunkenness, immorality, and excessive harshness in discipline. Units such as the Richmond Howitzers and Boston's 44th Massachusetts Infantry formed dramatic associations and presented plays in a manner that won hearty applause from both soldiers and civilians. The 44th Massachusetts gave a program consisting of songs by a quartet, musical selections by the band, a scene from *The Merchant of Venice,* and a concluding drama entitled *A Terrible Catastrophe on the North Atlantic R.R.*

Minstrels and comedies were the most popular of all the shows presented in camp. The 9th New York Regiment's Zouave Dramatic Club in June 1862 gave a burlesque *Combastus De Zouasio,* which a soldier observing rated as well-performed. He liked the singing and dancing and the concluding farce *Box and Cox.* He reported that the theater was crowded with local aristocrats, soldiers, and officers, among them General John P. Hawkins.

Both individuals and units derived much pleasure from pets. George Baxter of the 24th Massachusetts Regiment wrote from camp in Maryland in December 1861, "Last night I was on guard. . . . Towards morning a little black kitten came purring around my feet, so I picked her up and put her on my shoulder and continued pacing my beat, with a rifle on one shoulder and a cat on the other." In December 1863 a correspondent of the Army of the Cumberland reported, "One of the boys has carried a red squirrel through thick and thin over a thousand miles. 'Bun' eats hard tack like a veteran and has the freedom of the tent. Another soldier has an owl captured in Arkansas &

The need for wood was endless. (USAMHI)

James F. Gibson's spring 1862 image of the servants of the Prince de Joinville doing his chores for him. (KA)

named 'Minerva'. Another has a young Cumberland Mountain bear; but chief among camp pets are dogs, riding on the saddle bow, tucked into a baggage wagon, mounted on a knapsack [or] growling under a gun. . . . A dog, like a horse, comes to love the rattle and crash of muskets and cannon." Colonel Lucius Fairchild of the 2nd Wisconsin Regiment wrote from near Fredericksburg in July 1862, "We have . . . a big half bull dog . . . named McClellan & stolen from a secesh. He attends all drills . . . is always at dress parade, sometimes marches up & down in front of the regt with the band & always marches to the center with his officers & up to the Col. All this is done with becoming gravity." A Union private wrote his homefolk from Hilton Head, South Carolina, in 1862, "Co. B has got 3 pets in the shape of yong aligators . . . captured . . . in the swamp. . . . Our little dog has a big time with them. . . . Co. A has a yong coon, Co. K has a crow."

Soldiers whiled away many hours at cards, checkers, and dominoes, and almost every camp had a few chess enthusiasts. Meetings of Masons and other fraternal groups afforded diversion to a considerable number of men in both armies. Especially gratifying were the visits of wives and children, but these occasions were all too rare. The same was true of furloughs. A poor compensation for the lack of feminine association were the womanless dances at which soldiers and their bogus sweethearts whirled and stomped to fiddled renditions of such pieces as "Arkansas Traveler," "Billy in the Low Grounds," "The Goose Hangs High," "The Blue-Tailed Fly," and "Oh Lord God One Friday." These, like other social activities, sometimes were made more festive by copious draughts of "Oh Be Joyful," "Old Red Eye" and "Rock Me to Sleep Mother."

It is not surprising that many Yanks and Rebs sought relief from boredom in gambling. This was usually done with cards, and the most popular card games were poker, euchre, twenty-one, and faro. Soldiers used dice for craps and chuck-a-luck. They also gambled at keno, a game resembling bingo. Raffling was still another popular form of gambling. Rebel Sam Watkins stated that his comrades in the 1st Tennessee Regiment pitted vermin in trials of speed on tin plates. The owner of the louse that first vacated the plate was adjudged the winner. In one series of contests, one soldier's louse won so consistently as to arouse suspicion. An investigation disclosed that the winning Reb had been secretly heating his plate before each contest, thus giving his louse compelling reason to abandon it.

Gambling peaked in periods following payday. "Yesterday was Sunday," wrote a Mississippian shortly after a visit of the paymaster, "and I sat by the fire and saw the preachers holding forth about thirty steps off, and between them and me were two games of poker. . . . Chuck-a-luck and faro banks are running night and day with eager crowds standing around with their hands full of money. Open gambling has been prohibited but that amounts to nothing."

Visits to nearby towns and cities provided entertainment for many soldiers. Country lads derived special pleasure from these excursions. Zoos, large shops, tall buildings, and horse-drawn omnibuses were all new and exciting to men accustomed to a way of life devoid of all such attractions. Like soldiers of other conflicts, some of them freed for the first time from home restraints and knowing that the future was uncertain, yielded to the lure of a fling at the fleshpots. They visited grog shops and bawdy houses and in some instances paid a high price for their experimentation. The 10th Alabama Regiment, with a mean strength of 1,063, which went from the rural South in the early summer of 1861 to the environs of Richmond, had in July, according to the surgeon's report, a total of 62 new cases of gonorrhea and 6 of syphilis.

When visits to places beyond camp limits were made without leave, as they frequently were, apprehended offenders were subjected to punishment. Brief absences drew light penalties, prescribed by company or regimental commanders. These in-

The formal duties were ever-present in camp. Orderlies had to stand for inspection at the headquarters of the Army of the Potomac near Brandy Station in March 1864. (P-M)

Artillerists of the 1st Brigade of Horse Artillery, Brandy Station, in September 1863, studied their maps in off moments. (AMERICANA IMAGE GALLERY)

Signal corpsmen refined their skills, if somewhat lazily. A Brady & Company image from 1861. (CHS)

And there was always drill. (USAMHI)

cluded extra stints of guard duty, digging ditches, grubbing stumps, riding the wooden horse—a horizontal pole held aloft by two upright beams—standing in a conspicuous place on barrel, box, or stump, and cleaning company grounds. Unit commanders also punished other minor offenses such as petty theft, straggling on the march, excessive drinking, brawling, and neglect of duty. For these breaches of discipline Rebs and Yanks had to carry weights such as logs, rails, or cannonballs, wear placards specifying the offense, such as "I Stole a Shirt" or "I Am a Thief," promenade the parade ground in a "barrel shirt" with arms extending through holes cut in the sides, or wear a ball and chain, the ball being a cannonball weighing six to thirty-two pounds fastened to the ankle by a chain two to six feet long. One of the most painful penalties imposed by officers was to hang offenders by their thumbs from boughs or beams, with toes barely touching the ground for periods of time varying with the gravity of the disciplinary breach. This was a common punishment for soldiers who spoke disrespectfully to their superiors. Another loathsome punishment often imposed for "back talk" to officers and for other insubordinate behavior was bucking and gagging. This consisted of seating the offender on the ground, tying a stick in his mouth, fastening his hands together with a rope, slipping them over his knees and inserting a pole between the arms and knees. Sometimes artillery officers strapped a recalcitrant with arms and legs extended in spread-eagle fashion to the extra wheel carried on the rear of a caisson. This punishment was cruel enough when the vehicle was stationary and the soldier's head rested at the top of the wheel; but if the wheel was given a half-turn and the caisson driven over rough ground, the pain was excruciating.

Punishments of the sort mentioned above were sometimes dispensed by regimental or garrison

And more drill. (MHS)

courts-martial instead of by unit commanders. These bodies consisted of three officers, and their jurisdiction was restricted to enlisted men and to noncapital cases. They could not assess fines greater than a month's pay or impose hard labor sentences of more than a month's duration.

The most serious offenses, such as murder, rape, arson, desertion, cowardice in battle, striking a superior, and sleeping on sentry post, were tried by general courts-martial, summoned by commanders of separate brigades, divisions, and larger units. They consisted of from five to thirteen officers, and their jurisdiction extended to all types of cases including capital crimes. Army regulations authorized them to issue sentences providing for death, life imprisonment, solitary confinement on bread and water, hard labor, ball and chain, forfeiture of pay and allowances, discharge from the service, reprimand, and, in case of noncommissioned officers, reduction in grade. General courts-martial often specified a combination of legal punishments and sometimes they imposed penalties that violated the spirit if not the letter of the law, such as branding and shaving all or part of the head. The brand, stamped on with indelible ink or burned into the skin of hip, hand, forehead, or cheek, was usually the first letter of the victim's offense, such as "C" for cowardice, "D" for desertion, "T" for theft, and "W" for worthless. The Federals in August 1861 and Confederates in April 1862 enacted legislation prohibiting flogging, but these laws were sometimes ignored.

In both armies deserters, cowards, and other serious offenders who were sentenced to dishonorable discharge sometimes had their scalps shaved, had their buttons or insignia torn off, and were drummed out of camp to the tune of "The Rogue's March"—or in the case of Confederates, to the strains of "Yankee Doodle"—with soldiers fore and aft carrying arms reversed. Some capital offenders were hanged, but most Yanks and Rebs who paid the death penalty were shot by firing squads. Executions, which comrades of the condemned had to witness from a hollow square—a rectangle with one end open—made a tremendous impression. Private Thomas Warrick of Bragg's army wrote to his wife on December 19, 1862, "I saw a site today that made me feel mity bad. I saw a man shot for deserting there was twenty fore Guns shot at him they shot him all to pease . . . he went home and thay Brote him Back and then he went home again and so they shot him for that. Martha it was one site that I did hate to see But I could not helpe my self I had to do Jest as thay sed for me to doo." A Connecticut soldier reported that two of his comrades fainted while watching thirty executioners fire a fusillade that killed a deserter. Concerning an execution of six other deserters which he was forced to attend the next day, this soldier wrote that he stood within twenty feet of the victim sitting on the coffin nearest him. "They were all fired at the first time," he stated, "& 2 were killed instantly & 3 were shot the second time & the other one died while they were murdering the other three, for I call it murdering & I was not the olney one." Thomas Clark, a Pennsylvania Yank, registered no disapproval when in February 1864 he wrote his sister of the shooting of two deserters in Florida. "It was a great sight," he stated, "for it came on a Sunday and all of our regiment was out. . . . They where [were] hauled out in an opin wagon sitting on their coffins with a minister with each one of them and they looked and acted like they where going on an excursion. There was twelve men to shoot each one of them. The men was drawn up in a line nine paces from where the prisoners stood by their coffins. Four o'clock came and the order was given to fire and them and daylight was no more. There was nine balls went through one of their hearts and eleven passed through the other ones body. They did not live till the doctors came up to see if they were dead." If this report was accurate, the usual custom was not followed by loading only alternate rifles with live ammunition so that members of the firing squad might not know who fired the lethal shots. Clark attributed his indifference to the fact that the victims were recently recruited substitutes for whom "there was no pity."

Higher authorities on both sides showed a reluctance to approve death sentences. Apparently no Civil War soldier was executed for the capital offense of sleeping on sentry. Among Union forces totaling over 2,000,000 men, only 267 were executed and over half of these were deserters. Aggregate figures for Confederates are not available, but it is known that of 245 cases of court-martial convictions for desertion during the last six months of the conflict, mostly in the Army of Northern Virginia, death was prescribed in only 70 instances. President Davis's general amnesty of February 1865 set aside 31 of these sentences.

And still more. The New York Excelsior Brigade. (USAMHI)

But death, by whatever means, became commonplace to Yanks and Rebs as the war progressed. Whatever respite they obtained from it came chiefly in the society and distinctly American character of their life in the camps. There the friendships were made, loyalties built, and memories indelibly imprinted on their minds. Here, at the fire, the tent, the mess table, men North and South displayed the true commonality of all Americans in all wars.

George N. Barnard caught this company drilling amid its own quarters, behind a decidedly decorative fence. (NA)

When the drill and the duties were done, however, then came the time for food. Every Civil War soldier was an expert at eating. Here Captain James W. Forsythe—later a brigadier general—sits on the staple of the soldier diet, a box of "Army Bread"—hardtack. (NA)

Fresh bread came from the camp bakery, where the bakers let the dough rise in the sun. (INTERNATIONAL MUSEUM OF PHOTOGRAPHY)

They baked the loaves twenty at a time. (USAMHI)

And doled the loaves out to each mess's cook or servant, along with the ration of meat and vegetables. The meat was rationed by weight. (USAMHI)

No one was too bothered about sanitation. Keeping the bread in the same tent with the animal hay and letting a dog wander over both seemed not out of order. (USAMHI)

The armies brought their own herds with them, killing and butchering fresh beef daily when possible. These beef quarters have been salted and hung for drying. The salt residue lies on the boards below them. It would help preserve the beef—sometimes. (USAMHI)

Cutting the meat for the stew. Brady & Company published this image in 1861. (T. SCOTT SANDERS COLLECTION)

Doling out commissary stores at Camp Essex, weighing, carving, and—with the red tape so beloved of armies—recording who got how much of what and when. (MHS)

Weighing beef on Morris Island, South Carolina. The more tropical the climate, the more likely the soldier was to receive rancid meat—and eat it. (RONN PALM COLLECTION)

Boiled beef for the soldiers, cooked on the camp stove. (USAMHI)

Not the most nourishing meal, perhaps, but filling. Hardtack and butter on the plate, and bread in hand. Coffee would steam from the cup in good times. (LES JENSEN COLLECTION)

Like soldiers in all armies, Rebs and Yanks complained about their food. But they cooked and ate it nevertheless. (NA)

A few potatoes or other vegetables added variety to the salt pork and boiled beef. Always there was hardtack. A private of the 49th New York. (DALE S. SNAIR COLLECTION, RICHMOND)

Lieutenant Colonel F. M. Bache of the 16th United States Infantry and his mess in January 1864. He sits at left, with other members of the Army of the Potomac headquarters staff at Brandy Station. They dine well, served by a servant with a milk glass pitcher. Alexander Gardner's photograph. (USAMHI)

A noncommissioned officers' mess, Company D, 93rd New York, at Bealton, Virginia, August 1863. They dine with less style than the officers, but they still eat well. (MHS)

And the privates eat as they can, and as much as they can. Bread, hardtack, beef, and coffee are their staples. (COLLECTION OF MICHAEL J. MCAFEE)

After dinner, port and cigars for these men near Fort Monroe. (NYHS)

And now and then a picnic with sausages and bologna, cider, and sometimes chocolate. (COLLECTION OF MICHAEL J. MCAFEE)

The soldiers supplemented their uninteresting diet with delicacies bought from the sutlers—government-approved vendors—who followed the armies. Here a decidedly seedy-looking lot of them pose amid their wares of liquor and tobacco. (USAMHI)

They opened their stores wherever the tents and winter huts sprang up. Some, like A. Foulke, followed the same unit throughout the war. Brandy Station, Virginia, February 1863. (USAMHI)

The soldiers bellied up to the "bar" for their whiskey and beer. They bought Bibles and books at the same place. (USAMHI)

Fresh oysters were a real delicacy, and often not so fresh. Sutlers were frequently charged with selling rancid victuals. (USAMHI)

A "Fruit & Oyster House" in front of Petersburg in 1864. (USAMHI)

Some specialized solely in whiskey and tobacco, where the real money lay.
(USAMHI)

Others created virtual shopping centers like this area at Petersburg in early 1865. Sayer's Oyster House sold pipes, cigars, oysters, and soda water. Next door Mr. Shuz sold cakes, and his neighbor sold and repaired boots and shoes. Up on the hill sat an "Eating House," while on the left a clothier sold "Ready Made" army garments. In the center sits the wagon of Bates of New York City, who attached himself strictly to the 7th New York, and behind him stands a wholesale and retail condensed milk "depot." Behind that sits an outhouse.
(LC)

Both armies also relied heavily on "foraging," officially sanctioned theft from local farmers who were sometimes—but by no means always—paid in government scrip. G. W. Houghton captured this foraging expedition, decidedly ambitious, leaving to scour the Virginia countryside for edibles. (VHS)

More common was the individual foraging soldier, though there was certainly nothing at all common about this grinning lad, Billy Crump of Company I, 23rd Ohio Infantry. He was orderly to Colonel—later President—Rutherford B. Hayes. In February 1863 he borrowed Hayes's horse and pistol and set off from camp near Gauley Bridge in West Virginia. He traveled twenty miles in two days and came back laden with fifty chickens, two turkeys, one goose, twenty to twenty-five dozen eggs, and between twenty-six and thirty pounds of butter. Here was a good provider. (USAMHI)

Their hunger satisfied, the soldiers passed their leisure time as best they could. Reading was a favorite in both armies, and literacy was much higher than usually supposed. Those who could not read liked being read to. Gardner caught these news vendors in October 1862. (LC)

A. P. Muben, a somewhat gaily bedecked news vendor, with some of the New York illustrated weeklies so popular with the soldiers. (LC)

In Chattanooga, Tennessee, at the quarters of the 1st Engineers and Mechanics, they read and wrote letters. (MICHIGAN DEPARTMENT OF STATE, STATE ARCHIVES)

The small building in the middle, just left of the tent, is the 13th Massachusetts' library in their camp at Williamsport, Maryland. Few other regiments could boast such an establishment, yet many of the Bay State regiments were almost aggressively literate. (USAMHI)

In the camp of the 5th Georgia they wrote their letters. (JOE CANOLE, JR.)

Field post offices operated with most of the Federal armies, handling a huge volume of soldier mail. Here an unidentified brigadier general hands a letter to the postal clerk. (NA)

In winter quarters such as Brandy Station in February 1864, there were more permanent postal establishments, like this post office with a clerk perched on a mail bag. (USAMHI)

Neither snow nor rain nor gloom of night—not even the enemy—could stay the delivery of the mail to the soldiers. It was one of the single most important factors in preserving morale. Brandy Station in April 1864. (USAMHI)

Religious revivals frequently swept through the camps even faster than the mail. Devotion, as many soldiers confessed, helped fill idle hours, and sometimes local belles attended as well. Here the 50th New York Engineers built their own church before Petersburg. (P-M)

A group of IX Corps chaplains pose before their "Baltimore Cotton Duck Extra" tent, near Petersburg. (LC)

Mass at Camp Cass for the largely Irish 9th Massachusetts Infantry. Only the officers attend this service. (LC)

At Camp Griffin, Virginia, the 49th Pennsylvania worships as Chaplain Captain William Earnshaw uses stacked drums for an altar. (LLOYD OSTENDORF COLLECTION)

Father Thomas H. Mooney performs Sunday Mass for the 69th New York. Its colonel, Michael Corcoran, stands with folded arms just left of the cleric. Both North and South claimed divine endorsement. (LC)

When chaplains like this one found themselves conducting services in the presence of shot and shell and weapons of destruction, some were inclined to question whether the deity could possibly condone either side. Fort Darling in April 1865, the chaplain's quarters of the 1st Connecticut Heavy Artillery, photographed by J. Reekie. (LC)

With reading and religion exhausted, the soldiers turned to sport. Many opted for something cerebral like chess, but most, like those at the left, preferred cards. (USAMHI)

Gambling filled the long hours of boredom, and not a few pockets as well. Officers of the 82nd Illinois in camp at Atlanta, Georgia, in 1864 gambled with ease and comfort. Outrageous pipes, often handmade, were also the rage in the Western army. (CHS)

For the common soldiers, a blanket and a deck of cards were the only necessities. These sergeants belong to the 56th Massachusetts. (USAMHI)

A cockfight could also provide entertainment of a gruesome sort, and plenty of money changed hands on a rooster's feet. Even the brass took part. Brigadier General Orlando B. Willcox affects disinterest, looking at a letter, but he cannot help glancing at the start of a fight staged by former slaves George, on the left, and John, and their chickens. Taken at Petersburg in August 1864. (USAMHI)

When gambling failed there was always horseplay, often at the expense of the poor freedman. (LC)

A friendly spar for the camera was a favorite picture to send home. Boxing in camp, however, did not enjoy wide popularity. There was too much real fighting to be done. (DON W. MINDEMANN)

Their funning could take a macabre turn at times. Being so close to death, it helped to make fun of it. (T. GORDON, JR.)

Shamming for the camera was a favorite, and drinking seemed always the chosen topic, perhaps because it was so important a release for the soldiers. An excellent series ranging from the first toast in "Here is to the gal I love," to "Over the Bay," "Going Home," and finally "Good Night." Taken probably by H. Skinner of Fulton, New York, in 1862. (COLLECTION OF WILLIAM WELLING)

Whenever possible, however, camp life was mostly for relaxation. It was a picture that did not change no matter the year, the place, or the army. J. D. Edwards caught these men of the Perote Guards at Pensacola drinking, reading, drawing, gambling. It was a never-ending scene. (TU)

Edwards found the same scene with the 9th Mississippi in April 1861. (MUSEUM OF THE CONFEDERACY, RICHMOND)

General Robert O. Tyler and his staff presented much the same image two years later in Virginia. Tyler stands second from the right. (USAMHI)

Many fortunate officers North and South were joined in winter quarters by their wives, adding a dimension of domestic tranquility denied to most soldiers. (P-M)

Wives and daughters quickly became a focal point for attention, many men vicariously paying favor to loved ones at home through women with the armies. (USAMHI)

Many read and wrote letters for illiterate soldiers. Some, like the lady on the porch, even brought their babies. Hers has moved during the exposure, causing the blur with feet in her lap. (USAMHI)

The women's presence helped their men forget for a time that they were at war, especially when they had quarters like these in a casemate at Fort Monroe. (USAMHI)

The younger and prettier maidens became the belles of the armies, the object of every single officer's suit. This young lady attracts a host from an Illinois battery at Chattanooga in 1865. (CHS)

For one of these soldiers of Company G, 95th Illinois Infantry, camp life was more than exotic. It was a constant tension as he attempted to conceal a perhaps scandalous secret. For the soldier on the right, Private Albert Cashier, is in fact a woman. Born in Ireland, her feminine name was Hodgers, but all her life she was known as Albert J. Cashier. She not only successfully maintained her pose, serving well particularly at Vicksburg, but she eluded detection until 1911 when an automobile caused her hospitalization. It took a twentieth-century machine to expose the life-long sham of a patriotic woman who for so long fooled the men of her own century. (SPENCER H. WATTERSON, PONTIAC, ILLINOIS)

The soldiers made their camps as much like vacation spots as they could. The quiet moments were the best, like this one caught by Gardner in 1865. (P-M)

Intimate friendships made in camp lasted for life. Brevet Major General Charles H. T. Collis sits at left with a friend. He won the Medal of Honor for Fredericksburg. (NYHS)

Confederates like these of the 1st Texas at Camp Quantico, Virginia, in the winter of '61, formed especially firm associations, bound tightly together by the shared hardships of the later war years. This recently discovered image is published here for the first time. (ROSENBURG LIBRARY, GALVESTON, TEXAS)

The fellowship . . . (TONY MARION)

. . . the outrageous sense of fun . . . (KA)

. . . and the smiles of friends made the most memorable of war experiences. Smiling soldiers like Lieutenant John G. Hecksher of the 12th United States Infantry, at left, are rare indeed in Civil War photographs. The men preferred the more somber—nay, glum—aspect of his friend Captain William Sergeant. (P-M)

Camp life was for the generals, too, and they usually enjoyed it even more than their men. Brigadier General George Stoneman sits astride his charger watching men build their winter quarters—or his. (USAMHI)

Major General John Sedgwick, left, sits with Brigadier General George Washington Getty, seated at right, at their Brandy Station tent. (USAMHI)

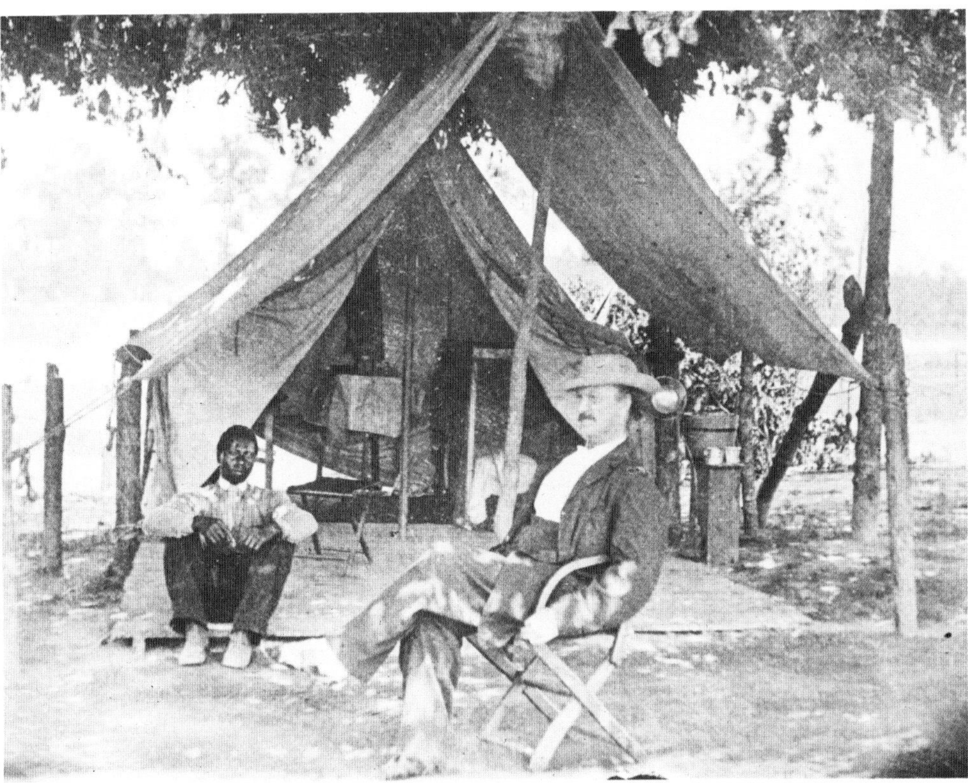

Major General Israel B. Richardson and servant pose in the summer shade in 1862. (USAMHI)

Brigadier General John A. Rawlins, Grant's chief of staff, was joined at City Point, Virginia, by his family in 1864. (USAMHI)

Brigadier General Marsena R. Patrick lived alone, as befitted Grant's chief policeman, provost-marshal general of the Army of the Potomac. (P-M)

Brigadier General Thomas W. Sherman lived in tropical tranquility on Hilton Head, South Carolina, when H. P. Moore took this image on March 8, 1862. (USAMHI)

Brigadier General Edwin V. Sumner was not so old he could not enjoy paying court to a young belle visiting camp. (LC)

And their entertainments were much the same as those of the men they commanded, including even an occasional sleigh ride. Here at Port Hudson, Louisiana, in January 1864, Brigadier General Cyrus Hamlin—son of Vice President Hannibal Hamlin—sits with a companion in the small one-horse sleigh at left. Behind him are the officers of the black regiment he was raising. (USAMHI)

Music proved a pleasant diversion for all. Here a member of the band of the 26th North Carolina Infantry, with his horn. (DALE S. SNAIR COLLECTION, RICHMOND)

Members of the band of the 26th North Carolina, missing only their compatriot of the previous image. Taken at Salem, North Carolina, around 1862. (MORAVIAN MUSIC FOUNDATION, INC.)

This Tennessee fiddler could enliven the coldest winter camp with the "Bonnie Blue Flag" or "Dixie." (TENNESSEE STATE MUSEUM)

Now terribly faded, this image of members of the Washington Light Infantry of Charleston once revealed the words "Music Hall" on the tent wall. A bugler stands at left and the soldier seated second from the right cradles a violin in his lap. This March 1861 photograph is ample evidence that music went to the camps with the very first Confederates. (WASHINGTON LIGHT INFANTRY, CHARLESTON, SOUTH CAROLINA)

Special ensembles like this group, with tambourine, banjo, guitar, violin, triangle, and bells, sprang up informally from among the members of several regiments. (T. SCOTT SANDERS COLLECTION)

The bands played for all sorts of occasions, the saddest being funerals and farewells to favorite generals being transferred to other commands. The band at left here serenades Major General Frederick Steele as he leaves Arkansas for another post, probably at the end of the war. Steele is standing second from the left between the columns immediately behind the band. (RONN PALM COLLECTION)

A typical Federal regimental band, this one composed of Pennsylvanians, photographed by S. R. Miller. (RONN PALM COLLECTION)

A concomitant to music was dramatics. This engineer battalion formed its own theatrical club, the "Essayons Dramatic Club," giving performances in a theater of their building at Petersburg in 1864. (USAMHI)

Photographers McPherson & Oliver took this image in Baton Rouge in 1863. It shows an improvised theater which at the moment is advertising a "Benefit to Lieutenant M. W. Morris" and presenting the Lady of Lyons and a Favorite Farce. (ILLINOIS STATE HISTORICAL LIBRARY)

Fraternal orders, chiefly the Masons, came with the army. Here Samuel Cooley photographs an improvised "temple" on Folly Island, South Carolina. (USAMHI)

Building and elaborate decoration occupied some, especially the ever-industrious 50th New York Engineers, who made their Petersburg headquarters a virtual arbor. (USAMHI)

The men trained pets, like the nationally famous "Old Abe," mascot of a Wisconsin regiment with whom it lived through the war. In battle the eagle would fly from its perch and remain aloft until the fighting subsided. (LC)

Dogs were the favorite. This one is supposed to be saying, "I am the dog that went through the army with the 25th Iowa Infantry." (CHICAGO PUBLIC LIBRARY)

And, of course, with idle time on their hands, the men would misbehave. That is where the provost came in. Here the Army of the Potomac's provost marshal's camp at Bealton, Virginia, in August 1863. (P-M)

Wherever the army went in numbers, so the provost went also. Mostly the men drank too much or disobeyed orders. (NA, U. S. WAR DEPARTMENT GENERAL STAFF)

When they did, the provost guard spirited them away to the guardhouse. Here the guard for the Army of the Potomac headquarters at Petersburg in 1865. Behind them is the picketed fence of their stockade. (USAMHI)

Minor offenders were fined pay or made to ride the wooden horse and other such essentially humiliating punishments. (ROBERT L. KOTCHIAN)

More serious cases spent time at hard labor in the heavy stockades like this United States Military Prison yard at Chattanooga. (NA, U. S. WAR DEPARTMENT GENERAL STAFF)

The worst cases went before courts-martial like this one meeting at Concord, New Hampshire. (USAMHI)

Another court-martial, at Chattanooga. If the offense was grave enough . . .
(TERENCE P. O'LEARY, GLADWYNE, PENNSYLVANIA)

. . . so was the punishment. Troops stand drawn into a three-sided square to witness a hanging near Petersburg in 1864. The mounds of earth right of the gallows mark the grave of the condemned already dug. (LC)

And like soldiers everywhere, the men of blue and gray loved to celebrate holidays. Here a Christmas feast appears ready for the men who will tightly jam the benches. Turkeys sit on the tables as well as relishes. The hot vegetables will be brought out and served, and every plate has a slab of bread or cake. (NA)

Another wreath-bedecked hall for Christmas. These diners will be a little less crowded. (USAMHI)

Washington's birthday, February 22, was a holiday in both North and South, and here the "New Forage House" ballroom in Beaufort, South Carolina, stands ready for an 1864 observance. (WRHS)

The speakers' stand for the Beaufort celebration, with flags and bunting aplenty. (USAMHI)

The Fourth of July was the greatest of all in the Union armies, and even some Confederates celebrated the day. Here the 50th New York Engineers revel in the day on July 4, 1864. Joining them, and seated at the extreme left, is Charles Francis Adams, Jr., historian, grandson of President John Quincy Adams, and future president of the Union Pacific Railroad. (USAMHI)

The Conquest of the Mississippi

CHARLES L. DUFOUR

The great river spawned great men to contest her waters

THE USS *Brooklyn* dropped anchor off the mouth of the Mississippi at 2 P.M. on May 26, 1861, and the Union conquest of the great river, so vital to the Confederacy, was underway.

It was the first implementation of General Winfield Scott's "Anaconda Plan," the purpose of which was not only the military envelopment of the Confederacy but its economic strangulation as well. As early as May 3, Scott had discussed his plan with General George B. McClellan, pointing out that a powerful Union movement, by land and by water, down the Mississippi together with an effective blockade of the river's mouth would "envelop the insurgent States, and bring them to terms with less bloodshed than by another plan."

The effectiveness of the Union blockade was almost immediately felt in New Orleans, the Confederacy's greatest city. On May 30, 1861, a ship loaded with Brazilian coffee was captured by the *Brooklyn* and the next day another New Orleans-bound vessel carrying foodstuffs was seized. From the moment the blockade was established, not a single ship reached the Confederate city until Farragut's attacking fleet ran past Fort Jackson and Fort St. Philip in April 1862. Although the Union blockading vessels prevented ships from entering the Mississippi, the river's five passes into the Gulf of Mexico offered avenues of escape to blockade-runners from New Orleans and several did make it to sea. The most significant escape was that of the Confederate raider *Sumter* commanded by Raphael Semmes, later of *Alabama* fame, which eluded the blockade on June 30 to prey relentlessly on American commerce vessels for more than six months.

The Confederate government was slow to realize the defenselessness of New Orleans and the absolute necessity of making an all-out effort to prepare the city for invasion. Four months after Louisiana seceded from the Union, a general officer had not yet arrived in New Orleans to take command. During that time, the city had been drained of troops; they had been ordered to Pensacola to reinforce Braxton Bragg. On April 10, two days before the guns sounded at Charleston, Governor Thomas O. Moore of Louisiana complained to Confederate authorities, "We are disorganized, and have no general officer to command and direct." Seven weeks went by before seventy-one-year-old General David E. Twiggs, veteran of more than half a century in the United States Army, reached New Orleans to take command.

Although the Common Council of the City of New Orleans praised Twiggs's "integrity, sagacity,

The USS Brooklyn, *the first ship to go on blockade off the mouth of the Mississippi. The warship and the river were to see a lot of each other in the years to come.* (NA)

and nerve so essential to a commander," it soon became evident that the enfeebled septuagenerian general was not the man to defend the South's greatest city from Federal attack. President Davis had already received complaints of the "infirmities of General Twiggs," when Governor Moore's plea for "an officer . . . who, with youth, energy and military ability, would infuse some activity in our preparation and some confidence in our people," reached Richmond in September. In closing this appeal to Davis, Moore begged that "this city, the most important to be preserved of any of the Confederacy, and our coast, the most exposed of all the states, be no longer neglected."

President Davis finally conceded that General Twiggs "has proven unequal to his command," but he shifted the blame for Twiggs's appointment to the people of New Orleans: "As in his selection I yielded much to the solicitation of the people of New Orleans, I think they should sooner have informed me of the mistake they had made."

When Major General Mansfield Lovell was assigned to New Orleans, Twiggs got the implied message and prevented an awkward situation by asking, on October 5, to be relieved from duty for reasons of health. Before leaving for New Orleans, Lovell conferred with both President Davis and Secretary of War Judah P. Benjamin and, with almost prophetic insight, declared that the only proper defense of New Orleans would require a unified command. He argued, but in vain, that the employment of naval as well as army forces should be under his direction. Fearing that Lovell had not fully understood the definition of his command responsibilities, Davis hurried off a letter to him stating, "The fleet maintained at the port of New

Major General Mansfield Lovell would never be fully appreciated in the Confederacy for his talents. Rather, he would be remembered as the man who lost New Orleans. (USAMHI)

Orleans and its vicinity is not a part of your command." This decision would prove fatal.

Lovell reached New Orleans on October 17 and found, as he reported to Richmond, "great confusion, irresolution, and want of system in every thing administrative." New Orleans was "almost entirely stripped of everything available in the way of ordnance, stores, ammunition, clothing, medicines etc." There existed a frightening shortage of powder, Lovell reported. So he established two powder mills in New Orleans, and moved a third mill from the Mississippi coast to the city.

Before leaving Virginia, Lovell met with his old army friend General P. G. T. Beauregard, a native of New Orleans who, for ten years before the war, had been in charge of the defenses of Louisiana. Beauregard reiterated to Lovell what he had told Louisiana authorities many months earlier, that Forts Jackson and St. Philip, miles downriver from New Orleans, could not prevent steam vessels from passing unless an obstruction in the river held the ships under the cross fire of the forts for half an hour. Such a barricade, talked about in February but not constructed until the summer, had been in place about a month when Lovell reached New Orleans. After inspecting this so-called raft, Lovell undertook to strengthen it.

On arrival, Lovell heard much of a recent Confederate naval victory at the Head of the Passes where a bold attack on a Yankee squadron routed it in what David Dixon Porter later described as "the most ridiculous affair that ever took place in the American Navy."

The heroes of this exploit were Commodore George Hollins and the ironclad *Manassas,* popularly known in New Orleans as the "Turtle." The latter, originally the twin-screw tugboat *Enoch Train,* had been purchased by a syndicate of businessmen for conversion into an ironclad to operate as a privateer against the blockaders. The cigar-shaped *Manassas,* covered with railroad iron three quarters of an inch thick, mounted one gun, which operated through a trapdoor forward. It had a

David D. Porter did heavy duty on the Mississippi. At the outset of the war, however, he ridiculed the Confederate success at Head of the Passes as a "ridiculous affair." (USAMHI)

Commodore George N. Hollins, who led the successful Confederate attack on the little Union squadron at Head of the Passes. (LSU)

heavy cast-iron prow, which extended below the waterline so that the vessel could operate as a ram.

Although the project was supposedly a secret one, reports of the "formidable instrument of destruction" the Confederates were building at New Orleans slipped into the Northern press. Fantastic stories, born of imagination and misinformation, told that the *Manassas* was equipped with a powerful auger which could bore holes in a ship below its waterline and that this "hellish engine" had twenty-four hoses with which boiling water could be played upon the crew of an enemy ship. The "Turtle" was, in fact, much more formidable in the Northern press than it proved in the water. Nevertheless, its owners had high hopes that, operating as a privateer, the *Manassas* would reap a rich harvest of prize money by capturing Union blockade vessels. But hardly had the *Manassas* been launched and given its trial runs than Commodore Hollins seized it for the Confederacy against the protests of the syndicate.

On the night of October 11–12, 1861, Hollins's little flotilla, consisting of the *Manassas, McRae, Ivy, Calhoun, Tuscarora, Jackson,* and *Pickens*—New Orleanians called it the "mosquito fleet"—attacked a Union squadron of four warships under Captain John Pope at the Head of the Passes, where the various mouths of the Mississippi leave the main stream.

What followed was a comic opera of naval warfare. The *Manassas* rammed the *Richmond,* and the ten-knot impact disabled the Confederate ironclad while causing panic aboard the Union flagship. In the confusion and darkness, three Union ships, *Vincennes, Preble,* and *Waterwitch,* on signals from Captain Pope, slipped their cables and began steaming down Southwest Pass, and the *Richmond* followed. A running fight of no actual consequence ensued, but the aftermath was farcical after the *Vincennes* ran aground on the bar. Commander Robert Handy, believing erroneously that Pope had ordered him to abandon ship, did so after ordering the lighting of a slow fuse to the magazine. Fortunately, a Union quartermaster, after lighting the fuse, cut off the burning end and tossed it into the river, and the *Vincennes* was thus saved. "Pope's Run" as the incident became known, was later characterized by Admiral Alfred T. Mahan as "a move which brought intense mortification to himself [Pope] and in a measure to the service."

Fully believing that he had sunk a Union vessel (he announced it as the *Preble*) in this weird affair at the Head of the Passes, Hollins hurried back to New Orleans with the morale-building news of a great victory. But the expedition had little significance beyond creating popular enthusiasm. Elise Ellis Bragg, writing her husband, General Braxton Bragg, said, "Our 'Turtle,' alias *Manassas* made a grand charge and would have done wonders if it had not been disabled. All these things make a sensation, but I fear they help our cause but little, and a dark and gloomy winter seems closing around us."

When General Lovell arrived, New Orleanians were still talking enthusiastically about the action at the Head of the Passes and also of the two giant ironclads *Mississippi* and *Louisiana,* which were under construction just above the city, and which were expected to be in operation in January.

The CSS McRae, *part of Hollins's "fleet."* (NHC)

The USS Richmond *was rammed by Hollins's ironclad* Manassas, *an action that did more damage to the ironclad than to the Federal warship. The* Richmond *served continually on the river in the years to come.* (NHC)

Ironclads were of interest to the Union naval authorities on the Mississippi. Captain John Rodgers was sent by the Navy Department to supervise the construction of the Benton-*class gunboats at Cairo, Illinois.* (NA, U. S. WAR DEPARTMENT GENERAL STAFF)

Meanwhile, the first Union preparations on the upper Mississippi had been made on August 2, when James B. Eads of St. Louis was authorized to construct seven ironclad gunboats of a new type for use on the western rivers. Three river steamers, the *Tyler, Lexington,* and *Conestoga,* had been converted into gunboats, and they became the nucleus of the Union naval forces on the Mississippi until Eads's ironclads were completed.

On October 7, the gunboats *Lexington* and *Tyler,* on a reconnaissance from Cairo, steamed toward Lucas Bend, Missouri, to engage Confederate shore batteries at Iron Bluff, not far from Columbus, Kentucky. On October 12, the same date of the ignominious "Pope's Run" from the Head of the Passes, the *St. Louis,* first Federal ironclad, was launched at Carondelet, Missouri.

Initial land operation by Union forces on the Mississippi proved abortive. On November 7, Brigadier General U. S. Grant descended from Cairo with 3,000 troops on transports supported by two wooden converted gunboats. Landing on the Missouri side, Grant seized the village of Belmont, across the river from Columbus, Kentucky. Grant held Belmont until Confederate reinforcements from Columbus crossed the river, and then he regained his transports and steamed back to Cairo.

Before 1861 ended, the first significant operation concerned with the conquest of the Mississippi occurred when 1,900 Union troops under Brigadier General John W. Phelps landed on Ship Island, in Mississippi Sound, twelve miles off the mainland and sixty miles from the mouth of the Mississippi.

With the coming of the new year, Union efforts on the upper Mississippi were stepped up. On January 14, three Union gunboats descended to the vicinity of Columbus and shelled Confederate encampments along the river. After the fall of Forts Henry and Donelson early in February, 1862, Columbus became the prime Union objective in the West. The Confederate government, recognizing its extreme vulnerability, ordered the evacuation of Columbus on February 20. Withdrawal of troops, guns, and material began at once and by March 2 the evacuation was completed. All but two of Columbus's 140 guns were moved south to Island No. 10 and its adjacent batteries. The next day, as Federal troops occupied Columbus, another force under General John Pope laid siege to New Madrid, Missouri. After a heavy bombardment of their works on March 13, the Confederates slipped out of New Madrid the next day and retreated to Island No. 10, leaving behind a substantial amount of guns and supplies.

Island No. 10, so named because it was the tenth island in the Mississippi south of its confluence with the Ohio, was assumed by the Confederates to be impregnable. Situated in Madrid Bend, between Tennessee and Missouri, Island No. 10 commanded the river in both directions. Earthworks, constructed for two miles along the banks, made Island No. 10 formidable for an attacking fleet, while virtually impassable swamps made a land attack on Island No. 10 unfeasible.

When Pope seized New Madrid, the Confederate naval force—six gunboats under Commodore Hollins—found itself much outgunned and withdrew to Tiptonville, thirty miles below Island No. 10 by river, but less than five miles by land. The

Naval stations at places like Mound City, Illinois, were organized and readied to construct new ships as well as to refit and repair those already in service. (WRHS)

Mound City remained in a bustle of activity during most of the war. (LC)

stage was now set for a combined army and navy operation against Island No. 10, with Pope attacking by land while Commodore Andrew Foote's flotilla, headed by Eads's formidable ironclad *Benton,* most powerful warship on the Mississippi, engaged the Confederate bastion from the river. While Pope was impatient to begin operations against Island No. 10 as soon as New Madrid fell, it was not until March 14 that Foote's flotilla left Cairo for the fifty-mile run down to Island No. 10. With seven gunboats and ten mortar vessels, and transports carrying troops to occupy Island No. 10 after its capture, Foote dropped anchor two miles from the Union objective on the morning of March 15. The next day, Foote's mortars opened fire on the Confederate works and on March 17 the *Benton* and Foote's other ironclads went into action, at a range of 2,000 yards.

Meanwhile, Pope had realized he needed transports to get his troops across the Mississippi if the joint operation were to be successful. In an official request, he promised that if Foote were to ". . . run past the batteries of Island No. 10 with two or three gunboats and reach here, I can cross my whole force and capture every man of the enemy at Island No. 10 and on the mainland." Foote immediately rejected Pope's proposal.

Pope's chief engineer, Colonel Josiah W. Bissell, then proposed that a canal be dug through the overflowed swamps to bypass Island No. 10. Pope approved the project when Bissell assured him that he could open a way for vessels of light draft to cut across the neck of land. He authorized Bissell to employ his entire regiment to open the canal. Working feverishly for nearly three weeks, Bissell cut a twelve-mile-long channel, fifty feet wide.

Before Bissell's canal was ready, Foote had a change of mind when Henry Walke, commander of the *Carondelet,* volunteered to run his ship past Island No. 10's batteries. In a thunderstorm on the night of April 4, the *Carondelet* ran the fiery gauntlet and reached New Madrid at midnight, a few hours after Bissell's engineers had completed the last stretch of the canal. Three nights later, during another storm, the *Pittsburg* ran past Island No. 10's guns and anchored at New Madrid. The same night, four shallow-draft steamers passed through Bissell's canal to provide Pope with the transports he needed to get his troops across the river to assault Island No. 10 from the rear.

Island No. 10 had been subjected to constant fire from Foote's ships, and a bold Union raid on April 1 by soldiers landing from small boats had succeeded in routing a Confederate guard and spiking six guns—driving soft nails into their touchholes so they could not be fired. Now, with a two-pronged all-out attack imminent, the Confederates began the evacuation of Island No. 10 on April 7. Retreat, however, was futile and seven thousand Confederates, including three generals, hemmed in by Union troops and the swamps, surrendered. On the same fateful date that Island No. 10 fell, the Confederate Army at Shiloh, having been repulsed in the second day's fighting, was preparing its retirement back to Corinth.

With Island No. 10 in Union possession, the only Confederate stronghold on the Mississippi above Memphis was Fort Pillow in Tennessee. Situated on bluffs about eighty miles upstream from Memphis, Fort Pillow consisted of a line of fortifications extended for seven miles along the river. Foote lost no time in putting Fort Pillow under fire and on April 14 he shelled the Confederate works as a preliminary to what he expected to be another combined operation. To Foote's surprise, however, Pope's troops were ordered to Pittsburg Landing, thus making impossible a joint army-navy movement against Fort Pillow.

Meanwhile, at the lower end of the Mississippi, Flag Officer David Glasgow Farragut was readying his campaign against New Orleans. Listed at thirty-seventh among navy captains, Farragut, a vigorously active sixty-year-old, had been in the service for more than half a century. As a boy, he

Its shops and ways echoed to the sounds of machinery and workmen. Here, in the foreground, blocks and tackle and lines are visible on the bank where ships were hauled out of the water for hull-scraping and repair. (USAMHI)

Tugboats like the little Daisy *plied the river constantly off Mound City.* (NHC)

was a midshipman in the War of 1812, and in the Mexican War he served on blockade duty. Secretary of the Navy Gideon Welles was impressed with Farragut, finding him "modest and truthful . . . self-reliant and brave," and decided he was the man to capture New Orleans. He summoned Farragut to Washington from a desk job in New York in December 1861 and offered him command of the New Orleans expedition.

Early in April, forty-seven days after he reached Ship Island to organize his expedition, Farragut had installed himself at the Head of the Passes with a formidable fleet of 17 warships with a total of 154 guns; a mortar flotilla of 20 schooners, each with a 13-inch mortar and a total of 30 guns; and 7 steamers with 27 guns. Difficulties in getting some of his larger ships over the bar caused exasperating delays, but by April 8, Farragut was nearly ready to strike.

Once in the river, Farragut was tireless in his preparations, overlooking no detail needed for success. He sent a geodetic survey team up the river to establish ranges to Forts Jackson and St. Philip from points where David Dixon Porter's mortar boats would be stationed. He had the hulls of his ships smeared with the tawny mud of the river as camouflage; he ordered bags filled with sand to strengthen bulwarks and protect the engines and other machinery; he had gun carriages and decks whitewashed to make easier the location of firing implements in the dark; he ordered iron-link cables suspended on the sides of the ships in the line of the engines; he had nettings made with large ropes spread above the decks to prevent injury from falling timber. Thus Farragut, by his energy, ingenuity, enthusiasm, and confidence not only prepared his ships superbly for the coming ordeal of passing the Confederate forts, but also infused into his officers and crew a high morale.

While confidence prevailed in the Union fleet at the Head of the Passes, New Orleans, with attack imminent, had become a jittery city. Spy fever, which had raged for weeks, was followed by an epidemic of wild rumors which the New Orleans press charged were circulated by "gossip-mongers or evil-disposed persons." The *Picayune* noted that "every day they hear one thousand alarming rumors," while the *Commercial Bulletin* complained that "every possible idea that could enter the head of credulous people seems to have been hatched up and enlarged."

General Mansfield Lovell had more serious matters than hunting spies and dispelling rumors to worry him. Although he was to have no control over the employment of the powerful warships *Louisiana* and *Mississippi,* he recognized them as integral to the defense of New Orleans and he viewed with considerable concern the way progress on the two ships was dragging.

Promised for service by January 1862, it was not until February 6 that the *Louisiana* was launched, with still considerable work left to be done in sheathing the vessel with armor and installing the machinery. The *Mississippi,* which had also been promised for January, was still on the way. Its woodwork was completed and its boilers were installed, but it lacked armor and machinery and the central shaft, which was slow in coming from Richmond's Tredegar Works.

Lovell, his hands already tied by Richmond's continued refusal to allow him to head a unified army-navy command, protested on being stripped of 5,000 troops which he was ordered to send to Columbus. To his complaint, Confederate authorities, seemingly totally oblivious of the threat to New Orleans posed by the Union naval build-up at Ship Island, replied that "New Orleans will be defended from above . . . the forces withdrawn from you are for the defense of your own command."

As if in compensation for withholding from Lovell command of the Confederate Navy at New Orleans, the War Department ordered him to seize fourteen steamboats for a River Defense Fleet, "not to be a part of the Navy . . . [but] subject to the general command of the military chief." This peculiar arrangement, with the steamboat captains in command of their vessels, was startling to Lovell.

New Orleans' morale sagged when word of the fall of Forts Henry and Donelson reached the city, to be followed shortly by the news that Albert Sidney Johnston's Kentucky line had collapsed with the evacuation of Columbus. Criticism of Confederate leadership, both in Richmond and in the field, was widespread among citizens and in the press. New Orleans was on the verge of panic when Lovell, acting on orders from Richmond, declared martial law in effect on March 15.

And frequently an entire fleet of ironclads and "tinclads" appeared at anchor in midstream. The USS St. Louis *rests in the center of the image, while in the distance behind its stern can be seen what is probably the USS* Tyler.
(USAMHI)

Brigadier General Johnson Kelly Duncan, who commanded at Forts Jackson and St. Philip, New Orleans' principal defenses, seventy-five miles downstream from the city, worked his officers and men to the point of exhaustion in preparing the bastions for Farragut's certain attack soon to come. Nearly 1,000 troops garrisoned the forts, which had 115 guns of various calibers—69 at Fort Jackson and 46 at Fort St. Philip.

The barricade, or raft, which had been made more secure by Lovell shortly after his arrival, was supported by enfilading fire from the forts. However, accumulated driftwood and the strong current proved too much for the barrier early in March. The main chains snapped, and the obstruction, so needed to hold enemy ships under the fire of the forts, ceased to exist. A makeshift barrier of parts of the original raft and some schooners, anchored and linked by chains, was hurriedly improvised. The schooners were anchored bow upstream, chained together stem, stern, and midships, with their rigging and cables trailing astern to be hazards to the propellers of enemy ships.

Nervous New Orleans received disheartening news from Shiloh's second day after exulting in the Confederate victory of the first day. The news of the fall of Island No. 10 followed fast, and the city then learned that a storm on April 9 and 10 had again dismantled the raft below the forts. Once more improvisation of a barrier was rushed.

To all of Lovell's worries there was added the continued incomprehensible unawareness in Richmond of the acute danger to New Orleans from Farragut's fleet at the Head of the Passes. Orders had come to send the still uncompleted *Louisiana* up the river, where President Davis and Secretary

Specialized craft like the hospital boat Nashville *were also needed to serve both the navy and the armed soldiers fighting along the river.* (LC)

Another hospital ship, the R. C. Wood, *on the wharf at Vicksburg in 1863.*
(OLD COURT HOUSE MUSEUM, VICKSBURG)

of the Navy Mallory amazingly believed the gravest danger to New Orleans lay. To Governor Thomas O. Moore's protest that "the *Louisiana* . . . is absolutely a necessity at the forts for the safety of New Orleans, and that it is suicidal to send her elsewhere," President Davis telegraphed back on April 17 the astonishing message: "The wooden vessels are below; the iron gunboats are above. The forts should destroy the former if they attempt to ascend. The *Louisiana* may be indespensible to check the descent of the iron boats."

This was not the only instance of Richmond's inexplicable blindness to the danger to New Orleans from the Union fleet in the river. When Commodore George N. Hollins, commander of the Confederate flotilla at Fort Pillow, asked permission on April 9 to steam down to New Orleans to participate in its defense, Mallory telegraphed back an emphatic refusal. Hollins, not waiting for Mallory's reply, however, reached New Orleans in the *McRae* and promptly urged by telegram that his fleet join him. Richmond's reply was a summons to Hollins to report at once in the Confederate capitol to head a board examining midshipmen. Thus was the best fighting man in the Confederate Navy on the Mississippi shelved at the most critical moment for New Orleans.

On April 18, Porter's mortar ships began their concentrated fire on the forts and for five days and nights, from a sheltered bend in the river, 13-inch shells were lobbed into Forts Jackson and St. Philip at regular intervals. General Duncan estimated that the Union mortar boats had thrown more than 22,000 shells at the forts before Farragut made his move.

When it became evident that the *Louisiana,* without its motive power in operation, could not go up the river as ordered, Commander W. C. Whittle, navy commander of New Orleans, finally responded to the importuning of Lovell and Duncan to have the ironclad towed down to the forts to serve as a floating battery. Despite the remonstrances of Duncan, the ironclad's captain refused to place the *Louisiana* below the barrier, where it could enfilade the Union mortar boats. He anchored it just above Fort St. Philip where it remained inactive against them. The same day that the *Louisiana* went down to the forts, the *Mississippi,* still far from completed, was launched.

On the night of April 20, Farragut sent Captain

Cairo, Illinois, also hosted an important naval station. Here its wharf boat lies moored on the shore. (USAMHI)

Henry Bell with two gunboats to sever the barrier and open a way for the ships to pass through. Bell succeeded in his mission and Farragut, never enthusiastic about the mortar ships' ability to silence the forts, determined to make his run on the night of April 23–24.

Everything was in readiness at the Head of the Passes, but disorganization prevailed among the Confederate defenders. That strange War Department instrument, the River Defense Fleet, refused to take orders from the navy; the navy showed no inclination to cooperate with General Lovell's defense plans; and, to top it, New Orleans was a city verging on panic.

At 2 A.M. on April 24, the *Cayuga* raised its anchors and steamed off into the moonless night, the vanguard of Farragut's attacking fleet. One by one, the warships followed. At 3:30 A.M., the *Cayuga* passed noiselessly through the breach in the barrier, unchallenged by any Confederate vessel and unthreatened by the fire rafts which were supposed to have been illuminated and sent down the river. Immediately, the guns of Fort Jackson and Fort St. Philip opened up as Farragut's other vessels moved into range, firing their broadsides at the forts. The flashes of their guns and the arching course of mortar shells lit the river in a spectacle of awesome grandeur. Three of Farragut's gunboats failed to make it through the breach in the barrier. The *Kennebec* entangled itself in the raft and the *Winona* suffered the same fate, and both freed themselves with difficulty and drifted out of action. The third, the *Itasca,* was badly crippled by gunfire from Fort Jackson and it retired downriver.

At the first fighting, the Confederate River Defense Fleet hurried off ingloriously, but three Rebel ships fought with valor. Hopelessly outgunned and outnumbered, the *Manassas* ("Turtle"), *McRae,* and *Governor Moore* were in the thick of the melee, each drawing the concentrated fire of several Union ships at various stages of the battle. The forts laid down tremendous barrages, but fourteen of Farragut's ships ran the fiery gauntlet successfully, although his flagship, the *Hartford,* was set ablaze by a fire raft while it was aground off Fort St. Philip. For a while, it was touch and

A river fleet at anchor off Cairo in 1865. (AMERICANA IMAGE GALLERY)

go for the *Hartford,* but discipline and engine power prevailed: The fire was extinguished by the crew and the flagship shivered and shook as it freed itself from the mud and steamed out of range of the forts.

At the peak of the battle, the roaring and flashing of the guns created a spectacular scene. One of General Benjamin Butler's officers wrote, "Combine all that you have heard of thunder, add to it all that you have ever seen of lightning, and you have, perhaps, a conception of the scene." To an officer on the *Hartford,* "it was like the breaking up of the universe with the moon and all the stars bursting in our midst." Farragut himself described it: "It was as if the artillery of heaven were playing upon the earth."

The *Manassas,* which had rammed the *Brooklyn* and *Mississippi* and fought at close quarter half a dozen other Union ships, was finally disabled and scuttled by its crew. The *McRae,* just as active in the unequal fight, had its tiller ropes shot away and made it with difficulty to the protection of Fort Jackson. The *Governor Moore* engaged the *Varuna* in a running battle, rammed the Union ship twice and sank it—Farragut's only loss in the passage of the forts. Beverly Kennon, commander of the *Governor Moore,* fired his ship, threw his sword overboard, and surrendered himself as half a dozen Union gunboats descended upon his horribly cut-up craft. The dead on the *Governor Moore* totaled fifty-seven—nine more than the combined dead in Farragut's fleet and in the two forts.

The *Louisiana,* still anchored above Fort St. Philip, received heavy firing at close range as Farragut's ships passed up the river, but the ironclad was practically undamaged. David Dixon Porter

At Cairo, soldiers boarded transports like the USS Brown *for the journey to the front at New Orleans or Vicksburg or Port Hudson.* (USAMHI)

noted in his journal that had Commander Mitchell, captain of the *Louisiana,* "possessed the soul of a flea, he could have driven us all out of the river."

The next day, April 25, Farragut pushed up the river to New Orleans. He was amazed at the sight that met his eye: "The levee of New Orleans was one scene of desolation, ships, steamers, cotton, coal, etc., were all in one common blaze," he wrote. "The *Mississippi,* which was to be the terror of the seas, and no doubt would have been to a great extent . . . soon came floating by us all in flames, and passed down the river."

Demands that the city surrender met with a scornful refusal by Mayor John Monroe, who pointed out to Farragut that as Lovell had evacuated his militia troops, New Orleans was defenseless and "the city is yours by the power of brutal force."

Meanwhile, down at the forts, mutiny broke out on April 27, compelling Duncan to surrender to Porter. During the signing, the *Louisiana* came drifting by ablaze, and moments later it blew up. All Confederate resistance below New Orleans was now ended. When the news reached Farragut he sent a party ashore to haul down the flag of Louisiana from the city hall flagpole and raise the American flag.

On May 1, Major General Benjamin F. Butler landed his occupation troops and New Orleans' days in the Confederacy were over. Mary Baykin Chesnut prophetically recorded the bitter fact in her diary: "New Orleans is gone, and with it the Confederacy! Are we not cut in two? The Mississippi ruins us if it is lost."

After Butler occupied New Orleans, Farragut was faced with a dilemma: What to do in the light of his original orders. These read: "If the Mississippi expedition from Cairo shall not have descended the river, you will take advantage of the panic to push a strong force up the river to take all their defenses in the rear. You will also reduce the fortifications which defend Mobile Bay and turn them over to the army to hold."

Farragut sent Porter and the mortar boats to Mobile Bay and dispatched Commander S. P. Lee with the *Oneida* and several smaller gunboats up the Mississippi, while he remained at New Orleans with the greater part of his fleet. Baton Rouge and Natchez, both undefended, were captured and the American flag was raised above their public buildings. At Vicksburg, however, Lee's demand for surrender was answered defiantly: "Mississippians don't know and refuse to learn how to surrender to an enemy. If . . . Farragut or . . . Butler can teach them let them come and try." Lee gave Vicksburg twenty-four hours to remove its women and children to safety, set up a blockade of the city, and awaited orders from Farragut.

When Farragut learned what was happening upriver, he was anxious to push up the Mississippi with his full command. On May 10, one of the few fleet actions of the war had taken place above Fort Pillow at Plum Run Bend when a much-outgunned Confederate flotilla of eight ships—the Confederate River Defense Fleet—with more valor than judgment attacked seven Union ironclads. With four of his ships disabled by the superior fire power of the Yankees' ships, Captain James Montgomery broke off action and retired downstream to Memphis. On May 23, Farragut's fleet, accompanied by 3,200 troops under Brigadier General

And packet boats carrying mail, like the Golden Era, *shared the stream with gunboats like the USS* Tyler *in the crowded waters off Cairo. Shipbuilder James B. Eads first used his skills to convert a steamer into the gunboat* Tyler. (CHS)

Thomas Williams, reached Vicksburg. Two days later, Colonel Charles Ellet's nine rams and two floating batteries, completed for the War Department in only forty days, made liaison with the Western Flotilla, now commanded by Captain Charles H. Davis, who had succeeded the ailing Commodore Foote.

Davis's reaction to Ellet's arrival was politely uncooperative. Ellet informed Davis that he was going to operate against Fort Pillow and asked for one gunboat to accompany him. Failing this, he invited Davis to assign some navy observers to the rams for this "daring and patriotic enterprise." Davis's reply reflected the age-old rivalry between military services: "I decline taking any part in the expedition . . . I would thank you to inform me how far you consider yourself under my authority; and I shall esteem it a favor to receive from you a copy of the orders under which you are acting." Ellet's reply was conciliatory: "No question of authority need be raised." But to Secretary of War Stanton he wrote, "Commodore Davis will not join me . . . nor contribute a gunboat . . . nor allow any of his men to volunteer . . . I shall therefore . . . go without him."

The fall of Corinth on June 3 made the Confederate evacuation of Fort Pillow inevitable and exposed Memphis to serious threat. At Memphis, the Confederates were building two powerful ironclads, the *Arkansas* and *Tennessee,* and their seizure was a Union objective. Two of Ellet's rams drew sharp fire from the works at Fort Pillow on June 3, but the Confederates had already begun evacuation, and during the night of June 4 it was completed. The only Confederate defense now between the Union vessels and Memphis was a weak Confederate flotilla at that city.

Union gunboats attacked this flotilla on the morning of June 6 in another of the rare fleet actions on the Mississippi. People of Memphis lined the bluffs to watch the battle when Commodore Davis sent five Union ironclads and four rams—a

And he did the same with the USS Lexington. *These gunboats were not very effectively armored, but they were a start.* (USAMHI)

Far more effective was the USS St. Louis, *launched at Carondelet, Missouri, the first Federal ironclad.* (NA, U. S. WAR DEPARTMENT GENERAL STAFF)

total of sixty-eight guns—against Montgomery's inferior flotilla of eight makeshift vessels mounting only twenty-eight guns. In the unequal struggle, which featured ramming and close-quarter fighting, the Confederates were decimated. Three Rebel ships were destroyed and four were captured, with only the *Van Dorn* escaping. The Union Navy now controlled the entire Mississippi, except at Vicksburg, Mississippi, and at Port Hudson in Louisiana.

The principal concern of the Union fleet on the Mississippi was the uncompleted Confederate ironclad, *Arkansas,* which, when Memphis was under threat, had been sent downriver to safety.

In the late summer of 1861, the Confederate Navy Department authorized the building of four powerful ironclads, easily the most formidable gunboats on the Mississippi. Devastating to the Confederate cause was the policy of "too little and too late" that prevailed with its gunboat building projects. The *Louisiana* and the *Mississippi,* as was stated earlier, were to have been completed at New Orleans by the end of January 1862. But neither was finished when Farragut attacked the forts below New Orleans in April, and the *Louisiana* was blown up and the *Mississippi* set afire.

About the time that work was begun on the *Louisiana* and *Mississippi* in New Orleans, two other formidable ironclads were started in a Memphis shipyard, the *Arkansas* and the *Tennessee.* Patterned on the *Louisiana* and *Mississippi* and perhaps even more formidable, the Memphis ironclads were to be ready by the end of December 1861.

The descent of the Mississippi by the Union fleet found work on both the *Arkansas* and *Tennessee* lagging, and on April 25, the same day Farragut's warships appeared at New Orleans, the *Arkansas* was launched. It was floated 300 miles down the Mississippi to the Yazoo River above Vicksburg and then was towed 200 miles up the Yazoo to Greenwood, where it was expected to be finished shortly. On orders from Richmond, the *Tennessee* was destroyed before launch.

A shortage of workmen, tools, equipment, timber, and other materials needed to complete the *Arkansas* resulted in interminable delays, despite the vigorous efforts of the ship's commander, Lieu-

Active operations on the Mississippi really begin with Brigadier General U. S. Grant, shown here as a major general. His attack on Belmont was staged from Cairo. (LC)

tenant Isaac Brown, who was charged with the *Arkansas*'s completion. Launch day finally came on July 4, but more than six months late, and the *Arkansas* steamed to Yazoo City.

It was Lieutenant Brown's intention to drive his ironclad through the entire combined Union fleet—Farragut had run Vicksburg's fortifications, and had joined Davis above the city—and anchor the *Arkansas* under the protection of the Confederate batteries.

Major General Earl Van Dorn, commanding at Vicksburg, impatiently awaited the *Arkansas,* which he expected to prove a formidable factor in defending the city. It was due on July 14, but it developed that a defective powder magazine admitted steam which dampened the powder. Lieutenant Brown lost a full day drying his powder on canvas spread along the bank. Underway once more, the *Arkansas* ran aground in the darkness. Instead of reaching the Mississippi by daylight, the *Arkansas* was still in the Yazoo when Brown picked up in his glass three Union vessels steaming toward him. They were the ironclads *Carondelet* and *Queen of the West* and the gunboat *Tyler.*

At 6:20 A.M. the *Carondelet* began to fire on the *Arkansas* at less than half a mile away, then turned and headed down the Yazoo, followed by the other two Union vessels. Stern guns opened on the pursuing *Arkansas* as the chase got underway and the Confederate ironclad was badly cut up. Lieutenant Brown was mistakenly believed to have been seriously wounded when struck in the head by a rifle ball. But the *Arkansas*'s guns had severely punished the *Carondelet,* shattering its steering equipment and cutting steam-escape, exhaust, and cold-water pipes. The *Carondelet* limped to the bank and did not return the *Arkansas*'s broadside and stern guns' fire as the Rebel ironside swept past, still in pursuit of the *Tyler* and the *Queen of the West.* The latter had fled hastily and its com-

The first real Union success came at Island No. 10, when Brigadier General John Pope cooperated with Foote's flotilla to force the Confederate bastion to surrender. (NA, U. S. SIGNAL CORPS)

In both defense and offense, cannons mounted on rafts and floated into position were used frequently on the river at places like Island No. 10. (NHC)

mander, James M. Hunter, was later denounced in the *Tyler*'s log for his "cowardly and dastardly" behavior. But the *Tyler,* in retreating, kept up its fire as the running fight brought the two vessels into the Mississippi and on toward Vicksburg.

Suddenly, on rounding a bend, the *Arkansas* came upon the combined fleets of Farragut and Davis—thirty-three ironclads, gunboats, rams, river steamers, and mortar boats—and quickly was furiously engaged. Lieutenant Brown reported later, "The shock of missiles striking our sides was literally continuous, and . . . we were now surrounded without room for anything but pushing ahead . . . I had the most lively realization of having steamed into a real volcano, the *Arkansas* from its center firing rapidly to every point of the circumference, without the fear of hitting a friend or missing an enemy."

For about two hours, the *Arkansas* fought its way through the Union fleets and at ten minutes before nine o'clock on July 15 it tied up at the Vicksburg wharf, "smokestack . . . shot to pieces . . . much cut up . . . pilot house smashed and some ugly places through our armor," as Lieutenant Brown later reported.

Elation in Vicksburg was unbounded and General Van Dorn, who had watched the fight from the top of the courthouse, said in his report that Brown "immortalized his single vessel, himself, and the heroes under his command by an achievement the most brilliant ever recorded in naval annals."

Farragut, not sparing himself in his criticism, wrote Davis, "We were all caught unprepared for him, but we must go down and destroy him. . . . We must go close to him and smash him in. It will be warm work, but we must do it." That night, Farragut made his run. Mortar fire on Vicksburg opened the action at 6 P.M. and forty-five minutes later the fleet was underway. At 8:20 P.M. it had passed the Vicksburg batteries and anchored below the city. But Farragut had not destroyed the *Arkansas;* in fact, only one of his ships, the *Oneida,* actually saw the Rebel ironclad. However, the *Arkansas* did not escape damage, for a shot passed through its armor, penetrated the engine room, and disabled the engine and also caused a severe leak. More casualties were added to the morning's toll of ten killed and fifteen wounded.

All efforts to destroy the *Arkansas* failed during the ensuing days—mortar fire directed at the Rebel craft, a direct assault by the *Essex* and *Queen of the West*. Captain Ledyard Phelps of the *Benton* summed it up in a letter to Andrew Foote: "The whole thing was a fizzle. Every day we heard great things threatened only to realize fizzles." Van Dorn, in a telegram to Jefferson Davis, characterized the attack on the *Arkansas* as a "failure so complete that it was almost ridiculous."

Farragut, chagrined, parted company with the *Arkansas* when he was ordered by the Navy Department to return to New Orleans with his fleet. Departing with Farragut was General Williams's force, which was so riddled with illness that barely a fourth of the 3,000-odd troops was ready for duty. Williams retired to Baton Rouge. With only his gunboats left at Vicksburg, Davis deemed it wise to steam upriver to the mouth of the Yazoo. For more than two months—sixty-seven days—Vicksburg had frustrated the efforts of two powerful Union fleets and more than 3,000 land forces.

Henry Gurney's image of the mightiest ironclad on the river, the USS Benton, *another of Eads's conversions. Foote made it his flagship. This photo was taken at Natchez in 1863 or later.* (JOAN AND THOMAS GANDY, NATCHEZ, MISSISSIPPI)

The 20,000 to 25,000 shells hurled at the city left Vicksburg undaunted.

Captain Brown took advantage of the respite to visit Granada, Mississippi, where he fell ill. Lieutenant Henry Stevens, left in command of the *Arkansas,* worked feverishly to repair the engines and to increase the ship's armor. General Van Dorn ordered Stevens to take the *Arkansas* down the river to Baton Rouge to support an attack on that city by Major General John C. Breckinridge.

On August 3 at 2 A.M. the *Arkansas* moved from the wharf and headed for Baton Rouge.

Commander Henry Walke, a Virginian by birth, ran his Carondelet *past No. 10's batteries to assist Pope's land assault.* (LC)

Throughout the day, the ironclad's engines functioned efficiently and an eight-knot speed was maintained. But shortly before midnight, the starboard engine broke down, and the *Arkansas* tied up while repairs were made throughout the night. At 8 A.M. on August 5, the *Arkansas* was apparently ready to participate in Breckinridge's attack, which was already underway. When the *Arkansas* was within eight miles of Baton Rouge, the engines went dead again. Once more repairs were rushed and once more the engines broke down. By 9:30 A.M. on August 6, the *Arkansas* seemed ready once again. At that time there appeared, steaming toward the *Arkansas,* four Union gunboats, the *Essex, Cayuga, Katahdin,* and USS *Sumter.* Stevens determined to make a fight of it, but the ironclad's port engine failed as the *Arkansas* headed to engage the enemy. A moment later the starboard engine gave way and the *Arkansas* drifted helplessly toward the advancing Union gunboats.

Both sides opened fire, but ineffectively, and Lieutenant Stevens realized he had no alternative to the destruction of the *Arkansas* to prevent its falling into the hands of the enemy. Ordering the crew ashore and commanding them to take off for the interior, Stevens, with seven officers and petty officers, prepared the *Arkansas* for its end and then abandoned ship, too. For an hour the *Arkansas* floated with the current, its loaded guns firing as the flames reached them, and shortly before noon, it blew up spectacularly.

"It was beautiful," recalled Stevens, "to see her, when abandoned by commander and crew and dedicated to sacrifice, fighting the battle on her own hook."

In a report to the Confederate Congress, Secretary of the Navy Mallory said, "Naval history records few deeds of greater heroism or higher professional ability than this achievement of the *Arkansas.*"

With the passing of the *Arkansas,* there passed also the last Confederate offensive challenge on the Mississippi. The Union now controlled the entire river except for the Rebel bastions at Vicksburg and Port Hudson, Louisiana.

Less than a year remained before these last two Confederate strongholds would fall, and the Father of Waters would again go, as Mr. Lincoln expressed it, "unvexed to the sea."

The USS Pittsburg *followed Walke's lead, and Pope's movement was ensured.* (LC)

Captures included the Confederate ship CSS Red Rover, *a barracks ship which the Federals turned into the first hospital ship in the navy.* (USAMHI)

The CSS De Soto *was captured as well, to become the USS* General Lyon. (NHC)

Flag Officer David G. Farragut will be much in evidence on the Mississippi, and nowhere more than in his reduction of Forts Jackson and St. Philip and the capture of New Orleans. (USAMHI)

Fort Jackson. The photograph was supposedly taken in 1862 but is probably early postwar. (WRHS)

The interior of Fort St. Philip looking toward the river, probably also a postwar image. The formidable command these forts exerted on river traffic is evident. (WRHS)

A front view of Fort St. Philip. (WRHS)

And here the much less known Fort Macomb, taken in 1863. The canal ran from Lake Borgne to Lake Pontchartrain in the rear of New Orleans. Colonel Francis Hesseltine and his wife stand with fishing poles in the foreground. (USAMHI)

Captain Napoleon B. Harrison commanded the USS Cayuga *when Farragut ran his fleet past the forts.* (USAMHI)

The mortar schooner USS C. P. Williams *took part with Porter's mortar fleet in the bombardment of the forts.* (WRHS)

And so did the USS Horace Beals. (USAMHI)

These monster mortars could throw a 200-pound shell from 3,000–4,000 yards. These were part of Farragut's fleet, later taken to rest here at the Philadelphia Navy Yard. (USAMHI)

To identify his ships from a distance in the confusion of battle, Farragut ordered numbers painted in letters six feet high on the stacks of each vessel. Number 2 was the USS Winona, *which served two years on the Mississippi before joining the blockade off Charleston.* (USAMHI)

Farragut's mighty flagship, the USS Hartford, *its midships sides still showing the chains draped over them as protection from enemy shot during the passage of the forts. A. D. Lytle, the outstanding photographer of Baton Rouge, made this view shortly afterward.* (CWTI)

Farragut and his executive officer Percival Drayton at the wheel of the Hartford. (USAMHI)

Men and officers of the Hartford *at the stern pivot gun, a massive Parrott rifle.* (USAMHI)

The gun deck of the Hartford, *looking aft.* (USAMHI)

The beautiful side-wheeler USS Mississippi, *built in 1839 under the eye of Commodore Matthew C. Perry. She was his flagship in the Mexican War and in his epic voyage to Japan in 1852. Farragut would send it upriver to pass the enemy batteries at Port Hudson the next year, and there it would run aground and be destroyed by its crew. The executive officer was the future Admiral George Dewey.* (USAMHI)

McPherson & Oliver's photograph of the crew of the USS Richmond *at quarters after the capture of New Orleans.* (USAMHI)

Brigadier General Morgan L. Smith, a native of New York, fought for the South and supervised New Orleans' defenses as well as leading troops there. (USAMHI)

The heart of the Crescent City, Jackson Square, showing St. Louis Cathedral and to the right of it, the Presbytère. The Andrew Jackson equestrian statue can be seen, and carved on its pedestal his declaration that the union "must and shall be preserved." (USAMHI)

Canal Street, running from Royal Street to the river. At the end can be seen the smokestacks of steamboats at the wharves. (USAMHI)

Chartres Street in the French Quarter. (USAMHI)

New Orleans' City Hall. Here Farragut raised the Union flag over the conquered city. (USAMHI)

Looking down the levee from Canal Street. The busy traffic, once interrupted by the war, now flows again. Bales of cotton await shipment. (USAMHI)

With the city taken, Major General Benjamin F. Butler and his troops began their controversial occupation. "Spoons" Butler they would call him, after accusations that he stole silver from the citizens. (USAMHI)

Before long New Orleans would be designated the headquarters of the new Department of the Gulf. Here officers serving in the department from several services, army, navy, and marines, gather for a group portrait in March 1863. Seated from the left are Lieutenant Edward Terry of the Richmond, *Captain James Alden commanding the* Richmond, *and Brigadier General Godfrey Weitzel. The rest are staff officers.* (USAMHI)

Soon after the fall of New Orleans, Farragut's ships took Baton Rouge and, shown here, Natchez. Then it was time to try for Vicksburg. (USAMHI)

Commander S. P. Lee led the small fleet that first tried to force the surrender of Vicksburg, but unsuccessfully. (USAMHI)

Farragut soon moved north to join Lee, bringing with him the 3,200 men of Brigadier General Thomas Williams, an almost universally disliked commander. The soldiers would attempt nothing, being shattered by disease. Williams retired to Baton Rouge, and there on August 5 he was killed in the Confederate attack. (USAMHI)

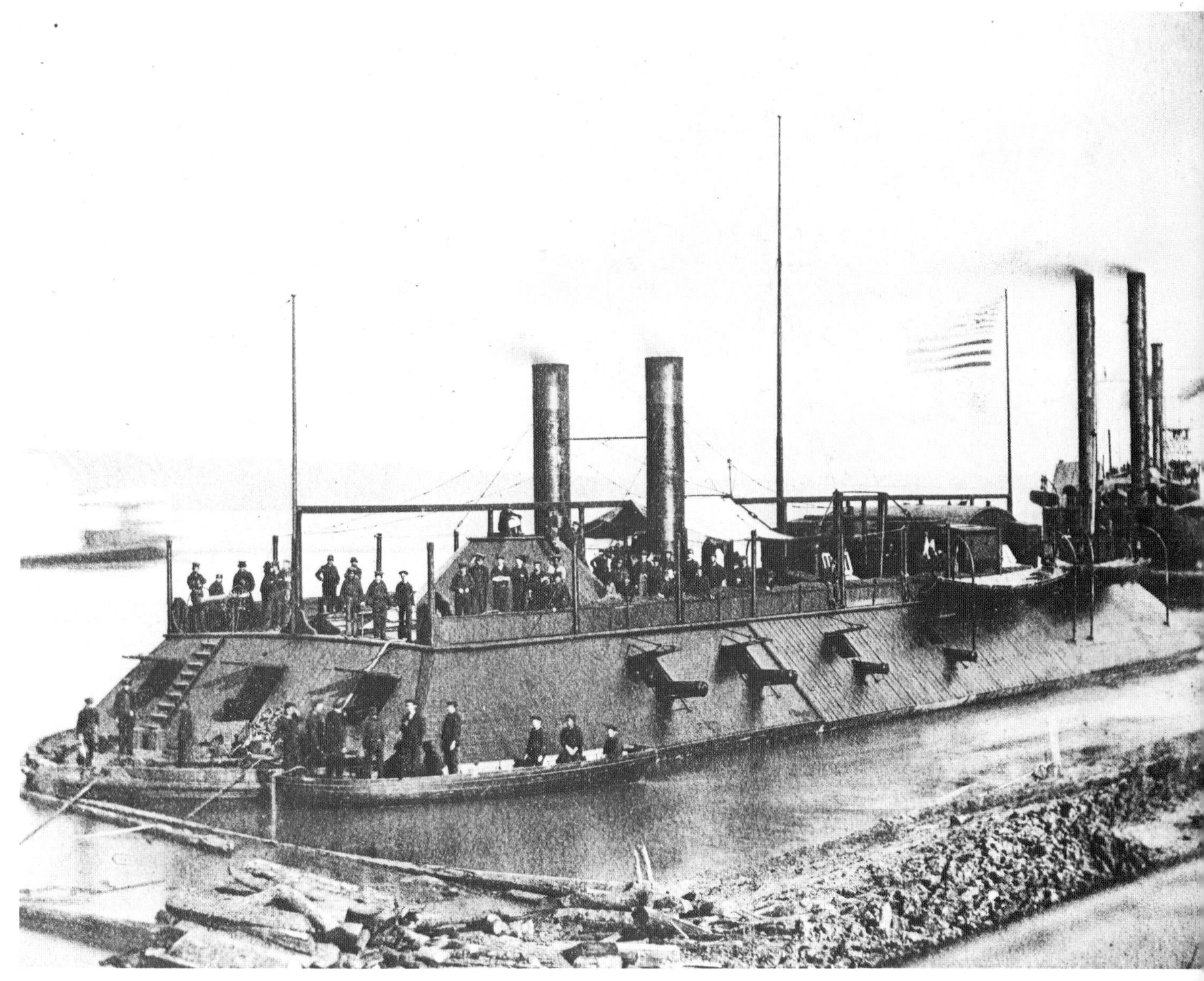

On the way to Vicksburg, Farragut learned of the Union fleet victory at Plum Run Bend, a victory won over ineffectual Confederate ships by gunboats like the USS Carondelet. (USAMHI)

The USS Louisville, *too, shown here at Memphis, made light work of the enemy River Defense Fleet at Plum Run Bend. It was, in fact, the largest fleet engagement of the war.* (NHC)

Brigadier General John B. Villepigue commanded the defense of Fort Pillow as best he could, until forced to abandon and destroy his fortifications. (P-M)

Then the Union Navy moved against Memphis. The only thing in their way was a little fleet commanded by the flamboyant M. Jeff Thompson who, though never promoted brigadier general, dressed like one anyhow. (DAVID R. O'REILLY COLLECTION)

Thompson's flotilla was obliterated, all but one captured or destroyed. The Little Rebel *was one of the captured, and it was later put into Federal service.* (TERENCE P. O'LEARY, GLADWYNE, PENNSYLVANIA)

The CSS General Price *had been a cotton-clad—bales of cotton stacked on her sides for protection—when she was sunk at Memphis. Raised and remodeled she became the USS* General Price, *commanded by . . .* (USAMHI)

. . . Acting Volunteer Lieutenant J. F. Richardson. (ROBERT G. HARRIS)

One of the ships of Ellet's ram fleet that destroyed Thompson's little flotilla. (NHC)

Alfred W. Ellet, later a brigadier general, succeeded to command of the ram fleet when his brother Charles died two weeks after the Battle of Memphis. (USAMHI)

And now Memphis belonged to the Union again. The city is shown here viewed from the levee. (USAMHI)

Here the Memphis levee itself, with Federal shipping and barges crowding the shore. (USAMHI)

The Memphis Navy Yard, where the mighty CSS Arkansas *was constructed.* (USAMHI)

Union Lieutenant John A. Winslow took command of the Memphis naval facilities, turning them to the purposes of Farragut's and Ellet's ships. (USAMHI)

Yet much of Memphis sat in ruins, the first Mississippi River city to feel the hand of destruction. (USAMHI)

Vicksburg became even more isolated. Its commander, the dashing Major General Earl Van Dorn, is shown here in an unpublished portrait. He expected the Arkansas *to come and redeem the city, and he was not disappointed.* (TU)

With Vicksburg secure, Van Dorn sent the Arkansas *downriver to cooperate with Breckinridge in the attack on Baton Rouge, the last real threat to Federal control of the lower Mississippi. Here the waterfront of Baton Rouge, with the state capitol to the right.* (LSU)

Brigadier General Halbert E. Paine commanded in Baton Rouge after Williams's death in battle, but refused to burn the city when ordered to do so by his superior, Butler. (LC)

Colonel Henry W. Allen was prominent in Breckinridge's attack on Baton Rouge until his leg was shattered by a bullet. He was crippled for the rest of his life. (LSU)

"Dirty Bill" Porter took his Essex *after the* Arkansas, *and later claimed credit for destroying the feared Confederate ironclad.* (USAMHI)

To be sure, the Essex *was a formidable ironclad. She appears here off Baton Rouge (which she helped defend) in March 1863. The* Richmond *and* Mississippi *can be seen off her stern.* (USAMHI)

A. D. Lytle's 1861 image of Baton Rouge, before the destruction of the war came to visit. (LSU)

Breckinridge was initially successful, but later he had to abandon Baton Rouge, which showed the effects of the battle. Most of this damage was done by Federal gunboats, chiefly the Essex, *as they attempted to support Williams's beaten troops.* (LSU)

Church Street in Baton Rouge, during the Federal occupation. (USAMHI)

Another view of Church Street. These views were made by the Baton Rouge firm of W. D. McPherson and his partner Oliver, whose first name is unknown. (USAMHI)

The Louisiana State House, taken by McPherson & Oliver. (USAMHI)

The Louisiana State Penitentiary, captured by Baton Rouge's other outstanding artist, A. D. Lytle. (USAMHI)

L. I. Prince's image of the Baton Rouge Arsenal. (ISHL)

Part of the arsenal grounds, by McPherson & Oliver. (USAMHI)

The courthouse as seen by McPherson & Oliver. It was turned into a barracks and later a hospital by the occupying Federals. (USAMHI)

Artillery covered as protection against rain on the grounds of the Jackson Barracks. (USAMHI)

Everywhere in the South, when the Union soldiers came, the slaves flocked to their camps. Here the headquarters of the contraband camps in Baton Rouge. (USAMHI)

General Williams's headquarters before the Battle of Baton Rouge. (USAMHI)

Here Farragut's fleet stands off the city in 1862, on its way north to Vicksburg. The stern of the USS Mississippi *is just visible to the left of the wood pile. The USS* Richmond *is in the center, and the USS* Winona *is to the left of it.* (USAMHI)

The Baton Rouge coaling yard, with the Winona *at right, and the* Richmond *next to it. The other vessels are part of the mortar fleet.* (LC)

Often erroneously identified as the Hartford, *this image shows the USS* Portsmouth *on the right and an unidentified warship astern of it.* (LC)

The Portsmouth *again, with one of the mortar schooners in the distance.* (LC)

Two of Porter's mortar schooners lie side by side against the bank at Baton Rouge, while a gunboat, perhaps the Tyler *or* Conestoga, *lies to the left with a damaged stack.* (LSU)

A similar view, showing the ruins of a factory at the water's edge. (CWTI)

The Hartford *lies off the Main Street levee in this McPherson & Oliver image.*

The same view, perhaps from Lytle's window, shows troops disembarking from the Sallie Johnson *in the spring of 1863.* (USAMHI)

The wharf boat at Baton Rouge, the Natchez, *operated as a warehouse, hotel, and even offered "Fresh Lake Fish" to the soldiers.* (USAMHI)

The Natchez *about to unload supplies from its "warehouse."* (USAMHI)

In March 1863 McPherson & Oliver photographed the Empire Parish *off Baton Rouge. Nathaniel Banks made the steamer his headquarters for a time.* (LSU)

A. D. Lytle's photograph of Federals at leisure on the Mississippi, apparently a celebration. (LSU)

Blacks drafted into service by the Federals worked within sight of the State House. (LSU)

And all around the city the white tents of the soldiers sprouted like mushrooms. (LSU)

Regiments drilled and reviewed constantly on the old arsenal grounds. (LSU)

And in front of the courthouse. (LSU)

And in front of the Jackson Barracks. (LSU)

And in a score of camps on the fringes of the city. Clearly, the Union was here to stay. (LSU)

One of the final acts of 1862 along the river was the Federal capture of Donaldsonville, Louisiana, in October. Unlike Baton Rouge, Donaldsonville suffered considerably from the fighting. Much of the town lay in ruins. Homes and businesses were burned or battered to pieces. (ISHL)

The Catholic church, damaged. (ISHL)

Everywhere scenes of destruction. (ISHL)

But the flag went up and the rebuilding began. (ISHL)

And by the dawn of 1863, nothing was more commonplace along hundreds of miles of Mississippi banks than the sight of Federal soldiers encamped, as here at Morganza, Louisiana. The Mississippi was truly conquered. Only Port Hudson remained, and Vicksburg. (NHC)

Jackson in the Shenandoah

ROBERT G. TANNER

A peculiar professor and a valley whose name meant "Daughter of the Stars"

IN THE SPRING OF 1862, the Union planned two invasions of Virginia. One is well known: McClellan's seaborne thrust to the Peninsula and Richmond. Less understood is the invasion that was to precede the Peninsula campaign and which was designed to make McClellan's campaign possible. That was the invasion of the Shenandoah Valley.

The Valley lay like a dagger across much of Virginia, running generally north and south between the James and Potomac rivers and bounded by the Blue Ridge and Allegheny mountains. At its northernmost rim, formed by the Potomac, the Valley was actually many miles north of both Washington and Baltimore, so that when Union commanders spread their maps to study the state they were always reminded that the Valley lurked behind them. Confederate forces occupied the northern portion of the Valley, from which they were always in position to thrust across the Potomac. The Baltimore & Ohio Railroad, one of the Union's main east–west highways, was severed by the northern tip of the Valley, as was the Chesapeake & Ohio Canal. The economic impact of the loss of those links was considerable. But worst of all was the fact that Winchester, headquarters of Rebel forces in the Shenandoah, was a scant sixty miles northwest of the Union capital. Geography alone dictated that Confederate forces in the northern Valley must be removed before McClellan launched his Peninsula invasion.

It was initially assumed that ejection of the Rebels posed no significant problem to McClellan's operation. Indeed this was looked upon as an invasion promising major returns for nominal risks. Confederate forces in Winchester were believed to be weak and dispirited after hard campaigning during a savage winter. Federal intelligence reports estimated that Union forces should encounter little difficulty in crossing the Potomac at Harpers Ferry and pushing southward as far as Winchester to destroy Confederate forces there. To ensure success, it was decided that the Federal invasion force would be bolstered by additional thousands of men from McClellan's main army. Once the entire northern Shenandoah had been liberated, garrison forces would be left behind, and the remainder of the invading host would shift east of the Blue Ridge Mountains to take up covering positions around Washington. By protecting Washington these forces would free McClellan to transfer the main Union Army to the doorstep of Richmond.

The two invasions seemed, on paper, to form a sound and perhaps even brilliant plan. And yet, if

The men who saved the Valley. Stonewall Jackson and his staff in 1862. The photograph of Jackson was made in Winchester; the composite including all of the portraits is the work of Richmond's distinguished portrait artists Vannerson & Jones. (VM)

Major General Nathaniel P. Banks, the perennial loser. Jackson outmaneuvered, out-thought, and outfought him in the Shenandoah, costing Banks 30 percent of his troops in casualties. (LOUIS A. WARREN LINCOLN LIBRARY)

the invasion of the Valley were disrupted or delayed, the shift of forces eastward would likewise be retarded, which could endanger the Peninsular campaign. Rarely in military history has a major military operation such as the Peninsular campaign depended so substantially for its success upon a seemingly minor and far-removed initial assault.

Rarely, too, has any important military operation been entrusted to one so utterly inexperienced in warfare as Major General Nathaniel P. Banks. Banks was a skilled politician, an ardent abolitionist, and an influential member of the Republican party; during only his second term in the United States Congress he had become Speaker of the House of Representatives. When South Carolina seceded he was retiring from the governor's mansion of Massachusetts; he knew virtually nothing of war, but unemployed governors had a way of finding themselves generals in the Civil War, and Banks was slated to lead the Union's drive into the Shenandoah.

That invasion began in February of 1862, as Banks's forces, totaling almost 40,000 men, spilled across the Potomac River and descended upon Winchester. The Federals advanced deliberately, brushing aside what seemed to be only token opposition. On the afternoon of March 11, 1862, Federal divisions converged upon Winchester from two different directions and found the Rebels drawn up in battle formation. A firefight ensued, and there was prospect of battle in the morning, but dawn found the Rebels gone and Winchester fell without a shot.

Banks trailed the Confederates southward from Winchester but was unable to bring them to a fight. They seemed, to Banks, to be running—just as had been anticipated. Within ten days the Rebels had moved far to the south, and Union forces were regrouping around Winchester. Thousands of Federals were already moving east of the Blue Ridge to take up their assigned positions around Washington. Banks even left the Shenandoah for a rest, a rest which was interrupted when, on the evening of March 23, 1862, the telegraph from the Valley began to crackle.

OPPOSING BANKS in the Shenandoah was the Confederate Valley Army, a force of perhaps 4,500 men rostered into three tiny infantry brigades, six small artillery batteries, and 600 poorly disciplined but splendidly mounted cavalrymen led by Colonel Turner Ashby. The Valley Army was commanded by Major General Thomas J. "Stonewall" Jackson, a West Pointer, retired United States Army Major, and former physics professor at Virginia Military Institute. Jackson was virtually unknown at this point of the war. Except for one brief hour of glory at the First Battle of Bull Run, he had contributed little to the Confederate struggle save a ruthless discipline of his men and a winter campaign in the Alleghenies that had killed or sickened hundreds of them.

But Jackson was full of fight, and that resolve was well adapted to his instructions. His task in the

Valley was to keep as many Federal soldiers pinned down there and as far away from McClellan as he could. It was the perfect mission for this fiercely stubborn man. Although outnumbered ten to one he had clung to Winchester even as Banks uncoiled around him; Jackson had even planned an attack on Banks for the night of March 11. He was prevented from striking only when his staff relayed his orders erroneously and moved the army out of position. Jackson retreated, but he left behind his cavalry commander Ashby to cover the rear and to search for openings to attack.

Ashby found an opening as Banks redeployed his forces east of the Blue Ridge to cover Washington in accordance with the overall Union strategy. His mounted scouts detected this eastward shift and relayed word to Jackson. Within hours, Jackson was pushing northward toward Winchester with the bulk of the Valley Army. On March 23, as Banks was reaching Washington for his rest, Jackson was nearing Kernstown, a hamlet three miles south of Winchester. His rapid march had left his troops exhausted and his ranks thinned by straggling; nevertheless, Jackson threw his men into the attack.

What followed was a confused stand-up soldiers' fight called the Battle of Kernstown. The Confederates made good initial headway, then were slowed by unexpected Federal strength. One Confederate wrote his father after the battle, "The crack of rifles and the whistling of balls soon told us what we must expect. Soon volleys of musketry seemed to shake the hills." When one of Jackson's aides reported sighting increasing Federal numbers, the General replied tersely, "Say nothing about it. We are in for it."

Jackson had blundered into at least 10,000 Federal troops under Brigadier General James Shields. Shields had kept most of his division hidden well enough to fool Ashby's scouts, and then fed them skillfully into the battle. His numbers allowed him to overlap the smaller Southern army on either flank, and by nightfall the Confederates were driven from the field in nearly total rout.

So the Battle of Kernstown ended as a Southern defeat—but a defeat which actually proved something of a victory. General Shields was impressed by Jackson's hard fighting; he believed that the Confederates had numbered at least 11,000 men who were the "very flower of the Southern Army."

Charlestown, Virginia, in 1862. Here and in the vicinity, the Federals who would face Jackson wintered and readied for the Valley campaign. (USAMHI)

The headquarters of Brigadier General Alpheus S. Williams, who commanded a brigade under Banks in the Valley campaign, taken at Darnestown, Maryland. (USAMHI)

Shields called for help from Northern forces moving east of the Blue Ridge after the battle; one large division was diverted back to the Valley at once. Shields's reports that the flower of the Southern army had emerged in the northern Shenandoah canceled plans for any further redeployment of Union forces from that area to Washington. Instead, the Union's invasion of the Valley had to begin anew.

Banks returned to the Shenandoah to handle operations there. His army was built up again to 25,000 men and he was directed to drive the Rebels as far south as Staunton. He would be assisted by Federal forces west of the Valley in the Alleghenies. Thus, Kernstown lured the Union to undertake an extended Shenandoah invasion. McClellan henceforth would be operating on one side of Virginia while Banks campaigned on the other; instead of one invasion of Virginia followed by another, the Union was now engaged in a dangerous two-pronged invasion. And every man who was in the Valley would be one man less for McClellan.

Confederate losses at Kernstown totaled almost 25 percent of those engaged; Jackson could not risk battle again for a month. During those weeks, while Federal forces were built up against him, he rebuilt his own battered army. Through March and April he retreated slowly southward up the Valley while he recruited, reorganized, and made his army ready for maneuvers.

In normal usage, because the top of a map represents the northernmost portion of the area depicted, to go *up* is to go *north* and, conversely, to go *down* is to go *south*. The idiom of the Valley is exactly the opposite because its streams drain generally northward and water routes were the principal early means of transportation. To go *down* the Valley is thus to go *northward* and, conversely, to go *up* is to go *southward*. The Shenandoah's *northern* region is the *lower* Valley, and the *southern* region is the *upper* Valley.

Before recounting these movements, a glance at the Shenandoah is essential. Up and down the middle of the region runs the great Valley Pike, a macadamized road which was one of the best highways of its time. Other roads in the area tended to be abysmal, so the principal towns clustered along the pike. From Martinsburg and Winchester in the north, the pike passed through Strasburg, New Market, Harrisonburg, and Staunton in the lower —northern—Valley. Staunton, which linked also with the eastern part of the state by the Virginia Central Railroad, served as Jackson's base of supplies. Another salient feature of the Valley is the great Massanutten Mountain. This is actually an interlocking system of ridges which rises precipitously just east of Strasburg and runs up the Valley for fifty miles. For this distance the Shenandoah is actually two valleys, the Luray Valley between the Massanutten and the Blue Ridge, and the Shenandoah proper between the Massanutten and the Alleghenies. There is only one pass through this tangled green wall, a winding and difficult road between New Market, in the Shenandoah, and the village of Luray, in the Luray Valley. From Luray a passable road ran northward to the little town of Front Royal and southward to the village of Port Republic. In the next few weeks Jackson would fight battles at both ends of that road.

While retreating southward after Kernstown, Jackson had not forgotten his primary mission of keeping Federal forces occupied in the Valley. Nevertheless, sheer Union numbers eventually forced Jackson to almost abandon the Shenandoah. By the end of April he had moved into Swift Run Gap, where he completed the reorganization of the Valley Army. He also received a major reinforcement from east of the Blue Ridge. This was the division of Major General Richard S. Ewell, a fine body of some 8,000 well-trained and well-equipped infantry. At the end of April Jackson and Ewell were concentrated within supporting range of each other in the vicinity of Swift Run Gap; their combined forces totaled 14,000 men.

The situation confronting Jackson was complex. Staunton, his base of operations, was threatened from two directions. Union Major General John C. Frémont—the "Pathfinder" of America's westward expansion to California—was approaching Staunton from the Alleghenies with an army of 10,000 to 15,000 men. His advance guard, under Brigadier General R. H. Milroy, was pressing forward vigorously against scattered Confederate

Camps of men of Banks's command at Darnestown. (KA)

strength. Banks, with 25,000 men, was located in Harrisonburg and threatened Staunton from the north. In simplest terms, Jackson's dilemma was how to keep Staunton secure and Fremont and Banks apart but still pinned down in the Valley. The resolution of that dilemma came through a series of dazzling marches and battles rarely equaled in military history.

On April 30, 1862, Jackson slipped out of his camps in Swift Run Gap and headed for Staunton. Ewell's division came across the Blue Ridge and occupied Jackson's camp, attempting thereby to conceal from Banks the start of a Confederate offensive. Winding in and out of the Blue Ridge, Jackson reached Staunton by May 3 with 6,000 men and then plunged westward into the Alleghenies. He soon linked up with the Confederate forces there and drove Frémont's vanguard back. On May 8 Milroy turned to fight near the little mountain town of McDowell. Like Kernstown, the Battle of McDowell was a stand-up soldiers' fight. The mountainous terrain made it impossible to give much direction to the fighting, which broke into small groups of men banging away desperately at each other. Jackson managed to seize the high ground overlooking the Federal camp, and this proved decisive. Though the Rebels suffered heavier casualties than the attacking Federals, they repulsed all attacks, and the next morning found the Union retreat accelerating.

Movement now exploded all around the Valley. Jackson pursued Milroy through the Alleghenies for several days. Banks abandoned Harrisonburg and retreated northward to Strasburg, a signal that the Union again had decided that the Shenandoah invasion was over. Due to Jackson's earlier with-

Here in Williamsport, Maryland, the Federals also awaited the order to march south. No one yet knew much about this fellow Jackson. (USAMHI)

The men of the 13th Massachusetts shown here at Williamsport soon had to leave the comfort of their winter quarters. (USAMHI)

drawal to Swift Run Gap, the Union high command had decided the Shenandoah was secure and Banks could retire to defensive positions along its northern borders and dispatch one division out of the Valley. Unlike the situation in March, however, Banks's redeployment this time was not merely defensive. Instead, Banks was to send Shields's division to Fredericksburg to join forces assembling there which were, in turn, to march south and link up with McClellan outside Richmond. The first step in achieving this redeployment was Banks's withdrawal to Strasburg.

The race began. Jackson hustled his troops back down into the Shenandoah and surged northward after Banks. The movements were rapid; marches of twenty miles a day were typical. The movements were also secret. Jackson had a mania for secrecy and told his subordinates—and his superiors—almost nothing of his location and intentions. His army seemed to simply drop from sight.

That Jackson disappeared during much of the Valley Campaign was true in one literal sense. His movements were such that there is almost no pictorial record of them. Burdened with unwieldy and very heavy equipment, photographers of the day needed a more stationary subject than Jackson's army to bring their talents into play. He simply moved too fast for them to arrive in time to take photographs of his operations. Such pictures as we have are of battlefields and not of the actual battles or marches, with the result that what we know of this campaign comes not from the camera but from the written word.

During May 1862, those words grew increasingly fatigued. "We are very wearied by the march, in fact, virtually worn down. A night's rest appears to do us no good—just as sleepy and languid in the morning as when we sleep in the evening," one Rebel recorded in his diary. Those who had started from Swift Run Gap with Jackson on

The surgeons shown here before their quarters in Williamsport would have plenty of work, thanks to Jackson. (USAMHI)

A brigade headquarters in Banks's command at Martinsburg, Virginia, in March 1862. (USAMHI)

Officers of the 2nd Massachusetts in 1861. They and their regiment would feel the full sting of Confederate might in the Shenandoah. (USAMHI)

the last day of April had marched more than 250 miles, most of the way across mountains and over horrible roads. But by force of will and much hard work the Valley Army kept coming. Jackson passed through Massanutten Gap with his forces and those he had collected in the Alleghenies and united around Luray with Ewell's division. He thus assembled all of the Confederates in the Shenandoah, perhaps 17,000 men and 50 cannons. Without a day's rest he turned northward on May 22 and marched to within 10 miles of Front Royal. There would be battle in the morning.

ON THE MORNING of May 23, Banks's forces in the Valley were concentrated in two small bodies: 8,000 men at Strasburg, with 1,000 men twelve miles east in Front Royal. Banks's remaining strength was spread along the Manassas Gap Railroad east of the Blue Ridge and beyond supporting distance. Shields's division had completed its shift to Fredericksburg, where it was resting for the march southward to attack Richmond. The Shenandoah had supposedly been secured, a redeployment of forces out of the Valley had been completed, and all available Federal forces were prepared to move on to Richmond. As had happened after Kernstown, however, Union plans were disarranged.

Around midday on the twenty-third, Jackson's 17,000 men engulfed the Union garrison at Front Royal, comprised principally of the 1st Maryland Infantry. As it happened Jackson also had a regiment recruited in Maryland, and he used it as his shock troops. The Marylanders squared off in a brief but fierce skirmish, interrupted by arrival of a freight train that chugged into town between the opposing battle lines. The Rebels swept up the train, the town, and almost one thousand prisoners. Only a few dozen Federals escaped to bring Banks word of the onslaught.

Banks reacted to the situation poorly, first underestimating and then exaggerating Southern strength. His subordinates urged him to evacuate Strasburg at once, but he refused to do so until midmorning of the next day. He then ordered an immediate retreat, with the result that a near frantic collection of wagon trains, cavalry columns, and infantry poured down the pike for Winchester. The column was subjected to repeated Confederate cavalry raids and occasional shellings. Around Middletown the Federal column was severed, and hundreds of Yankees fled to the south and then the west as Rebels fanned out after them.

Banks, meanwhile, reached Winchester by evening with the bulk of his forces. He put them into line of battle on the hills south of Winchester and

Colonel John White Geary of the 28th Pennsylvania in an unpublished portrait by McAllister of Philadelphia. Formerly the first mayor of San Francisco and the governor of Kansas Territory, he was, like Banks, a politician turned commander. Unlike Banks, he proved to be a man of genuine military talent. In March 1862 he captured Leesburg before the campaign had fairly begun. (CWTI)

began to wire Washington frantically for reinforcements. But there was no time for help to arrive.

The Rebels hit again at first light on May 25, and Banks saw his army dissolve. Within two hours his brigades were swept from their positions in total rout. The Federal flight continued throughout the day, carrying them almost to the Potomac that night.

In two days of running battle, Banks had been swept out of the Valley. Three thousand Federals were prisoners. More than nine thousand rifles, warehouses of urgently needed medical stores, herds of cattle, and tons of other stores had been captured from Strasburg to the Potomac. Confederates gloated that the Federal rout was more complete than that at Manassas; total Southern casualties from Front Royal to Winchester were less than four hundred killed and wounded. One Rebel veteran summarized this highlight of the war long after when he wrote, "We had no general engagement, and our loss was small; it being a kind of one-sided fight all the time. General Jackson 'got the drop' on them in the start, and kept it."

THE EFFECT of Jackson's onslaught was immediate. President Lincoln was seriously disturbed by events in the Shenandoah, and he responded with orders to capture or crush the Valley Army. Studying his map of Virginia, Lincoln noted that Jackson had moved dangerously north of both Frémont and the Union forces around Fredericksburg; the Rebels were, in fact, moving into a trap. Even as the Confederates were herding Banks out of the Shenandoah, Lincoln directed Frémont to drive into the Valley from the Alleghenies, while Shields was ordered to retrace the march he had just made and return to the Valley from the east with 20,000 men. Both halves of this pincer were to enter the Valley well south of Jackson so as to cut off his escape.

Lincoln's bold plan, which was, in effect, a third invasion of the Shenandoah, was purchased at the price of assistance to McClellan. With Shields leading 20,000 men back to the Valley, the remaining Union forces at Fredericksburg were too weak to lunge southward, which is just what Jackson desired. Jackson had fulfilled his mission to keep as many Federal troops as possible tied down in and around the Shenandoah. Overall, some 50,000 to 60,000 Federals across northern Virginia were concentrating on the Valley Army instead of Richmond.

Jackson, meanwhile, pushed northward to Harpers Ferry at the end of May and made a vigorous demonstration before a well-entrenched Union garrison hoping to multiply the shock value of his sudden appearance in the lower Valley. But his own situation was now critical. By May 30, Jackson learned he was almost surrounded by Federal columns from the west (Frémont), east (Shields), and north (Banks's reorganizing army

Harpers Ferry, Virginia, showing the remnant of the United States Arsenal. Here Banks anchored his army at the outset of the campaign. (USAMHI)

David B. Woodbury's October 1862 image of Federal troops camped on ground which once held the armory buildings. (USAMHI)

The charred remains of a canal boat and steam engine at Harpers Ferry, the scene of repeated destruction in 1862. (USAMHI)

and the garrison at Harpers Ferry). Jackson's response was calm and to the point: He ordered his men to turn around and march southward very fast. In two days of heroic effort he covered the fifty miles from Harpers Ferry to Strasburg with all his captured stores and prisoners. He collided with Frémont just outside of Strasburg and drove him back into the Alleghenies, clearing the way for the last of his stragglers to slip through the Union ring.

Throughout the first week of June, the Valley Army withdrew from Strasburg under terrific pressure. Frémont trailed the Rebels along the Valley Pike, while Shields pushed his divisions southward into the Luray Valley. Rain poured down in crackling streams. Units lost their wagon trains, officers lost their commands, regiments became intermingled, and confusion reached epidemic proportions. The courageous cavalry leader Turner Ashby was killed protecting the army's rear in a heavy skirmish. The retreat demanded the courage of a battle and was far more costly. The Valley Army had lost four hundred men fighting its way from Front Royal to Winchester; it lost thousands of stragglers and sick on this retreat. One Rebel wrote, "I never saw a Brigade so completely broken down and unfitted for service as our Brigade. . . . I am satisfied that the Brigade has lost at least 1,000 men broken down, left on the way and captured."

By June 7, Jackson had turned southeastward from Harrisonburg to slip around the Massanutten to the village of Port Republic. There he would stand between Frémont and Shields, and around this village were to occur scenes as thrilling as any of the Valley Campaign.

These events erupted on the morning of June 8, as a surprise Union cavalry raid stormed into Port Republic and almost captured Jackson and most of his staff. Other Union cavalrymen probed to within a few hundred yards of the huge Confederate wagon train. A courageous stand by a dozen sentries stalled the Union raiders just long enough to allow Jackson to move in reinforcements and eject them.

As if in echo, Frémont's guns began to pound Confederate positions west of Port Republic. Jackson feared that he was about to be struck from two sides at once and built up his positions around the village; he left the handling of Frémont to Ewell's division. Ewell did his job well. In what has be-

Past this sawmill at Kernstown, Jackson advanced against Shields in the Battle of Kernstown, first engagement of the campaign. An 1885 photograph. (USAMHI)

Colonel John Echols was severely wounded leading his 27th Virginia at Kernstown. Three weeks later he was promoted brigadier, and would become—though unsung—one of the finest subordinates in the army. At 6 feet, 4 inches, and weighing 260 pounds, he was a wonderful target. (USAMHI)

Jackson, with something of an affinity for stone walls, formed his line of battle on the near side of this one at Kernstown. (USAMHI)

Captain Pinckney D. Bowles led a company of the 4th Alabama in Jackson's army. Like many junior officers of talent, he gained from the ravages of the bullet, which gave him plenty of opportunity for advancement. He finished the war an unconfirmed brigadier. (USAMHI)

come known as the Battle of Cross Keys, Ewell sparred with Frémont throughout the day, repulsing every Union attack and driving the Federals back several miles by nightfall. During the day Shields's advanced guards showed themselves briefly to the east of Port Republic but made no advance.

Emboldened by Frémont's weak showing, Jackson planned the most ambitious battle of the campaign for the next morning. He would maneuver all available men across the two small rivers that joined around Port Republic to crush Shields's advance guard east of those streams, then return to rout Frémont. His timetable allowed only four hours to thrash Shields before he would have to rejoin the thin covering force he would leave behind to bluff Frémont. There was equally little time to prepare the attack; Jackson was able to span the river obstacles with only primitive temporary bridges, and this was to cost more valuable time.

Before dawn on June 9, Jackson's maneuver brigades were on the march, and things promptly began to go wrong. Delays were encountered crossing Jackson's hastily erected bridges, batteries came up without ammunition, and the Confederate attack began piecemeal about 7:00 A.M. It stalled at once and during the next several hours Jackson was outnumbered and on the defensive. Shields's men, recalling Kernstown, attacked furiously and at one point shattered the main Southern line. The dramatic arrival of Ewell with several fresh regiments reversed the flight, but more anxious minutes passed before Jackson finally assembled an overwhelming numerical superiority and drove Shields's forces back handsomely. Kernstown was revenged by the Battle of Port Republic but Confederate losses were severe, and Jackson abandoned any further hope of attacking Frémont. Instead, he coiled his forces along the slopes of the Blue Ridge out of enemy reach. He need not have worried, for both Frémont and Shields retreated the next day.

The Valley campaign comes to an end with those retreats. Jackson made preparations to join Lee around Richmond as soon as he learned of the enemy withdrawals. As he laid his plans, Jackson found himself something of a hero of the South. Since leaving Swift Run Gap on April 30, he had marched almost four hundred miles. He had inflicted approximately seven thousand casualties on the Union, half of them prisoners, and captured enormous quantities of supplies. His own losses had been less than half of those of the enemy, light losses indeed when compared to the ghastly casualty lists from other encounters of this war. Most important of all, the Valley Army's weeks of marching had been weeks of victory which stalled the Union drive on Richmond. Jackson's successes reinspired a South parched for victory. Robert E. Lee expressed the feelings of the Confederacy when he wrote to Jackson, "Your successes have been the cause of the liveliest joy in this army as well as in the country."

It seemed almost unfair that with so much Confederate talent in the Shenandoah, the Federals enjoyed so little. A case in point is Brigadier General Robert H. Milroy. In 1863 he had almost an entire brigade captured in the Shenandoah, and he did little better against Jackson in the earlier campaign. (USAMHI)

A few days after Jackson's victory at Front Royal, a photographer caught these Confederate prisoners awaiting transport to prison. They keep a respectful distance from their guards and their stacked arms. (LC)

Brigadier General Alpheus S. Williams advanced from brigade to division command at the Battle of Winchester. Few Federals won laurels there. (P-M)

A street in Winchester showing Taylor's Hotel, the building with the columns, where Federal officers made their headquarters in April before the battle. Winchester changed hands in this war fifty-two times. (USAMHI)

Main Street in Winchester, probably taken after the war. Winchester saw more marching armies than any other town in the war. (USAMHI)

Brigadier General William B. Taliaferro, seated left, commanded a brigade for Jackson. He had been in command of the Virginia Militia, as shown here, when it mustered to put down John Brown's attack on Harpers Ferry. (MUSEUM OF THE CONFEDERACY, RICHMOND)

Francis T. Nichols led the 8th Louisiana at Winchester, and there took a wound which cost him his left arm. Promoted to brigadier—as shown here—a few months later, he later lost a foot at Chancellorsville. (NYHS)

A ford on the Shenandoah River, crossed and recrossed by Jackson many times in the course of his campaign. (USAMHI)

A postwar view of the Massanutten Mountain, key to Jackson's brilliant success in the Shenandoah. (USAMHI)

Jackson's brilliant cavalry leader, Brigadier General Turner Ashby, made major contributions to the defense of the Valley. It cost him his life on June 6, 1862, just two weeks after he received his general's stars. The only known photograph of him in uniform is this one, taken in death. (CHS)

Colonel Beverly Robertson succeeded to command of Ashby's cavalry at his death, and three days later he was made a brigadier. (VM)

Brigadier General John P. Hatch commanded Banks's cavalry in the futile attempt to contain Ashby. Shown here in an 1865 portrait made in Charleston, South Carolina, he failed to distinguish himself. (USAMHI)

The battlefield at Cross Keys. (USAMHI)

The ever-present Brigadier General Louis Blenker had to make a torturous march with his division in March 1862, going from McClellan's army to join the Federals in the Valley. It took six weeks and the War Department forgot to supply him with anything. Cross Keys was his last battle. He fell from his horse during the war, and in October 1863 he died from the effects of the fall. (P-M)

Colonel Wladimir Krzyzanowski, a Pole by birth, led the 58th New York at Cross Keys. "Kriz" rose to brigade command within a year. (P-M)

Brigadier General George H. Steuart, called "Maryland Steuart," thanks to his birthplace, led a Virginia brigade and was badly wounded at Cross Keys. At Winchester he had declined to obey an order from Jackson because it did not come through the proper chain of command, and this may have cost the Confederates the chance to entirely destroy the Federals. (SOUTHERN HISTORICAL COLLECTION, THE UNIVERSITY OF NORTH CAROLINA AT CHAPEL HILL)

Colonel Thomas T. Munford led the 2nd Virginia Cavalry under Ashby and at Cross Keys. Like many of these Virginians, Munford found that the dashing Valley service appealed to the romantic in him. (CWTI)

Brigadier General Arnold Elzey distinguished himself and his brigade at Port Republic. His horse was killed under him and he took a painful wound in the head. (VM)

Port Republic, in a photograph taken fifty years after the battle in which Jackson effectively completed the Valley campaign in victory. (USAMHI)

The Second Bull Run

DAVID LINDSEY

To Manassas once again, another battle, another defeat

AS UNION Major General George B. McClellan's Peninsular campaign sputtered out in the heavy fighting of the Seven Days Battles, the opposing armies drew apart. McClellan backed off his 100,000-man Army of the Potomac to a new base at Harrison's Landing on the James River, where Federal Navy control assured protection, supplies, and future mobility. The newly named commander of the 75,000-man Confederate Army, General Robert E. Lee, had succeeded in beating back the Union drive on Richmond. Both sides now paused, catching their breath, pondering how to proceed next.

From Washington a disappointed President Abraham Lincoln came in person to McClellan's headquarters to assess the situation. When McClellan handed him a lengthy note giving blunt advice on matters of policy, Lincoln kept his own counsel, while mulling over what to do with his balky general and the well-trained, well-equipped army. In a move to pump new blood and spirit into the eastern theater command, Lincoln now brought bewhiskered Major General John Pope from the west to command a newly organized Army of Virginia that combined the forces of Major Generals Nathaniel Banks, John Frémont, and Irvin McDowell. Pope's credits included some earlier victories in the west, strong antislavery views, and an aggressive attitude toward the enemy. He talked too much and had criticized McClellan's "indisposition to active movements." Also from the west came Major General Henry W. Halleck, clean-shaven and bug-eyed, whose large forehead inspired his nickname "Old Brains," to be installed as General-in-Chief of all Union armies.

Where McClellan fitted in the new command picture remained undetermined by Washington. Clearly "Little Mac" was extremely popular with his soldiers, one of whom wrote, "the real man of the army is Little Mac. No general could ask for greater love and more unbounded confidence than he receives from his men. . . . everywhere among his boys, as he calls them, . . . he is received with enthusiasm." For himself, McClellan says of his plans for midsummer 1862, "I would have crossed to the south bank" of the James River and seized Petersburg from which "I would have operated against Richmond and its communications from the west, having already gained those from the south." Perhaps. McClellan wrote this years later, knowing with hindsight that General U. S. Grant used precisely that approach in 1864–65. At least one of his soldiers thought it possible, agreeing with McClellan that the administration had not given adequate support, noting, "We want 300,000 men raised and sent down here immediately. We've been fooling about this thing long enough. . . . The army and the people demand such a vigorous prosecution of the war as shall give some hope of ending it."

But the Lincoln Administration decided otherwise by early August. On August 3 Halleck ordered McClellan "to withdraw your army from the Peninsula to Aquia Creek" on the Potomac, some thirty miles south of Washington. McClellan protested, arguing, "Here is the true defense of Washington; it is here on the banks of the James that the fate of the Union should be decided." But Halleck insisted McClellan get moving. But "Little Mac" as always moved with caution, sending first the wounded, followed by the able-bodied troops, on transports down the James, up Chesapeake Bay and the Potomac to Aquia Creek and Alexandria. All of this took time—too much time as it turned out.

During July Lee watched intently from Richmond seeking to fathom the next Federal move. He learned of Pope's taking command of the new 40,000-man Army of Virginia. If Pope should begin moving south toward Richmond and McClellan should punch again at Richmond from the east, the combined 140,000 Union force would put Lee in deep trouble. To remain inactive was to risk envelopment. Weighing the risks carefully, Lee decided on July 13 to move boldly by sending Major General Thomas J. "Stonewall" Jackson with 12,000 troops sixty miles northwest out of Richmond to Gordonsville. Here where the Virginia Central Railroad crossed the Orange & Alexandria Railroad was the critical point the Confederates had to hold—whether Pope decided to move south or Lee decided to move out from Richmond.

Octagon House in Arlington, Virginia, headquarters for Major General Irvin McDowell in the early summer of 1862, when Lincoln held his corps back from McClellan on the Peninsula. (USAMHI)

Then once again McDowell marched south into Virginia's heartland, past scenes remembered from his campaign of the year before, scenes like Falls Church. (USAMHI)

When the Federal command made no immediate response, Lee then sent Major General A. P. Hill's "light division" of 12,000 men forward to join Jackson, saying, "I want Pope to be suppressed." When Jackson probed forward north of the Rapidan he found a small advance Union force of about 8,000 men under Banks drawn up along a small stream near Cedar Mountain. Characteristically, on August 9 Jackson attacked immediately—probably too soon, since he had only about half his men in position. Banks's troops fought back fiercely, repulsing the first Confederate assaults and pummeling the celebrated Stonewall

Brigade (that had won Jackson his nickname at Bull Run a year earlier). But Jackson succeeded in rallying his men, hurried A. P. Hill's division into action, and drove the Federals from the field. After a brief pursuit Jackson withdrew south of the Rapidan.

In itself Cedar Mountain meant little. But overall it meant the military initiative was shifting away from the Federals, who only two months earlier were threatening Richmond. Now Lee, assuming the offensive, would step up pressure on Pope's army. On August 13, learning that McClellan's army was starting to embark from its James River position, he ordered Major General James Longstreet with 25,000 men forward to Gordonsville. Two days later he left some 25,000 soldiers to protect Richmond and he himself moved out to lead the Army of Northern Virginia in person.

General John Pope from his Culpeper headquarters fifteen miles north of the Rapidan River surveyed the military situation. Earlier on arriving from the west, he had issued some bombastic proclamations urging his army to fight tenaciously, not show their backs to the enemy, and not retreat. At mid-August Pope's command of about 55,000 men (including 8,000 of General Ambrose E. Burnside's corps led by Major General Jesse Reno) were encamped north of the Rapidan with the Orange & Alexandria Railroad, their main supply route, running southwest from Alexandria some sixty miles distant. Pope was following Halleck's instructions to remain there until joined by the Army of the Potomac. Some 70,000 to 100,000 of McClellan's troops, withdrawing from the Peninsula via the Potomac and Aquia Creek, were expected shortly to line up alongside Pope's position. At that point, Pope thought, Halleck would come from Washington and take personal command in the field.

Seeking the weakness in Pope's position north of the Rapidan, with the Rappahannock in his rear, Lee calculated that fast-moving Confederate cavalry could knife swiftly across the Rapidan, drive north, and destroy the rail bridge over the Rappahannock, thus cutting Pope's supply line. But, Lee knew, the strike would have to be lightning fast because McClellan's troops would be reaching Pope within about ten days. On August 18 the Confederates tried it, but signals got crossed. Part of the cavalry missed an assignment. A river crossing was left unguarded, and a Federal patrol in a surprise raid south of the river just missed capturing Gen-

Photographer Timothy O'Sullivan's wagon on the road leading into Culpeper. (USAMHI)

Culpeper's important railroad depot on the Orange & Alexandria. (USAMHI)

eral "Jeb" Stuart but did get his famous plumed hat and silk-lined robe. More important they seized a junior officer carrying Lee's orders. As a result Pope, now aware of Lee's strategy, pulled his troops back to the north bank of the Rappahannock and set strong units at each of the river's fords.

During the intermittent rains of the next few days Lee probed for a crossing of the Rappahannock and pushed farther upstream. Stuart's cavalry crossed after dark on August 22, snaked swiftly through the foothills, and then swinging eastward pounced on Pope's headquarters at Catlett's Station on the Orange & Alexandria Railroad. There Stuart seized a stack of Pope's military papers including an important dispatch book, took personal revenge for the loss of his plumed hat by carrying off Pope's uniform coat, and after trying in vain to fire the rain-soaked rail bridge, withdrew to the Confederate lines.

As the days passed, Lee saw his chance of a quick victory diminishing. From Pope's papers he learned that McClellan's V Corps under Major General Fitz John Porter, having landed at Aquia Creek, was marching to join Pope on the upper Rappahannock. Major General Samuel P. Heintzelman's III Corps was scheduled to follow shortly. Lee figured Pope had 70,000 troops within call on August 25 with more on the way. Already outnumbered, Lee would find attack futile if he postponed it even a few days. In fact, it was perhaps already too late for a pitched battle, unless Pope could be maneuvered off balance. Lee was willing to give it a try.

On August 25 Lee sent Jackson with 23,000 "foot cavalry" scurrying out on a long sweep west and north. This division of the army in the immediate presence of the enemy, contrary to all conventional military wisdom, posed a serious military risk. Had Pope pulled all his units together and

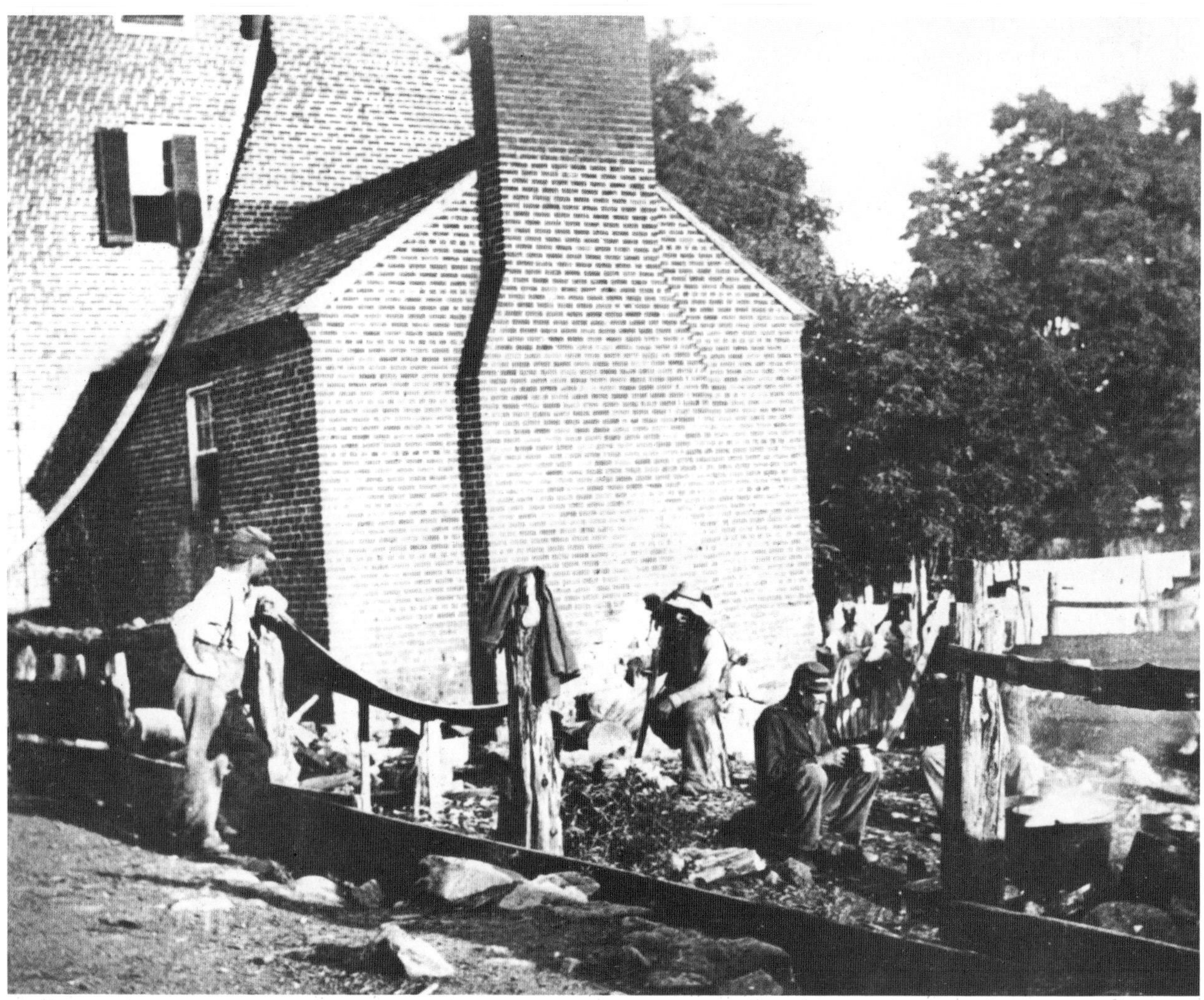

Inside Culpeper McDowell's soldiers made themselves comfortable for what they hoped might be a long stay. (USAMHI)

concentrated on Lee's force remaining south of the Rappahannock, the Rebels might have been badly whipped. But Lee took the gamble, counting on Pope not to move quickly while Jackson circled behind the Bull Run mountains out of sight and around Pope's right flank. If all went well, Jackson would swing in behind and cut Pope's supply and communication lines.

Shedding knapsacks and surplus paraphernalia, Jackson's men sliced swiftly north to Salem Village on the west side of the mountains, then turned east through Thoroughfare Gap in the Bull Run mountains. Having covered a remarkable thirty miles by evening of the first day's march, Jackson proudly watching his columns file forward was heard to murmur, "Who could fail to win battles with such men as these?" The gap, unguarded by Federal troops, was readily negotiated. From its eastern summit the Confederates surveyed the rolling farmland interspersed with woods stretching eastward, with Gainesville lying directly east on the main turnpike that ran northeast to Centreville and southwest to Warrenton. No Federal forces lay in sight on that road. Ten miles beyond lay the Orange & Alexandria rail line, Pope's supply artery and Jackson's target. Pouring out of the mountains, Jackson's troops pushed on swiftly and seized Bristoe Station by dusk on August 26. Capturing most of the astonished garrison, they destroyed the rail bridge over Broad Run, tore up the tracks, cut the telegraph wires, and wrecked two trains. But two trains escaped, one going north to Alexandria, the other south to Warrenton to spread the alarm. Jackson's two forward regiments captured Ma-

But they would not be there long. In August their wagons loaded to roll toward the enemy. (USAMHI)

nassas Junction by midnight, and he followed with the rest of his force by morning of August 27.

Manassas Junction, as the main Union supply depot, offered a rich harvest to the tired and hungry Rebels. Here were tons of supplies, hundreds of loaded freight cars, streets of bulging warehouses, fields filled with barrels, boxes, and piles of munitions. After the captured whiskey was carefully destroyed, Jackson's famished men—who had been on short rations for days—tore into the rich stores of food. An enormous picnic resulted as men gorged themselves not only on staples of bread, salt meat, and coffee, but also on canned lobster, oysters, boned turkey, pies, and other delicacies. Shoes, trousers, shirts, toothbrushes, combs, and more were appropriated. The revelry continued all through the day of August 27. Before the bloated army marched that evening, torches were applied to the remaining, unconsumed supplies and munitions, which burned and exploded like fireworks all night.

Meanwhile General Pope with his troops on the north side of the Rappahannock found himself in a position that was both a risk and a challenge—it offered a good opportunity if Pope could seize it, but unless he managed well he would be in increasing danger. Of the three corps comprising his army at the outset, Pope saw McDowell's corps as the only one worth much. Major General Franz Sigel, he thought, was incompetent. Banks's corps, badly mauled at Cedar Mountain, with only 5,000 survivors, was of reduced effectiveness. From McClellan's army, one-armed Major General Phil Kearny brought a reliable division of Heintzelman's corps.

There was a new commander in Virginia, Major General John Pope, a hero from the western campaigns who promised he would lead this army to victory. He led the army first toward Cedar Mountain. Pope here appears as a brigadier. (LC)

Other troops were reported to Pope as at hand or nearby—Heintzelman's other division under Joe Hooker, Reno with most of Burnside's men, and John Reynolds's division from Porter's corps. The rest of Porter's command was reported moving to join Pope. This gave Pope over 70,000 men in the vicinity. If coordinated they could throw overwhelming power against Jackson. At the least they could plug Thoroughfare Gap and thereby prevent Lee and Longstreet's combined force of 30,000 men from using that route to come to Jackson's support. But to do these things, Pope would have to get a good many separate units to do some fast marching under coordinated direction in conditions that would change as the movements of Jackson and Lee changed. Since Pope's wire dispatches to Washington were not reaching Halleck because Jackson had cut the telegraph, Washington had only a faint idea of what was happening in the countryside beyond Manassas Junction. Messages carried by mounted couriers were uncertain. Many slips were possible—Pope could misread enemy movements, his orders to subordinates could be misinterpreted or poorly obeyed, delay and confusion could set in. If any of these things occurred, Lee's gamble would pay off.

From John Buford's effective cavalry Pope learned of Jackson's march west of the mountains—but at first Pope somehow concluded that Jackson was heading for the Shenandoah Valley. Even when he discovered that Jackson's army was coming east through Thoroughfare Gap, Pope seemed unable to deal effectively with the information. Not that Pope was slow or lazy. If nothing else, he was a man of vigor. His response was understandably vigorous. When word reached him of Jackson's sacking of Manassas, Pope pulled his troops back from the Rappahannock to positions running roughly from Gainesville about five miles east of Thoroughfare Gap on the Alexandria–Warrenton turnpike to Warrenton Junction about twenty miles south on the Orange & Alexandria Railroad. This was a well-conceived move.

From Gainesville Pope sent James B. Ricketts's division of McDowell's corps west to cork the bottleneck at Thoroughfare Gap. But from this point forward Pope dispatched curious orders that were often incomprehensible or contradictory or self-canceling. Porter's corps, for example, was marched at top speed for ten miles under a broiling August sun only to be rushed back at the same fervid pace to the point it came from. Heintzelman's III Corps tramped eighteen miles to reach a point only three miles from where it started. Federal troops were being worn down by marching and countermarching on reduced rations, since the Manassas stores had been burned.

Pope pushed other Federal units forward to Manassas Junction to smash Jackson. There they found nothing but smoldering ruins. Leaving after dark the night before, Jackson had sent three columns forward—one across Bull Run and northwest toward Centreville, a second across Bull Run and northwest to Sudley Springs, the third up the west bank of Bull Run. Next day, August 28, he brought all three together near Groveton in a wooded area a short distance west of the Warrenton pike. Puzzled over the invisible Jackson, Pope concluded the enemy was heading north toward the Potomac and ordered troops forward to Centreville to head off such a move. But Jackson wasn't there either. Figuring Jackson was now desperately trying to escape, Pope determined to concentrate his forces on Jackson when he found him.

In making Jackson the sole target of his drive, Pope somehow forgot about Lee and Longstreet. The Federal plug came uncorked from Thoroughfare Gap as Ricketts moved his men back from their forward position there. This was exactly the reverse of what was needed for a Union success. Ricketts should have been strengthened to thwart a juncture between Lee and Longstreet from coming through the pass and joining Jackson. Somehow Pope erroneously developed the notion that McDowell's unit, "ordered to interpose between" Jackson and the enemy's "main body . . . moving down through Thoroughfare Gap" had "completely accomplished" its mission by driv-

On August 9, 1862, the armies clashed at Cedar Mountain. That same day O'Sullivan caught this battery fording a tributary of the Rappahannock on its way to the fight. (USAMHI)

The battlefield at Cedar Mountain, taken a few days after the fight (NLM)

ing Longstreet "back to the west side" of the gap. This totally false impression led Pope into mistaken planning for the next day, August 28.

Arriving at Bristoe by dusk August 27, Pope convinced himself he had Jackson trapped. Out went orders to subordinates to march "at the very earliest blush of dawn" in order to concentrate forces between Gainesville and Manassas and "we shall bag the whole crowd. . . . Be expeditious, and the day is our own."

In pulling his forces away from Manassas Junction Jackson had ultimately chosen his position well. He brought his various columns together on the western edge of what had been the Bull Run battlefield of a year earlier, under the cover of a wooded area a short distance west of Groveton just off the Warrenton pike. His left was anchored on Bull Run at Sudley Springs, his right on a hill roughly two miles southwest toward Gainesville. His front was protected by a low wooded ridge and a steep embankment of an abandoned railroad line. Here he could rest his men concealed in the shade of the woods, but in a commanding position difficult to assail and with a potential escape route via Aldie Gap in the mountains to his rear. And yet he was close enough for Lee and Longstreet to reach him when they passed through Thoroughfare Gap a dozen miles to the southwest. Here on August 28 Jackson waited in the woods and watched as units of McDowell's corps trudged along the pike to Centreville, past the Stone Bridge to Jackson's left.

Finally as evening approached Jackson determined to make Pope stand and fight rather than let him withdraw to a strong position on the Centreville side of Bull Run. The column of Rufus King's division approached along the pike in the late afternoon heat. "Stonewall" Jackson, after riding out in front of his hidden troops, eyed the Yankees through his glass, then wheeled, galloped back to the ridge, and barked an order. Confederate artillery batteries rolled out and began firing. From the woods Rebel troops charged "with a hoarse roar . . . like wild beasts at the scent of blood," red battle flags gleaming under the sinking sun. Forming the line of battle they started shooting.

On the Union side Brigadier General John Gibbon's four brigades took the initial shock of the enemy attack. Green, never under fire before, they should have panicked. Instead they wheeled about coolly into their own line of battle and stopped the Rebel attack. Joined by men from Abner Doubleday's brigade, 2,800 Federals faced nearly twice as many Confederates in one of "the hardest close-quarter fights of the whole war." The contending battle lines stood face to face "as if they were on parade awaiting inspection, and volleyed away at the murderous range of less than one hundred yards." For two solid hours the deadly firing continued until darkness closed in. By nine o'clock the lines drew apart. On both sides the losses had been staggering. Two of Jackson's generals, William Taliaferro and Richard Ewell, were carried from the field severely wounded. Gibbon's midwestern farm boys, already called the "Black Hat Brigade," won laurels that day and would soon be rightly known as the "Iron Brigade."

By nightfall August 28, Pope, now aware of Jackson's position, decided to destroy Jackson's force the next day. Again orders went to division commanders to move "at the earliest dawn." But as Pope moved his headquarters forward to a hill near the famous Stone House, well-remembered from the first Bull Run battle's intense fighting, he was still fuzzy on several crucial factors. For one, he did not know the current location of McDowell or that Ricketts had moved to Bristoe Station. He still held to his delusion that Lee and Longstreet had been repulsed at Thoroughfare Gap. In addition, his men, after much marching and little eating, were tired and sluggish.

From dawn on August 29 Federal artillery blasted away at Jackson's position in the woods just northwest of the Warrenton pike, while infantry units moved closer. Again, if Pope could get all his forces concentrated, he figured to outweigh Jackson's battered 20,000-man army by three to one. Chance for victory looked bright. Anxious to open the attack, Pope moved hastily while many of his units were still on the road and out of touch.

Cedar Mountain itself sits in the distance, seen here from the Union position. (USAMHI)

Major General Nathaniel Banks. A failure in the campaign against Jackson in the Shenandoah that spring, he was defeated by Jackson again here at Cedar Mountain. (USAMHI)

After the artillery blasts drove in Confederate skirmishers, Sigel's 11,000 men were ordered to attack the center of Jackson's defense line. As a Confederate observer reported, "The Federals sprang forward with a long-drawn 'huzzah' ringing from their 10,000 throats. On they went until half the distance to the [railroad] cut and then the smoke, flash and roar of 4,000 well-aimed guns burst from the Confederate entrenchment, and a wild, reckless and terrifying Southern yell echoed and reechoed through the woodlands." Two more Yankee assaults were made on the center and repulsed.

The attack then shifted to Jackson's left where Pope sent Kearny and Hooker with 12,000 Army of the Potomac veterans aided by Reno's 8,000 seasoned veterans. But organization, timing, and coordination were lacking. Federal units went into action piecemeal, bit by bit, and the full effect of such a massive blow was lost. Besides, the Rebel line here was defended by some of Jackson's best troops under A. P. Hill. The Confederate line bent and at one point snapped temporarily under the impact of six separate attacks, punctuated with vicious hand-to-hand bayonet fighting. Hill's ammunition supply was almost gone and his casualties were enormous, but he managed to hang on as dusk fell.

Meanwhile some 30,000 Union troops nearby had failed to get into action. These men under Porter and McDowell, moving from Manassas toward Gainesville to hit Jackson's right, sighted large clouds of dust ahead. Figuring that Confederate reinforcements were arriving, Porter and McDowell slowed, paused, and shifted course toward Groveton, beyond which fighting raged. Because of their slowness few of McDowell's and none of Porter's troops got into battle before the day's fighting ended. Porter would later be court-martialed and cashiered for holding back here.

Also sitting out the action of August 29 were Longstreet's 30,000 soldiers. They had emerged from Thoroughfare Gap early, marched forward, contacted Jackson's right by noon, and took position just south of the Warrenton pike by 3 P.M., where they blocked Porter's line of advance. Poised to attack the Federal left flank, Longstreet persuaded Lee to wait, arguing that his men needed rest after a long march and that delay might produce new Federal blunders. Toward evening Longstreet sent a reconnaissance unit forward on the pike only to clash with McDowell and to pull back to await the next morning. That night Lee reported to President Davis, "My desire has been to avoid a general engagement, being the weaker force, and by maneuvering to relieve a portion of the country."

That night at his headquarters on a hill close to the Stone House at the junction of the Warrenton pike and the Manassas–Sudley road, the husky Pope with the usual cigar in hand reviewed the day's action with some satisfaction. Jackson, as Pope saw it, was badly bruised, was cornered, and could be captured next day. Annoyed by Porter's failure to advance when ordered, he dismissed as nonsense Porter's claim that Longstreet barred his path with three times his numbers. Reporting optimistically, Pope told Halleck, "We fought a terrific battle . . . which lasted with continuous fury from daybreak until dark. . . . The enemy is still in our front, but badly used up. . . . The news just reaches me that the enemy is retreating toward the mountains."

On August 30 Pope's actions defy comprehension. During the morning he planned cautiously in the belief that Jackson, badly cut up, was pulling out of his position leaving only a rear guard—and of course that Lee and Longstreet were not in the vicinity. But if the Federals' task were simply to mop up the remaining Rebels, why wait until midday to start the process? True, Federal troops were tired after much marching and fighting and they had limited supplies; but the same applied to the enemy. As Pope eyed the situation, the railroad embankment, scene of yesterday's heavy fighting, seemed virtually empty, only a few Rebel sharpshooters replying to the Federal outposts' firing. (Jackson had his men out of sight getting some rest on the wooded hillslope above.) Systematically Pope disposed his units, pulling Porter's corps in on the left to close up with McDowell for a two-pronged drive along the pike, sending Heintzelman to drive west from the pike against Jackson and "press him vigorously during the whole day."

As Pope was concentrating his forces, Lee kept Jackson firm on his left and had Longstreet fan his five divisions out on the right to form the lower mandible of a giant jaw. Into this maw Union troops were now marched. About noon Stuart reported to Lee that bluecoats were massing in front of Jackson. Lee forwarded the warning to Jackson, who alerted his men, but kept them concealed in the woods.

At noon without warning Federal troops charged forward in three waves—much heavier than the day before. Rebels rushed to man their line along the railroad bank and fought back doggedly. Determined Yankees slogging forward got within a few yards of the defense position. Confederates, running out of ammunition, began heaving rocks at their attackers. Hill's line wavered, broke, then reformed. Jackson signaled an appeal to Lee for reinforcements.

As Porter's units surged forward on the Union

The Robinson House near the center of the battlefield at Cedar Mountain. Banks enjoyed some initial success on this line before Jackson smashed him. (USAMHI)

Brigadier General John White Geary, hand in blouse, stands with his staff at Harpers Ferry. He fought well for Banks and took two wounds from the field. (LC)

left, Longstreet's men coming out from their forest cover absorbed the first fury of the attack, then began pivoting on a hinge close to Groveton and positioned their artillery for enfilading fire. One observer wrote, "gunners leaped to their pieces . . . , bowling their shots along the serried rows of Federals who up to now had been unaware of the danger to their flank. The effect was instantaneous. Torn and blasted by this fire, the second and third lines milled aimlessly, bewildered, then retreated . . . whereupon the first line soldiers [seeing] . . . their supports in flight, also began to waver and give ground." South of the Warrenton pike two New York volunteer regiments guarded the base of a knoll on which a six-gun Union battery was stationed. As Longstreet swept forward these men caught the brunt of the assault. One regiment was quickly overrun. But the second —Zouaves, nattily dressed with white spats, tasseled fezzes, blue jackets, and fancy scarlet trousers —stood firm while the battery flailed the attackers and then limbered—hitched the guns to their teams—and got away, the New Yorkers then withdrawing. The cost was enormous—of 490 Zouaves, 124 lay dead, 223 wounded when it was over.

By 4 P.M. Porter found his men fighting for their lives on their front and left flank with a prospect of being enveloped by Longstreet. A withdrawal began with Longstreet in hot pursuit. As Porter reeled backwards, Lee ordered his whole army to advance—Jackson's units to drive east and south to block Federal retreat along the Warrenton pike toward the Stone Bridge. Jackson's revived lines surged forward down the embankment and out onto the plain. Shrieking the Rebel yell, they charged against the backdrop of the setting sun, said a Northern observer, like "demons emerging from the earth."

Federal forces rallied on the high ground of Henry House Hill, where Jackson had won his nickname thirteen months earlier. Sigel's and Reno's troops joined Gibbon's "Black Hat" boys to form a firm shield for the retreating Federal units. Some feared the withdrawal might turn to panic and rout, as it had in July 1861 on this very same ground. Riding up to Gibbon, Phil Kearny, empty sleeve flapping in the breeze, cried, "It's another Bull Run!" When Gibbon said he hoped not, Kearny replied, "Perhaps not. Reno is keeping up the fight. . . . I am not stampeded; you are not stampeded. . . . My God, that's about all!" At any rate, battling bluecoats on the hill held the charging Rebels long enough for Pope's army to reach and cross the Stone Bridge over Bull Run. The bridge was then blown up. As darkness and rain came on, these troops, grumbling about their inept leaders, slogged on four muddy miles to camp long after nightfall in positions on the heights of Centreville. These were entrenched fortifications left by Confederates from July 1861. What might have been a disastrous Union rout came off as an orderly withdrawal, quite in contrast to first Bull Run. As Pope saw it in his report that night to Halleck, "The battle was most furious for hours without cessation, and the losses on both sides very heavy. The enemy is badly crippled, and we shall do well enough."

But another observer assessed Pope's situation differently, pointing out he had been "kicked, cuffed, hustled about, knocked down, run over and trodden upon. . . . His communications had been cut; his headquarters pillaged; a corps had marched into his rear . . . ; he had been beaten and foiled in every attempt he had made to 'bag' those defiant intruders; and, in the end, he was glad to find refuge in the intrenchments of Washington."

That night Lee reported proudly if a bit inaccurately to Richmond, "The enemy attacked my left, under Jackson, on Thursday [August 28], and was repulsed. He attacked my right, under Longstreet, on Friday, and was repulsed; and on Saturday I attacked him with my combined armies, and utterly routed" the Federals "on the plains of Manassas."

Casualties on both sides were severe. Lee's losses included 1,481 killed, 7,627 wounded, 89 missing; Pope's, 1,724 killed, 8,372 wounded, 5,958 missing. Some 7,000 Federals appear to have been captured, not counting several thousand wounded left on the field. Over a three-by-five-mile stretch of the Manassas plain, dead and wounded men lay strewn, in some places in heaps. The day after the battle Longstreet's men worked to aid the wounded and bury the dead. Confederate surgeons were so busy with their own as to have no time for Yanks. Shortly Federal ambulances were permitted on the field. Some 3,000 Union wounded were brought to

Here the home of the Reverend Mr. Slaughter, an appropriate name for Cedar Mountain. Banks's losses were almost twice those of Jackson. (USAMHI)

makeshift facilities at Fairfax, where aides, doctors, and nurses were rushed from Washington. Clara Barton, seeking to get medicines and supplies there, estimated that 3,000 wounded men still lay on the straw-strewn ground at Fairfax a week after the battle. "All night," she wrote, "we made compresses and slings, and bound up and wet wounds, when we could get water, fed what we could. . . . Oh, how I needed stores on that field!"

As Pope's wounded were gathered at Fairfax, Union hope, which had been high only a few months before during the drive on Richmond, now lay dashed and broken. All the marching, maneuvering, fighting, dying, sickness, broiling in the Virginia sun had come to nothing by the end of August 1862. Federal troops were back where they had started—resentful, bitter, feeling betrayed and misled by military incompetents. Among Pope's soldiers, noted an officer, "Everyone had an unwashed, sleepy, downcast aspect . . . as if he would like to hide his head . . . from all the world." One newsman caught the mood: "We have been whipped by an inferior force of inferior men, better handled than ours."

From the Confederate viewpoint Lee had achieved a miracle—drawing a larger army than his own away from Richmond, running circles around the enemy and then administering a smarting defeat even in the face of superior Union numbers. Southern military fortunes were now at their highest as Lee plunged across the Potomac in early September to invade Union territory. Prospects for European aid to the Confederacy seemed brighter than before, even a possible European intervention that might assure Confederate independence.

In the North a crisis was at hand. Endless lists of wounded and dead filled newspaper pages. Morale sagged. Military leaders and Lincoln's administration were denounced by the surging political opposition. Prospects grew that Republicans would lose control of Congress in the upcoming midterm election, as voters tired of the war. Perhaps some kind of armistice leading to a negotiated peace, some thought, was preferable to continued slaughter and suffering. Obviously Lincoln's plans for wartime emancipation of the slaves—formulated in July—would have to be postponed. Gloom settled over a grim North as the people faced an uncertain future.

Yet Jackson, too, paid a heavy price. Brigadier General Charles S. Winder commanded Jackson's old division in the furious fighting, and in the battle a shell brutally mangled him. He died hours later in this house. (USAMHI)

Officers of the 10th Maine Infantry survey the field of battle some days later. (USAMHI)

The toll in animals, too, proved heavy. O'Sullivan caught this scene a few days after the fight. (USAMHI)

Simple homes became field hospitals, this one for Confederate wounded. (USAMHI)

Men like Brigadier General Samuel W. Crawford—once the surgeon at Fort Sumter—saw their commands almost destroyed. Crawford's brigade suffered 50 percent losses. (NA)

The captured were taken back to Culpeper. Here O'Sullivan photographed several Confederates in their rather informal "prison" in Culpeper Court House. (LC)

The Union dead, 314 of them, were buried on the field, in sight of the mountain whose battle killed them. (USAMHI)

Though they lost the battle, the Federals held the field, and here at Cedar Mountain Pope and McDowell made their headquarters. In the background left of the house stands the field wagon for reporters of the New York Herald *who followed the army.* (LC)

On August 18, Pope began to move his army north of the Rappahannock to meet the threat posed by Lee. His engineers had to build several bridges to accomplish the movement. This one crosses the North Fork of the Rappahannock. (USAMHI)

The Hazel River, a tributary, afforded a crossing already in place and not destroyed by the Confederates. (USAMHI)

But most bridges had to be built. O'Sullivan took a series of fine images of Franz Sigel's corps crossing this bridge on August 19. (P-M)

Wagons and baggage cross. (LC)

Then horsemen and part of the army's beef herd. (USAMHI)

Many of the Federals camped at Rappahannock Station, where they skirmished with the enemy on August 23. (LC)

Meanwhile, at Catlett's Station, Lee's cavalry captured Pope's baggage, including vital information on reinforcements coming to him from McClellan. (USAMHI)

The pace of the campaign accelerated quickly. Jackson, occupying Manassas, evacuated just as Pope was set to attack. All he found was ruins, some like these dating to March 1862 and the first Confederate evacuation. George N. Barnard photo. (LC)

All that remained were enemy winter huts and earthworks, and at least one outhouse. (USAMHI)

The Barnard & Gibson views taken in March are almost all that survive to give a picture of Manassas. It looked much the same when Pope marched in. (USAMHI)

The fortifications were extensive. (USAMHI)

And so was the clutter and debris. The horse appears to have been hobbled before it was killed, and several pieces of a steer are scattered about it. (USAMHI)

Pope's Federals faced a big task just in cleaning up after the Confederates. (USAMHI)

They occupied the old earthworks. (AMERICANA IMAGE GALLERY)

They restored and refurbished them. (WRHS)

O'Sullivan's July 1862 image shows the eastern range of earthworks at Manassas. (USAMHI)

And this photograph, probably taken by A. J. Russell, reveals Confederate Fort Beauregard. The Federals did not retain the name. (USAMHI)

Then Pope heard the enemy was at Centreville, and off he went, leaving behind some destruction of his own. Rolling stock of the Orange & Alexandria was burned to the wheels rather than be allowed to fall into Confederate hands. (USAMHI)

Engines were pushed over the railroad embankments. It would take a major effort to right this one. (USAMHI)

And then came another battle at Bull Run. Here Blackburn's Ford is shown on July 4, 1862, a few weeks before the battle. (USAMHI)

Some familiar faces were here again. Major General Richard S. Ewell played a minor role at the first Bull Run. Here at the second he was in the thick of the fighting and lost a leg. (VM)

Brigadier General William B. Taliaferro took a bad wound in the preliminary fighting at Groveton. (USAMHI)

William A. Wallace succeeded to the colonelcy of the 18th South Carolina on the field when its commander was killed. This later image shows him as a brigadier general. (USAMHI)

Major General David R. Jones, called "Neighbor" by friends, was a veteran of the first battle here. During the present campaign he made a major contribution to victory when he took Thoroughfare Gap. (SOUTHERN HISTORICAL COLLECTION, THE UNIVERSITY OF NORTH CAROLINA AT CHAPEL HILL)

And, of course, there was meandering Bull Run. Here the ruins of the Stone Bridge, taken by Barnard & Gibson in March 1862. (USAMHI)

Stone Bridge and the heights beyond once again shook with the sound of guns. (USAMHI)

McDowell's engineers had to build bridges to span Bull Run a few days before the battle. (USAMHI)

At the southern end of the field, near Union Mills, the Orange & Alexandria crossed Bull Run. (USAMHI)

But the real fighting took place where it had before, around Henry Hill and along the Warrenton Road. Here a part of the battlefield. (USAMHI)

It must have seemed déjà vu *for McDowell. Another Bull Run, another defeat.* (USAMHI)

A. J. Myer, the signal officer who could not get his balloon aloft at first Bull Run, operated a more effective signal office for McDowell at the second. Here O'Sullivan's image of Myer in his headquarters in late August. (LC, H. J. MYER COLLECTION)

Sending intelligence to the front, though little good it did. (LC, H. J. MYER COLLECTION)

The 2nd United States Sharpshooters, led by officers like Lieutenant B. S. Calef, saw their first real action at Second Manassas. (USAMHI)

Brigadier General Abram Duryée, formerly commander of a flamboyant Zouave regiment, took two wounds in the battle while he led a brigade. (USAMHI)

Reuben L. Walker fought with distinction at Second Bull Run, working A. P. Hill's artillery. (VM)

A face familiar to the fields along Bull Run, "Shanks" Evans, hero of the first battle. His command, called the "Tramp Brigade," seemed to be everywhere. A year from now his drinking would get him into trouble. (VM)

The Stone House on the Warrenton Turnpike would be used as a hospital again, as a year before, when the armies were done fighting around it. (USAMHI)

And the Widow Henry's house was no more. The war is simply too much for it. (NA, U. S. SIGNAL CORPS)

Few of Pope's high commanders distinguished themselves in the fight. Franz Sigel, commander of a corps, almost never distinguished himself. (USAMHI)

Brigadier General Robert C. Schenck was an exception. He led a brigade in Sigel's corps with distinction until a bullet removed him from further field command. (WRHS)

Samuel P. Heintzelman ended his active field service with an unsuccessful attack on Jackson at Groveton in the opening of the battle. He was photographed here with his staff just a few weeks before the battle. (WRHS)

A new name attracting much attention was Joseph Hooker, called "Fighting Joe" by the Northern press after his performance on the Peninsula. He led a division for Heintzelman, and would shortly replace Sigel at the head of the I Corps. (USAMHI)

"Portici," the house that had been headquarters for Johnston in July 1861, saw the armies in its fields once again. (MANASSAS NATIONAL BATTLEFIELD PARK)

Another Manassas house, again the scene of encamped armies, this time Federals. (USAMHI)

Men of Second Bull Run. Company A, 10th New York Infantry. It was the first regiment hit by John B. Hood's Texans in Longstreet's attack on August 30. A year from now it would be so depleted by battle that it would be redesignated a battalion. (ROBERT MCDONALD)

The 21st Massachusetts. Its officers, like Lieutenant Henry H. Richardson of Company K, are there as well. (USAMHI)

The 73rd Ohio Infantry, shown here leaving Chillicothe in 1862, saw its first battle at Second Manassas. They would go on to march through Georgia with Sherman two years later. Photograph by J. A. Simmonds. (WRHS)

This battle was the undoing of Major General Fitz John Porter. Devoted to "Little Mac," he was used in Pope's vendetta against McClellan and charged with disobedience of orders and disloyalty. In January 1863 he was dismissed from the army. Exoneration did not come until 1886. He appears seated here on August 1, 1862, at Harrison's Landing, less than a month before the battle. (USAMHI)

Micah Jenkins had moved up since leading his 5th South Carolina at First Manassas. He is shown here as a colonel, but a severe wound at this second battle interrupted his career for several months. (LC)

Another promising younger officer, William Mahone, called "Scrappy Billy." Shriveled, dyspeptic, weighing less than one hundred pounds, and furiously combative, he was one of Lee's most active brigadiers. (USAMHI)

David A. Weisiger was officer of the day in Taliaferro's Virginia Militia at the hanging of John Brown. At Bull Run he led a regiment in Mahone's brigade. He was seriously wounded but recovered to become a brigadier as shown here. The Confederacy had no distinction of insignia among the various grades of general—brigadier, major, lieutenant, and full general. All wore three stars in a wreath. (USAMHI)

Colonel Jerome Robertson took a wound while leading his 5th Texas Infantry in its attack on the 10th New York. He became a brigadier a few months later. His son Felix also became a brigadier. A war criminal, accused of the murder of Negro soldiers at Saltville, Virginia, in 1864, Felix was to be the last surviving Confederate general, living until 1928. (P-M)

An unusual bearded portrait of Brigadier General Henry Slocum, promoted to major general just before the battle. He materially aided in covering Pope's retreat after the defeat. (NA)

There was a small engagement at Chantilly, the final echo of the Second Manassas battle, and there one of the Union's most promising officers, Brigadier General Philip Kearny, rode accidentally into enemy soldiers. While attempting to escape he was shot and killed instantly. Winfield Scott called him "the bravest man I ever knew." He lost his arm in the war with Mexico. (USAMHI)

Brigadier General Isaac I. Stevens, once governor of Washington Territory, head of the Breckinridge campaign in 1860, died after the Battle of Second Manassas was virtually done, at Chantilly, on September 1. The Union lost great potential in his death and Kearny's. It recognized the loss in the unusual act of promoting Stevens to major general posthumously. (USAMHI)

And so, defeated, Pope retreated to Centreville, and here he stood briefly. There was no rout this time. A Barnard photo from March 1862. (NLM)

Six months before, jubilant Union soldiers had posed gaily here in the old Confederate earthworks. (USAMHI)

Now these fortifications, designed to protect from an attack from the north, were of little use to them against an enemy that might pursue from the south. (USAMHI)

The "Quaker guns" once used by the Rebels to fool the Federals were now a taunt. With the bitter memory of two defeats at Bull Run, Union soldiers were not saddened to continue their retreat to Washington. (USAMHI)

The War on Rails

ROBERT C. BLACK, III

Spiderlike the rails spread over the land, carrying the war everywhere, and feeding its voracious appetites

THE IRON HORSE was not bred, on this continent, for war.

Indeed, American railroads have seldom been planned for military purposes. For over a century and a half they typically have been built to serve the economic convenience, either of the public, or of those interests which found it useful to associate their private aspirations with the public good. No railroad was ever designed to create a Southern Confederacy—or to save the Union. The original lines were established for local reasons; subsequent projects remained oblivious to the possibility of war. That such enterprises should have found themselves engulfed in the first significant railroad conflict in all history was as fortuitous as it was unexpected, and it was inevitable that the railroad facilities of 1861 should in few respects perfectly fulfill the wartime needs of either the United or the Confederate States.

At the dawn of the nineteenth century, Americans still thought of transportation in terms of waterways; even when facing inland, they sought out naturally navigable streams and lakes. Canals and steamboats, which came two decades later, were little more than elaborations upon the water concept. Highways were significant chiefly as land bridges, transcending inconvenient terrain between places of navigation. Railroads, when they appeared, were regarded as a special variety of highway, and they assumed for some time a kind of bridge role—Mohawk & Hudson; Baltimore & Ohio; Richmond, Fredericksburg & Potomac; Western & Atlantic—the western waters were meant. That railroads possessed the capacity to supersede waterways was understood at first by almost no one, and even at the outbreak of the Civil War the idea still lacked universal acceptance. As a result, American railroad enterprise was subject for a long time to local influences, frequently petty in nature, that did much to inhibit the growth of anything like a national *system;* indeed, neither of the famous sections, Northern or Southern, could boast of anything like a unified network.

There did exist, albeit in embryo form, a number of trans-Appalachian railroad routes that straggled across the map between the east coast and the Mississippi River. Three were unquestionably Northern: the New York Central (Albany to Buffalo) and its connections; the Erie (Piermont, New York, to Dunkirk, New York) and its connections; and the Pennsylvania (Philadelphia to Pittsburgh) and its connections. Another was of uncertain status—the Baltimore & Ohio (Baltimore to Wheeling, Virginia) with connections west, which

The railroad, like the camera, came of age just as the nation went to war. Even as the armies were ready to march, so were the routes and rolling stock ready to carry them. Here a locomotive of the Raleigh & Gaston Railroad in North Carolina, around 1850. The South lay far behind the North in its rail system. (NORTH CAROLINA MUSEUM OF HISTORY)

ran so close beneath Mason's and Dixon's line that it found itself, during much of the Civil War, in a kind of no-man's-land; as a *carrier* it would serve the Union sometimes, the Confederacy never. Authentically *Southern* trackage, east to west, coalesced at Chattanooga into the single line of a single company, the Memphis & Charleston, a road destined to early fragmentation.

Though Northern superiority in terms of number of "routes" was clear, none of the routes could as yet be classified as trunk lines. The tradition of localism continued to be evident in even so fundamental a matter as the distance between the rails of a track. It is true that many Northern companies had adopted the classic British gauge of 4 feet, 8½ inches; moreover, there was an equally strong tendency in the South to use a gauge of 5 feet. But Northern practice could vary; the Erie was committed to an expansive 6 feet. The South contained considerable mileage of the British sort and in other places fancied an unconventional width of 5 feet, 6 inches. Connecting lines, even of an identical gauge, did not always represent unobstructed arteries. In many instances (but particularly in the South) there existed no physical contact between the roads that served a single city or town. Gaps of this sort were naturally cherished by hackmen and drayers, who saw to it that municipal ordinances discouraged their elimination.

The carriers themselves nursed restrictive notions. Many of them—and once more this was most conspicuous in the South—shrank from releasing their rolling stock to the lines of a "foreign" company. Even in the North, railroad executives were happier when such interchanges involved the property of a third company—the germ of the car-line idea. North or South, the advantages of the through trains were as yet only dimly perceived.

. . . Herman Haupt, a near-genius who graduated from West Point at age eighteen and thereafter dazzled the railroad industry with his achievements. Stanton made him chief of construction of the United States Military Railroads with the rank of brigadier general. He worked wonders. (NA, U. S. SIGNAL CORPS, BRADY COLLECTION)

Secretary of War Edwin M. Stanton, learning from the bitter lesson of the First Battle of Bull Run, which was lost when the enemy used railroads to combine troops against McDowell, knew the vital role to be played by the railroads. As a result, soon after taking his portfolio, he brought to Washington . . . (USAMHI)

Speaking very generally, it may be said that the railroad equipment of the Civil War period, both Union and Confederate, reflected a kind of American standard; that is, nearly *all* locomotives were of the 4-4-0 classification—two sets of four wheels front and center, and none under the cab—and burned wood; most rails were of wrought iron and weighed no more than 40 pounds to the yard; while the load limit of the average boxcar was established at about 16,000 pounds. This was only natural; most—though not all—of the engines and cars were manufactured in the North, while most—though not all—of the rails were rolled either in

Tenuous lifelines, like this viaduct on the Baltimore & Ohio at Relay House, Maryland . . . (MHS)

the North or in England. But if the Confederacy entered the Civil War with roughly similar patterns of railroad material, it typically possessed less of everything. The South counted 9,000 line miles of track; the North had 21,000. The Pennsylvania Railroad—in 1861 it ran from Philadelphia to Pittsburgh only!—owned more locomotives—220—than did all the lines of secessionist Virginia. The South Carolina Railroad possessed the greatest number of cars of any Confederate property—849. The leading company in the North was the Delaware, Lackawanna & Western with more than 4,000 cars.

Furthermore, if the Southern railroad plant was deficient at the outset, its capacity to grow, or even to maintain itself, was minimal. Confederate inferiority in the metallurgical arts and the steadily more constrictive effects of the Federal blockage are abundantly documented. But it must also be observed that these factors were rendered much worse by an unimaginative public policy, which prevented the most effective use of what the Confederacy did have.

One must, of course, be fair. At the outset, the United States authorities were as naïve with respect to the administration of railroads as were the Confederate. Both opponents had sprung from a common military background, and they now faced each other with a common baggage of notions. Prior to 1861, the steam locomotive had played a scant role in American military activity; army transport had depended upon animal-drawn wagons, moving under the orders of commanders in the field and administered by a quartermaster organization whose traditions were as rigid as they were ancient. Enter the iron horse, offering greatly superior speed and almost unimaginable capacity. That the new beast would be useful was obvious, yet the wagon continued to afford an advantage that the boxcar could not match: it was not confined to a track and therefore, like its motorized descendant, provided a greater flexibility of movement. This flexibility had conditioned, over the centuries, the very *mores* of military transport. But now, whenever a field commander applied the traditional procedures to a railroad, the anticipated flood of supplies and reinforcements abruptly ceased. Official wrath would thereupon descend upon the railroaders concerned; "wretched" was an early and probably laundered epithet applied by General Joseph E. Johnston to the Confederate management of the Orange & Alexandria, and it is likely that other comments never saw official print.

The causes of such difficulties quickly became obvious to intelligent railroad men. One was understandable: military authorities were prone to dealing with train crews as if they were teamsters enlisted under the Articles of War, ordering them about without thought of the consequences. Another was inevitable: the temptation to regard rail-

. . . and the Orange & Alexandria here at Union Mills on Bull Run, were vital to supply and transportation for the armies. A March 1863 image by A. J. Russell. (USAMHI)

Sometimes they could be protected by a detachment of soldiers, as here near Union Mills in a G. W. Houghton photograph. (VHS)

road cars as convenient storehouses, and the disinclination of field units to unload and release them became notorious. Still another was the absence of any well-understood official relationship between the carriers and the military. None of these problems was ever to be perfectly resolved, but experience brought considerable improvement, especially on the Union side.

Of these principal difficulties, the absence of a formal railroad-army relationship was paramount. Until this was assured, there could be no dealing with the storehouses or the *ad hoc* train orders.

During the first year of the war, both administrations, Federal and Confederate, simply muddled through, relying largely upon quartermaster departments of the conventional kind. True, each side commissioned and inserted into the traditional structure certain knowledgeable railroad officials; the Pennsylvania's Thomas Scott and William S. Ashe of the Wilmington & Weldon are primary examples. But in neither organization were these men given appropriate authority: in the administrative bureaus their advice was overlooked; in the field it was flouted.

The Federal authorities finally moved, early in 1862, to attack the railroad problem in a serious way. First came a cleansing at the top: Edwin M. Stanton was appointed Secretary of War in place of the dubious Simon Cameron. Mr. Stanton has not enjoyed a universally favorable press; he could be an unpleasant colleague, and his political honesty remains cloudy to this day. But he was both intelligent and efficient, and he was devoted to the proposition that the Confederacy should be subjected to utter defeat. Shortly after Stanton's arrival, an administration railroad bill was pushed through Congress and received President Lincoln's signature on January 31, 1862. Its text was brief: it granted to the President of the United States the authority to assume, whenever the military situation warranted, full control over any railroad in the country. In the face of such a statute, the subordinate status of the railroad industry was clear.

To enact a law is one thing; to carry it out with imagination and dispatch is another. Even under Stanton an effective implementation required a lengthy period of trial and error. The substance of the act was published as a general order of the Adjutant General's office as early as February 4, and on the eleventh the widely respected general superintendent of the Erie, Daniel C. McCallum, was appointed military director and superintendent of railroads in the United States with very broad powers, based upon the statute and its derivative order. But the troubles persisted; they had penetrated so deep that their elimination would require not only an enlightened supervision but also Herculean labors in the field.

The labors were performed by Herman Haupt, a civil engineer of impeccable reputation, who was charged late in April with the restoration of reliable railroad service in the northern Virginia theater. Haupt was a humorless man, born to controversy. Although a graduate of West Point, he utterly lacked a sense of subordination, and his confrontations with certain braided martinets were memorable. He was, in fact, precisely the kind of man the situation demanded. His professional abilities were vast; they embraced every aspect of railroad construction, maintenance, and operation. He furthermore could usually depend upon the support of both McCallum and Stanton. Amid the Virginia disasters of 1862, he pounded out the fundamentals of an organization, the United States Military Railroads, divided specifically into construction and operating corps, and managed upon carefully stated principles perfected by himself. In the course of his service Haupt underwent repeated fits of the sulks, and after the Gettysburg campaign he stamped home to Massachusetts for good. But his military railroad ideas would be enormously and, for the Federals, happily expanded. They would be much recorded by Yankee photographers.

Though the wartime railroad law conveyed sweeping powers to the Lincoln government, this did not mean that every carrier in the United States was subjected to seizure and operation by the Union Army. So Draconian a process was wisely reserved for emergencies—Gettysburg is an example—and was routinely applied only to occupied Confederate properties. The statute did, however, inspire a healthy cooperation by Northern companies.

Behind the Confederate lines, the railroad situation continued to be in woeful contrast to the improvements on the Union side. Underequipped for the burdens of wartime traffic, hard pressed even to sustain themselves, the Southern carriers were subjected, until nearly the end, to an official policy that can only be pronounced irresponsible. Nothing that was faintly similar to the establishment of McCallum and Haupt was ever achieved. Local, even private, rights were deemed sacrosanct; facts were brushed aside. The South possessed a wealth of natural waterways, especially in the West, but these tended, like the Mississippi, to run in directions favorable to the enemy. The South also enjoyed the means to develop a respectable system of wagon transport, but this was quite inadequate to the supply, over great distances, of the large defensive armies that had become necessary in the face of even larger enemy forces. These, in their turn, had been made possible by both the waterways and the new railroads! Nevertheless, Confederate rails did provide an imperfect skeleton of interior lines, and this just possibly might have been used to so prolong Confederate resistance that the Northern will to fight—always the *supreme* factor in this war—might have crumbled.

But the Southern leadership failed to make sophisticated use of what was available. It was not until December 1862 that the Richmond government went so far as to bring into its military structure a railroad man of a stature equivalent to that of McCallum and Haupt. This was William M.

But not always. Here, Barnard & Gibson's March 1862 picture of a ruined rail crossing near Blackburn's Ford on Bull Run. (USAMHI)

Wadley, who currently was associated with a half-finished enterprise in Louisiana, but who could look back upon a large and fruitful experience with a number of other companies in Georgia and Mississippi. He was, in a professional sense, probably the ablest railroad man in the Southern Confederacy. Wadley was noted for the brevity of his speech and, though not so brusque as Herman Haupt, was deficient in certain military niceties. His Southern loyalties were intense, but he had been born and raised in New England, a circumstance that aroused embarrassing suspicions. But his most serious difficulties were derived from the fact that he had been given rank—a full colonelcy—but no power over either the carriers or over any segment of the military. He tried earnestly to improve matters, but he quickly found himself enmeshed in the thankless role of "ombudsman" between the railroads and the government, neither of which proposed to yield an inch to the other. He did contrive to organize, without clear authority, a quasi-independent Railroad Bureau, with informal lines of communication to a variety of Confederate points. He resigned his commission seven months later, when the Confederate Senate refused, for reasons unspecified, to confirm his appointment.

The activities, such as they were, of the Railroad Bureau were inherited by Wadley's principal assistant, Captain—later Lieutenant Colonel—Frederick W. Sims. Sims enjoyed neither the background nor the reputation of his predecessor, but he was by no means incompetent, and he was en-

Posing behind the embankment and pretending to defend the bridge after the fact was of little use. Other means, preventive means, had to be found.
(AMERICANA IMAGE GALLERY)

dowed with a happy ability to endure frustration. Like Wadley, he carried responsibility without authority, yet he served to the very end as the Confederacy's principal rail transportation officer, devising ineffective "miracles" and accomplishing nothing of lasting consequence. He was invested at last with the kind of power that he and Wadley should have received at the beginning, but the requisite legislation was approved, with open reluctance, by President Jefferson Davis only on March 9, 1865, precisely a month before Appomattox.

Yet the Confederates could sometimes demonstrate a certain brilliance in their use of railroads. On at least three occasions they managed to improvise a steam-powered mass transit system in order to accomplish a particular strategic purpose.

The first took place in the late spring of 1862, when the divisions of W. H. C. Whiting and Jackson were shunted in bewildering sequence between Richmond and the Valley of the Shenandoah and finally were concentrated upon Lee's left wing in the Peninsula. The episode involved at least 20,000 troops, and though they at times exceeded the capabilities of the Virginia Central Railroad, their commanders did achieve a commendable harmony with its operating personnel. The results, from the Confederate viewpoint, were satisfying.

The second occasion came a few weeks later. It witnessed the removal of the greater part of Braxton Bragg's army from Tupelo, in the northeastern part of Mississippi, and its reconcentration at Chattanooga, Tennessee. Like the Virginia episode

Haupt built blockhouses, frontier-style forts to protect bridges in Virginia and Tennessee. Here one overlooks the Orange & Alexandria crossing of Bull Run. (USAMHI)

it was locally conceived and executed—and was carried out with a minimum of fuss. It was a major undertaking; involved was the movement of more than 20,000 men over the tracks of five railroads by a circuitous route through Mobile, Montgomery, and Atlanta. Yet it was completed in little more than two weeks. The consequences were considerable: the disruption over many months of the entire Federal offensive west of the Appalachians.

The third entailed the famous transfer, in September 1863, of Longstreet's corps from Lee's army in Virginia to Bragg's command in northern Georgia. It was a complex affair, organized under difficult circumstances and carried out under the general supervision of Sims's railroad bureau. Federal activities in eastern Tennessee denied to the Confederates the logical routing via Knoxville, and they were obliged to resort to a series of awkward passages through the Carolinas and Atlanta; the situation was further confused by certain unrelated movements in the direction of Charleston. Nevertheless, the thing was brought off successfully. The weather was pleasant, most schedules were kept, and perhaps half the troops arrived in time to participate in the Battle of Chickamauga. The statistics of the operation remain uncertain; the best estimates suggest that the total number completing the journey cannot have much exceeded 12,000. But their presence undoubtedly contributed to the Confederate victory and to a subsequent glimmer of Confederate hope.

The most significant result of Chickamauga, however, was the Union response to it. Hardly had the plight of the defeated General Rosecrans, now trapped in Chattanooga, become clear when plans were being drafted to rectify the situation with massive reinforcements. The most suitable available units were all in northern Virginia; they must proceed by rail, beginning at once and upon an emergency basis, to the vicinity of Chattanooga. The substantive preparations were completed in a single day: General McCallum, President John Garrett of the Baltimore & Ohio, and Thomas Scott assumed the responsibility for specific segments of the route, which was necessarily long and roundabout. It passed through Washington, Benwood—on the Ohio River in West Virginia—then to Indianapolis, south to Louisville and Nashville, and then to Bridgeport, Alabama, on the Tennessee River. Needed cooperation was ensured by reminding participants of the railroad law of 1862, and behind the law stood a no-nonsense administration and a steadily growing U.S. railroad capability.

The first train puffed away from the Virginia encampments on September 25; the last crept down the winding grade into the Tennessee Valley on the evening of October 6. In eleven and one half days, 25,000 infantry, 10 batteries of artillery, and 100 carloads of miscellaneous equipment had been carried 1,200 miles over the lines of a half-dozen railroads without a single serious delay or notable interference by the enemy.

Although the reinforcing of Rosecrans at Chattanooga was the most spectacular incident of its kind over the whole course of the Civil War, it was not, in a technical sense, the most impressive. The United States Military Railroads organization was not to be presented with its supreme challenge until the following spring, when it was charged with the supply, over hundreds of miles of single track, of General William T. Sherman's Atlanta

Even this was not foolproof, as the same blockhouse, now burned, demonstrates. (USAMHI)

But usually they were effective. Here a more elaborate blockhouse built on the East Tennessee & Georgia line to guard the Hiawassee bridge, largely from raiders like Nathan B. Forrest. (USAMHI)

campaign. This represented more than a rigorous exercise in logistics; thanks to the renewed activity of enemy guerrillas, very extensive portions of the route required constant rebuilding. The effort—physical and administrative—was staggering, but Sherman and his 100,000 men never lacked for rations or ammunition. Superintending the miracle were three officers of the Military Railroads—W. W. Wright, Adna Anderson, and E. C. Smeed. The Confederates were simply bewildered, and as they were thrust relentlessly back upon Atlanta they wondered aloud whether the Yankees were not carrying their bridges and tunnels with them in their knapsacks.

During all this, the officers of the United States Military Railroads were always pleased to have their accomplishments recorded photographically. This pleasant liaison between photographer and military railroader in the Civil War was a natural development; railroad gear "held still" frequently enough to serve as a subject for the slow and inconvenient emulsions of the day; moreover, railroad matters enjoyed, in the 1860s, a distinctive appeal to the picture-buying public.

The photographs that follow remind us of something more than the discussions in the text. They are nearly all *Northern* images and depict *Northern* activity. To suggest that there nowhere exists a photograph of an authentic *Confederate* railroad train would be taking a risk, but such a photo has yet to surface.

The South lacked boiler tubes for its locomotives. It also lacked developer and fixer. Consequently Confederate photographers could not undertake to record everything, and likenesses of loved ones must have always been more sought after than prints of the trains that carried them off to battle. Furthermore, the final catastrophe brought grievous disruption to Southern records in all categories. It was therefore inevitable that surviving views of Confederate railroads should be the work of Northerners and that they should portray scenes of occupation and ruin.

It is a fascinating coincidence that the American Civil War should have been the first conflict to encompass, in an extensive way, the techniques of both photography and railroading. And if railroads contributed to the victory of the Union, contemporary railroad photographs dramatically suggest the reasons.

And here Barnard's 1864 image of a fortified bridge on the Louisville & Nashville crossing of the Cumberland River. Giant fortress doors could close each end of the bridge, turning it into a stronghold. (LC)

It was men like Brigadier General John D. Imboden that Haupt sought to defeat. Though they were were usually troublesome to their superiors, on independent command they were skilled at destroying railroad equipment and installations. Imboden wreaked terrible damage on the Baltimore & Ohio in 1863 and 1864. (USAMHI)

So did Major Harry Gilmor and his 2nd Maryland Cavalry. On an 1864 raid on the B & O he not only stopped a train, but also robbed the passengers, a feat which got him suspended from command. This portrait was made in Columbia, South Carolina, by W. Weain. (USAMHI)

The Baltimore & Ohio shops at Martinsburg, Virginia, a favorite target of Confederate raiders. Probably an image from the 1850s. Shown are camelback locomotives and several "iron pot" coal cars. (BALTIMORE & OHIO RAILROAD)

A somewhat retouched photo showing the junction of the Baltimore & Ohio and Cumberland & Pennsylvania Railroads with the Chesapeake & Ohio Canal at Cumberland, Maryland. The mules are moving the coal cars into position to dump their contents into the canal barges. Another place exceedingly vulnerable to Confederate raiders. (B & O RAILROAD MUSEUM)

Here the Chattanooga depot at Nashville, Tennessee, shows the effects of a Rebel raid. (HERB PECK, JR.)

And Manassas Junction, Virginia, is repeatedly disrupted by the passing of the armies. (USAMHI)

Keeping the U. S. Military Railroads running would be a massive task for the innovative Haupt. He proved equal to it. Here he paddles a small pontoon boat of his own design, used for inspecting bridge foundations. (USAMHI)

Carrying out Haupt's instructions were engineers like these of the Construction Corps, photographed with their tools in Chattanooga in 1864. (LC)

And commissioned to follow the railroads was one of the few officially commissioned military photographers—perhaps the only one—Major A. J. Russell. Here the headquarters of his operations at Petersburg, near City Point, in the summer of 1864. (ROY MEREDITH)

Haupt moved mountains of material over long distances to maintain old lines and build new ones as needed. Here Russell's image of tons of iron rails at Alexandria, ready to go where needed. (USAMHI)

At Burnside's Wharf on Aquia Creek, the Construction Corps joined the rails with the waters to transport supplies. (NA)

The lines of tracks seem endless. Haupt brought his rails to the very water's edge on the James, below Richmond, in 1865. Photograph by Russell. (USAMHI)

Here, opposite Richmond, even locomotives were brought from ship to roadbed at the war's end. (USAMHI)

In the summer of 1864 Russell captured this scene of the camp of the workers of the Construction Corps at City Point, Virginia, their tents bordering the very ties of their tracks. (USAMHI)

All along the vital arteries of supply Haupt's men could be found. One, at least, proved indifferent to the camera and, turning his back to it, had a mate shine his shoes. (ROY MEREDITH)

A Russell image of a Construction Corps camp on the outskirts of Richmond after the surrender. The Virginia state capitol appears on the skyline at left. (LC)

A Russell view of rolling stock and camps in Virginia. (NA)

Haupt's innovative mind produced many oddities, including the "shad belly" bridge, easily transportable, and speedily assembled. (ROY MEREDITH)

Here in 1863 one such bridge is tested. (ROY MEREDITH)

His "beanpole" bridges made him famous, attracting the admiration of President Lincoln. This bridge over Potomac Creek was built in forty hours, utilizing two old piers from its destroyed predecessor. An A. J. Russell image from May 1864. (USAMHI)

Two days before, this creek was an impassable barrier for trains. Now a train can cross in safety. (LC)

Russell's 1863 print of Bull Run and a bridge under construction in the distance. (KA)

The Bull Run bridge a-building. (LC)

And completed. The first train crosses. Russell took this scene in the spring of 1863. (KA)

Later there would be time to elaborate and refine the bridge, once it was passing traffic again. The makeshift undergirding of the previous photo is replaced by a sturdy "shad belly" superstructure, complete with ornamental eagle above the entrance. (SOUTHERN RAILWAY SYSTEM)

The same wonders were worked out West. The 1st Michigan Engineers, with Construction Corps help, built the Elk River bridge near Pulaski, Tennessee. It was 700 feet long and 58 feet high. (CHICAGO PUBLIC LIBRARY)

A similar "beanpole" bridge near Chattanooga. (MHS)

And a magnificent bridge built over the Tennessee at Chattanooga in 1864, mighty Lookout Mountain brooding in the distance. (MHS)

The Howe Turn bridge over the Tennessee at Bridgeport, Alabama, a marvel of Construction Corps engineering. Here, in October 1863, it was just being rebuilt. (MHS)

And here it is almost finished, with still some temporary shoring at the old piles. (USAMHI)

By January 24, 1864, it is complete, passing regular traffic, and something of a marvel. (MHS)

And at every major river and creek between Tennessee and Virginia, similar unheralded feats occurred regularly as Haupt kept the railroads running. (LC)

Conductors and engineers like these actually ran the trains. An A. J. Russell image. (USAMHI)

Their engines were frequently the best that the factories of the North could produce, splendid machines like the Gen. Haupt *built by William Mason of Taunton, Massachusetts.* (USAMHI)

Their engineers sometimes decorated their locomotives. (USAMHI)

And sometimes the Confederates did the decoration for them. In this Russell photo the men point to enemy shell damage in the stack and tender of the Fred Leach. (USAMHI)

Most major cities soon got—if they did not have them already—major rail yards. Alexandria, at the terminus of the Orange & Alexandria, became the most important in the east by virtue of the O & A's necessary part in supplying armies in Virginia. (USAMHI)

The roundhouse at Alexandria, shown in this Russell image, spun scores of locomotives in the constant traffic moving south. (USAMHI)

The offices of the Orange & Alexandria, photographed by Russell from the top of the roundhouse. (NEIKRUG PHOTOGRAPHICA, LTD.)

Mountains of scrap collected at Alexandria for melting into new rails and wheels. (NA)

Nashville's Chattanooga depot acted as a principal link in the rail system supplying the Federals in the West. (KA)

Lesser depots like this one at Culpeper, Virginia, also played their part. (KA)

And always there was the constant motion of engines and cars. Here a puff of smoke and a blur give testimony to one of hundreds of iron horses at its task. (KA)

A variety of special pieces of equipment came out of the needs of war. Here a private car sits on a siding at City Point in 1864. (ROY MEREDITH)

And here a more elaborate Presidential car, caught by Russell in the Orange & Alexandria yard in 1865. It will take Lincoln home to Illinois, in his coffin. (NA)

Iron boxcars like this one were built to safely haul ammunition over the Baltimore & Ohio. (ARCHIVES OF THE B & O RAILROAD MUSEUM—CHESSIE SYSTEM)

Car barges like these operated on the Potomac River, shifting trains where bridges could not cross. (NA)

Improvised rail splices like this made quick repairs to old or sabotaged track. (NA)

Haupt was not the only innovator, either. The Confederates, with far more limited means, are believed to have created this railroad battery near Petersburg. Such quickly mobile armored artillery could be very useful, if only the rails went to the right places. (USAMHI)

The Union, too, put guns on rails, and none greater than the mighty 13-inch mortar "Dictator." It weighed 17,000 pounds and performed well at Petersburg. Only rails could move the behemoth gun. (SOUTHERN RAILWAY SYSTEM)

It is unfortunate that so little survives to illustrate the role of Confederate railroads in the war. What does remain is from the cameras of Union photographers, like this tranquil image of an engine of the Atlantic & North Carolina line. Behind it is a "conductor's car." (USAMHI)

And here at Port Hudson, Louisiana, McPherson & Oliver caught two dilapidated pieces of equipment of the Clinton & Port Hudson Railroad. As in so many other areas, the South simply could not compete with the North's industry in railroading, and as shown, was hard pressed to maintain what it already had. (ISHL)

The Contributors

WARREN W. HASSLER, JR. is a longtime professor of history at Pennsylvania State University. A highly regarded and prolific historian in the field of American and Civil War military history, he has authored *General George B. McClellan,* which won him the "Southern Book of the Year Award" for 1958, *Commanders of the Army of the Potomac* (1962), and *Crisis at the Crossroads: The First Day at Gettysburg* (1970), as well as many articles and book reviews in scholarly journals. His essay on the Siege of Yorktown deals with one of his foremost interests, the Army of the Potomac.

WILLIAM N. STILL's two-year duty with the navy in the 1950s may have triggered his insatiable love for the maritime and its history.

Currently a professor of history at East Carolina University, Greenville, North Carolina, Still has authored numerous articles in historical journals and periodicals as well as *Iron Afloat: The Story of Confederate Ironclads and Confederate Shipbuilding.*

EMORY M. THOMAS has authored four books dealing with the Confederacy and Reconstruction, *The Confederacy as a Revolutionary Experience, The Confederate Nation, The Confederate State of Richmond: A Biography of the Capital,* and *The American War and Peace, 1860–1877,* as well as many articles and book reviews in journals and periodicals. Thomas is professor of history at the University of Georgia and has been a recipient of several awards and grants for his work in history.

The late BELL I. WILEY's essay "In Camp with the Common Soldiers" reflects his solid interest and lifelong studies of the life of the soldier in the Civil War. Other fields that he has written on include the Civil War lives of blacks, women, and Southerners. His outstanding reputation earned him many awards, fellowships, and associations with uncountable learned societies, and a seat on the National Archives Advisory Council that he held from 1968 until his death.

CHARLES L. DUFOUR is a New Orleans native, a retired newspaperman with fifty-five years of service, thirty of which he spent writing a daily column for the New Orleans *States-Item.*

A graduate of Tulane University with a Doctor of Humane Letters honorary degree awarded him in 1978 from the same institution, Dufour is also author of eight books, three of which dwell on the Civil War. He is also past president of the Louisiana Historical Association as well as one of the founders of the Civil War Round Table.

ROBERT G. TANNER is a young, new historian who hails from Los Angeles. A graduate of Virginia Military Institute in 1969 and of Wake Forest University School of Law in 1973, Tanner is currently an attorney in Atlanta.

His main interests lie in the Shenandoah Valley campaign of 1862. He authored *Stonewall in the Valley* (Doubleday, 1976) which was selected by the Military Book Club and History Book Club in 1977.

DAVID LINDSEY, author of seven books including

Americans in Conflict: The Civil War and Reconstruction, is well known for his lively writing style and wide range of interests in American history. He has been professor of history at California State University, Los Angeles, since 1956.

ROBERT C. BLACK is a retired professor of history at Colorado Women's College whose special interest has always been transportation. He served in the Army Transportation Corps during World War II and his essay on the railroads of the Civil War reflects his background as well. He is the author of *The Railroads of the Confederacy.* A graduate of Williams College and the University of Denver, Black received his Ph.D. from Columbia University in 1951.

Abbreviations

CHS	Chicago Historical Society, Chicago, Ill.
CWTI	Civil War Times Illustrated Collection, Harrisburg, Pa.
ISHL	Illinois State Historical Library, Springfield
KA	Kean Archives, Philadelphia
LC	Library of Congress, Washington, D.C.
LSU	Louisiana State University, Department of Archives and Manuscripts, Baton Rouge
MHS	Minnesota Historical Society
NA	National Archives, Washington, D.C.
NHC	U. S. Naval Historical Center
NLM	National Library of Medicine, Bethesda, Md.
NYHS	New-York Historical Society, New York
P-M	War Library and Museum, MOLLUS-Pennsylvania, Philadelphia
TU	Tulane University, New Orleans
USAMHI	U. S. Army Military History Institute, Carlisle Barracks, Pa.
VHS	Vermont Historical Society
VM	Valentine Museum, Richmond, Va.
WRHS	Western Reserve Historical Society, Cleveland, Ohio

Index

Abercrombie, Brigadier General John J., 144
Adams, Charles Francis, 254
Adams, John Quincy, 254
Adams Express Company, 92, 93
Agamenticus (double-turreted monitor), 55–56
Ajax (monitor vessel), 56–57
Albemarle (ironclad), 60, 61, 81
Alden, Captain James, 291
Aldie Gap, 356
Alexandria, Va., 349, 352; iron rails at, 417; railroad scrap, 437; rail yards, 435; roundhouse at, 435
Alexandria–Warrenton turnpike, 354
Allegheny Mountains, 322, 324, 327, 328, 331, 332, 334
Allen, Colonel Henry W., 302
"All Hail the Power of Jesus' Name" (hymn), 189
"Amazing Grace" (hymn), 189
Amphitrite (double-turreted monitor), 56
Amy, Captain L', 23
Anaconda Plan, 255
Anderson, Adna (officer), 410
Anderson, Brigadier General Samuel R., 31
Andersonville prison, 82
Appalachians, 408
Appomattox Court House, 20, 62
Aquia Creek, 349, 350, 351; Burnside's Wharf on, 418
Archer, Brigadier General James J., 158
Arkansas, 195, 244
Arkansas (ironclad), 49, 60, 255, 272, 273–74, 275–76, 277, 299, 300, 301, 302; destruction of, 50
"Arkansas Traveler" (song), 196
Arlington, Va., 349
Arlington House, 17; McDowell at, 18
Army of Northern Virginia, 123, 187, 201, 350
Army of the Cumberland, 195
Army of the James, 191
Army of the Potomac, 11–13, 19, 86, 239, 350; near Brandy Station, 197; Cumberland Landing, 120; Peninsula campaign, 112–72; Petersburg headquarters, 249; provost marshal's camp at Bealton, Va., 248
Army of Virginia, 348, 349
Ashby, Brigadier General Turner, 324, 325, 334, 342, 343, 346
Ashe, William S., 404
Atlanta, Ga., 226, 408
Atlanta campaign, 409–10
Atlanta (ironclad), 83, 84
Atlantic (magazine), 188
Atlantic & North Carolina Railroad, 444
Ayers, Captain Romeyn B., 33

Bache, Lieutenant Colonel F. M., 210
Baltimore & Ohio Railroad, 322, 399–400, 409, 412–13, 414; iron boxcars, 441; 1864 raid on, 412; at Relay House, Md., 402; shops at Martinsburg, Va., 412
"Baltimore Cotton Duck Extra" tent, 222
Banks, Major General Nathaniel P., 315, 358; background of, 324; Second Bull Run, 348, 349, 353, 358, 359, 360, 361; in the Shenandoah, 324–26, 328, 329, 330, 331–32, 343
Barnard, George N., 34, 35, 37, 38, 40, 42, 86, 202, 370, 396, 411
Barnard & Gibson, 371, 379, 406
Baron De Kalb (ironclad), 51, 57
Barry, Brigadier General William F., 21, 118
Barton, Clara, 362
Baseball, 191–92
Baton Rouge, La., 50, 246, 271, 291; Church Street, 305; coaling yard, 310; contraband camps, 309; courthouse, 308, 317; Farragut's fleet, 310; Federals at leisure on the Mississippi, 315; gunboat damage to, 304; *Hartford* off Main Street levee, 313; Jackson Barracks, 308, 318; mortar schooners anchored in, 311–12; soldier tents, 316; State House, 306, 316; Union camps, 318; Union conquest of the Mississippi and, 276, 277, 285, 291, 292, 301–18; waterfront, 301; wharf boat at, 314
Baton Rouge Arsenal, 307, 317

Battery No. 1, 37; earthworks at, 43, 44; Farnholt House behind, 45
Battery No. 4, 44
Baxter, George, 195
Bay Point, S.C., 97–98; machine shops at, 97; United States Marine headquarters, 97
Beal, J. H., 77
Bealton, Va., 210; provost marshal's camp (Army of the Potomac), 248
Beaufort, S.C., 86, 87–98, 253; at Bay Point, 97–98; Bay Street, 92, 93, 94; commissary storehouse, 91, 94; Cooley's gallery, 87–88; Cooley's photographs of, 87–96; fishing tackle and general provisions store, 91, 94; Fyler's store, 90; Fuller House, 89; hospital for "contrabands," 95; post office, 90, 92; quiet street scene, 95; from the river, 89; west side of Bay Street, 94
Beaufort Arsenal, 96
Beaufort Hotel, 92, 94
Beaumont, Colonel, 23
Beauregard, Brigadier General Pierre G. T., 257
Beaver Dam Creek, 119
Bell, Captain Henry, 267–68
Belmont, Mo., 260
Benjamin, Judah P., 256
Benton (ironclad), 51, 55, 262, 276
Berdan, Colonel Hiram, 30
Bible, 188
Big Bethel, Battle of, 11
"Billy in the Low Grounds" (song), 196
Birney, Brigadier General David B., 143
Birney, James G., 143
Bissell, Colonel Josiah W., 262, 263
Black, Robert C., 448
Blackburn's Ford, 376; ruined rail crossing, 406
"Black Hat" boys, 360
Black Hat Brigade, 357
Blake, W., 104
Blenker, Brigadier General Louis, 19, 344
Blockade runners, 107, 111
Blockades, 175, 284; effectiveness of, 255; Mississippi River, 255, 256
Blockhouses, railroad, 408, 409, 410
Blue Ridge Mountains, 322, 324, 325, 326, 327, 328, 331, 337
"Blue-Tailed Fly, The" (song), 196
Boatswain's Swamp, 121
"Bonnie Blue Flag" (song), 242
Boston *Journal,* 187
Bowles, Captain Pinckney D., 336
Box and Cox (farce), 195
Brady, Mathew B., 34, 47, 121, 133, 140, 142, 144, 165
Brady & Company, 20, 21, 36, 47, 198
Bragg, Major General Braxton, 177, 201, 255, 258, 407, 408
Bragg, Mrs. Elise Ellis, 258
Brandy Station, Va., 198, 210, 212, 220, 221, 237; Army of the Potomac near, 197
Breckinridge, Major General John C., 277, 301, 302, 304, 396
Brick House Point, 19
Bridgeport, Ala., 409, 429–31
Bristoe, Va., 356
Bristoe Station, 352, 357
Broad Run, Va., 352
Brooke, John, 61, 80
Brooke guns, 61
Brooklyn (ship), 255, 256, 269
Brown, D. A. (musician), 106
Brown, Lieutenant Isaac, 273–74, 275, 277
Brown, John, 340, 394
Brown, Joseph, 53
Brown, Sam, 106
Brown (transport), 270
Buchanan, Franklin, 84
Buford, John (commander), 354
Bull Run, First Battle of (1861), 11, 12, 17, 112, 144, 324, 361, 401
Bull Run, Second Battle of (1862), 348–98; bridge a-building, 424–25, 426; bridges and river crossings, 367, 368, 380; casualties, 357, 358, 360, 361–62, 363, 366; Cedar Mountain battlefield, 349, 350, 353, 354, 355, 356, 357, 358, 359, 366; at Centreville, 352, 355, 356, 361, 375, 396–97; Chantilly engagement, 395, 396; field hospitals, 364; fortifications and earthworks, 397; intelligence operations, 382–83; "Quaker guns," 398; railroads, 349, 350, 351, 352, 354, 355, 376, 380; at Rappahannock Station, 369; sacking of Manassas, 352–53, 370; at Stone Bridge, 356, 360, 361, 379
Bull Run Mountains, 352
Bureau of Ordnance and Hydrography (Confederate Navy), 61
Burnside, Major General Ambrose E., 350, 354
Burnside's Wharf (on Aquia Creek), 418
Bushnell and Company (C. S.), 54
Butler, Major General Benjamin F., 11, 269, 270–71, 301; in New Orleans, 270–71, 290
Byrd, William, 172

Cairo, Ill., 262, 271; gunboat construction at, 260; ironclads at, 57; naval station, 268; river fleet at anchor, 269; soldiers boarding transports, 270
Cairo (ironclad), 51
Calef, Lieutenant B. S., 384
Calhoun (ship), 258
Camanche (monitor-type vessel), 55, 66; engine room of, 71
Cameron, Simon, 16, 405
Camp Cass, mass at, 222
Camp Ella (Bishop, Ky.), 186
Camp Essex, commissary stores at, 206
Camp Griffin (Virginia), 223
Camp life, 173–254; absent without leave, 197–98; bouts with "the sh-ts," 186; butchering fresh beef, 174, 205; card-playing, 191, 196, 224, 225; clowning and horseplay, 190, 226–27; commissary store red tape, 206; Confederate huts, 184; courts-martial, 200, 251; desertions and serious offenders, 200–1; dramatic clubs, 245, 246; drills, 184, 199, 200, 201, 202; executions, 201, 254; female soldier (Private Albert Cashier), 233; floggings, 200; food concerns, 173–77, 202–16; foraging, 176, 216; fraternization with the enemy, 189–90; friendships, 234–36; gambling, 196–97, 225, 229; for the generals, 237–40; glee clubs, 184; health concerns, 186; at Hilton Head (New Hampshire boys), 103–7; holiday festivities, 192, 252–54; homemaking proclivities, 179–81; hunger, 173, 176; hymn singing, 188–89; impromptu diversions, 190–91; inspection, 197; laundering and washdays, 177; letters and letter-writing, 185–86, 218, 219, 231; liquor drinking, 184, 213, 228, 249; mail call, 185–86, 220–21; medical care, 184, 192; minstrels and comedies, 195; music, 184–85, 191, 241–45; need for wood, 195; newspapers and reading, 186–88, 217, 218, 229; officer quarters, 180, 182–83, 187, 230; officers' mess, 210; parades, 184; pet animals, 195–96, 247–48; picnics, 212; punishment, 197–200, 249–51; ration supplements, 176, 204; religious activity, 188–89, 221–24; sham courts-martial, 195; shamming for the camera, 228; shelter and quarters, 174, 178, 179–84, 192; sports and games, 191–95, 196, 226; Sunday reviews, 184; sutlers, 212–13, 214–15; tent interior (officer's), 179; unpopular officers, 190; visits to towns, 197; winter enjoyment, 188, 192, 194–95; winter quarters, 181–82, 183, 185, 186, 188, 220; womanless dances, 196; women's presence, 231–32; work tasks, 193

Camp Quantico (near Dumfries, Va.), 189, 235
Camp Winfield Scott, 23, 45
Canonicus (monitor vessel), 56–57
Carondelet, Mo., 56, 260, 273
Carondelet (ironclad), 51, 262–63, 274, 277, 293
Carondelet Marine Railway, 56
Casco (light-craft monitor), 77
Cashier, Private Albert J., 233
Catawba (ironclad), 56–57, 65
Catlett's Station, 351, 370
Catskill (ironclad), 55, 67–70; anchor well of, 67; in Charleston harbor (1863), 67; engine room of, 70; officer's cabin, 68; turret machinery, 69
Cayuga (gunboat), 268, 277, 282
Cedar Mountain, 349, 350, 353, 354, 355, 356, 357, 358, 359, 366; from the Union position, 357
Centreville, Va., 352, 355, 356, 361, 375, 396–97; winter houses at, 185
Challeron, Lieutenant, 194
Chancellorsville, Battle of, 341
Chantilly, Va., 395, 396
Charleston, S.C., 9, 55, 62, 284, 408; naval attack (1863), 49, 72
Charleston Harbor, 80
Charleston (ironclad), 61
Charlestown, Va., 325
Chartres, Duc de (Robert Philippe Louis d'Orléans), 23, 24
Chattanooga, Tenn., 173, 174, 177, 218, 232, 250; "beanpole" bridge near, 428; court-martial at, 251; railroads and, 400, 407–8, 409, 416, 428, 429
Chattanooga Daily *Rebel,* 187
Chesapeake & Ohio Canal, 322, 414
Chesapeake Bay, 12, 349
Chestnut, Mary Baykin, 271
Chicago *Times,* 187
Chickahominy River, 116–17, 121, 135, 151, 153, 155, 161; bridge on Mechanicsville road, 155
Chicamauga, Battle of, 408–9
Chickasaw (ironclad), 58, 65
Chicora (ironclad), 61, 80
Chillicothe (ironclad), 53–54
Chimo (light-draft monitor), 74
Choctaw (ironclad), 51–52, 59, 61
Cincinnati *Gazette,* 187
Cincinnati (ironclad), 51, 57
City Point, Va., 20, 238, 416, 419; private railroad car at, 439
Civil War: camp life, 173–254; introduction to, 9–10; invasion of the Shenandoah Valley, 322–47; ironclads, 49–85; Peninsula campaign, 112–72, 322–23; railroads, 399–445; Second Bull Run, 348–98; siege of Yorktown, 11–48, 115; Union conquest of the Mississippi, 255–320
Clark, Thomas, 201
Clinton & Port Hudson Railroad, 445
Cockfights, 226
Coles, Captain Cowper, 54
Collins, J. W., 92
Collins & Company (J. W.), 92
Collis, Brevet Major General Charles H. T., 234
Columbia (ironclad), 61
Columbus, Ga., 62
Columbus, Ky., 260
Columbus, Mo., 265
Combastus De Zouasio (burlesque), 195
Commissary storehouse (Beaufort, S.C.), 91, 94
Common Council of the City of New Orleans, 255–56
Concord, N.H., court-martial at, 251
Conestoga (gunboat), 260, 312
"Confederate coffee," 175
Confederate Congress, 49, 277, 406
Congress (frigate), 50
Connor, Colonel James S., 157
Constitution (ship), 140
Construction Corps, 416, 418, 419–20, 427; camp of the workers, 419
Continental Army (Revolutionary War), 11
Continental Iron Works, 55, 74
Contrabands, 95, 133, 309
Cooke, General Phillip St. George, 121
Cooley, Samuel, 246; with assistants and photographic wagon, 88; background of, 86; Beaufort gallery, 87–88; photographs of South Carolina, 87–99
"Cooley's" (Beaufort, S.C.), 87–88
Coppen, Gaston (commander), 168
Corcoran, Colonel Michael, 222
Corinth, Miss., 263; fall of, 272
Cornwallis, Lord Charles, 11, 36, 46
"Cornwallis' Cave," 46, 47
Crawford, Brigadier General Samuel W., 364
Cross Keys, Battle of, 334–35, 344, 345, 346
Crump, Billy, 216
Culpeper, Va., 350, 352; railroad depot at, 438
Culpeper Court House, 113, 365
Cumberland, Md., railroad-canal junction at, 414
Cumberland & Pennsylvania Railroad, 414
Cumberland Landing, 116, 120, 121, 124; panorama showing army at camp, 122; panoramic view of troops, 124
Cumberland River, fortified bridge on, 411
Cumberland (sloop-of-war), 50
Cushing, Lieutenant William B., 81
Custer, Captain George Armstrong, 152
Cyrus (servant), 103

Dahlgren smoothbores, 38, 42, 54, 55, 57
Daisy (tugboat), 264
Dalton, Ga., 194
Darnestown, Md., 326; camps of men of Banks's command, 327
David (torpedo boat), 54
Davis, Captain Charles H., 272–73, 274, 275
Davis, Jefferson, 11, 17, 18, 55, 112, 113, 115, 117, 118, 149, 276, 358; decision for a naval force, 49; general amnesty of (1865), 201; New Orleans defense and, 256–57, 266–67; railroad legislation, 407
DeChanal, Colonel V., 25
Delamater Iron Works, 75
Delaware, Lackawanna & Western Railroad, 402
Department of the Gulf, 291
De Soto (ship), 279
Dewey, Admiral George, 286
Dictator (ironclad), 57, 74–76; launch of, 75–76
"Dictator" (railroad battery), 443
Dix, Dorothea, 36
"Dixie" (song), 242
Donaldsonville, La., Federal capture of, 319–20
Doubleday, Captain Abner, 357
Drayton, Percival (officer), 285
Drewry's Bluff, naval battle at, 52, 54, 115, 116
Dufour, Charles L., 447
Dumfries, Va., 189, 235
Duncan, Brigadier General Johnson Kelly, 266, 267, 270
Dunderberg (armored cruiser), 54
Du Pont, Rear Admiral Samuel F. I., 54, 59, 72
Duryée, Brigadier General Abram, 384

Eads, James B., 56, 57, 58, 79, 260, 271, 276
Earnshaw, Chaplain Captain William, 222
East Tennessee & Georgia Railroad, 410
Echols, Colonel John, 333
Eckert, Thomas T., 141
Edisto Island, Seabrook plantation, 107–10
Edwards, J. D., 168, 229
18th South Carolina, 378
8th Louisiana, 341
82nd Illinois, 226
Elk River bridge, 427
Ellet, Brigadier General Alfred W., 297
Ellet, Colonel Charles, 272, 297, 299

Ellison's Mill, 153
Eltham's Landing, Battle of, 19, 48, 115
Elzey, Brigadier General Arnold, 157, 346
Empire (blockade runner), 107
Empire Parish (ship), 315
England, 49
Enoch Train (tugboat), 257
Ericsson, John, 54, 55, 56, 57, 58, 63, 64, 74, 79
Erie Railroad, 399, 400–1, 405
Essayons Dramatic Club, 245
Essex (ironclad), 51, 58, 59, 276, 277, 302, 303, 304
Evans, Brigadier General Nathan G. "Shanks," 385
Ewell, Major General Richard S., 327, 328, 331, 357, 377; Cross Keys battle, 334–35

Fairchild, Colonel Lucius, 196
Fairfax, Va., 362
Fairfax Court House, house at, 14
Fair Oaks, *see* Seven Pines, Battle of
Falls Church, Va., 349
Farnholt House, 16, 18; behind Battery No. 1, 45
Farragut, Flag Officer David Glascow, 50, 84, 255, 263–64; conquest of the Mississippi, 255, 263–64, 266–76, 279, 282, 284, 289, 291, 292; flagship of, 284–86; flotilla of, 264
Favorite Farce (play), 246
Fellows, Colonel C. Q., 108, 109
Field, Dr. J. T., 58
15th New York Engineers, 170
V Corps, 351
5th Georgia, 218
5th New Hampshire, 135
5th South Carolina, 393
5th Texas Infantry, 394
5th Vermont, in camp in 1861, 176
50th New York Engineers, 221, 254
58th New York, 345
55th New York, 171
55th New York Engineers, 247
51st New York, 192
56th Massachusetts, 226
Fingal (blockade runner), 83
1st Brigade of Horse Artillery, 198
1st Connecticut Heavy Artillery, 20, 47, 181–82; chaplain's quarters, 224
I Corps, 12, 14, 388
1st Engineers and Mechanics, 218
First Manassas, *see* Bull Run, First Battle of (1861)
1st Maryland Infantry, 331
1st Massachusetts Artillery, 169
1st Michigan Engineers, 427
1st North Carolina Infantry, 154
1st Pennsylvania Light Artillery, 136
1st Rhode Island Light Artillery, 192
1st Tennessee Regiment, 197
1st Texas, 189, 235; "Wigfall Mess" of, 194
1st United States Cavalry, 163
Fletcher, Colonel, 23
Florida, 201
Folly Island, S.C., 86, 246
Foote, Commodore Andrew, 55, 262, 263, 272, 274, 276
Forsythe, Captain James W., 202
Fort Beauregard, 375
Fort Darling, 224
Fort Donelson, fall of, 260, 265
Fort Fisher, naval battle at, 54
Fort Henry, Battle of, 260, 265; ironclads at, 51
40th Massachusetts Infantry, 174
Fort Jackson, 50, 257, 264, 266, 267, 268, 279, 280
Fort Macomb, 281
Fort Monroe, 11, 12, 13–14, 15, 20, 114, 115, 211, 232; exterior of officers' quarters, 13
Fort Pillow, 263, 267, 271; Confederate evacuation of, 272, 295
Fort Richardson, 135
Fort St. Philip, 255, 257, 264, 266, 267, 268, 269–70; front view of, 281; interior of, 280
Fort Sumter, 364; naval attack at (1863), 59
Fort Wells, 111
44th Massachusetts Infantry, 195
49th New York, 209
49th Pennsylvania, 222
Foulke, A., 212
4th Alabama, 336
4th Georgia, 166
Fox, Gustavus, 54
France, 49
Franklin, Brigadier General William B., 115, 117, 118
Fredericks, Charles D., 116
Fredericksburg, Battle of, 234
Fredericksburg, Va., 12, 194, 196, 329, 331, 332
Fredericksburg (ironclad), 61
Fred Leach (locomotive), 434
Fremantle, Colonel Arthur, 28
Frémont, Major General John C., 327, 328, 332, 334, 348; Cross Keys battle, 334–35
Front Royal, Battle of, 327, 331, 332, 334, 338
Front Royal, Va., 327, 331
Fuller House (Beaufort, S.C.), 89
Fyler, John S., 90

Gaines House, 33, 156
Gaines's Hill, Va., 140
Gaines's Mill, Battle of, 121, 123, 155–61
Gainesville, Va., 352, 354, 356, 358
Galena (ironclad), 51, 52, 54, 115
Galveston, Tex., 62
Gardner, Alexander, 86, 120, 153, 217, 234
Garrett, John, 409
Gauley Bridge, 216
Geary, Brigadier General John White, 332, 360
General Grant (ironclad), 63
Gen. Haupt (locomotive engine), 433
General Lyon (ship), 279
General Price (cotton-clad), 297
General War Order Number One (Lincoln), 112
George (slave), 226
Georgia, 117, 391, 406
Getty, Brigadier General George Washington, 237
Gettysburg, Battle of, 159, 405
Gibbon, Major General John, 360–61
Gibson, James F., 24, 26, 29, 43, 45, 52, 53, 114, 128, 130, 131, 135, 136, 137, 138, 139, 147, 160, 162, 196
Gibson, Brigadier General John, 357
Gill, Mrs. Bettie and Callie, 186
Gill, Robert M., 186
Gilmor, Major Harry, 412
Gloucester Point, 13, 14, 15, 42; Federal capture of, 19
Golden Era (packet boat), 271
"Goose Hangs High, The" (song), 196
Gordonsville, Va., 349, 350
Gorman, Brigadier General Willis A., 144
Gorman, Mrs. Willis A., 144
Gosport Navy Yard, 50
Governor Moore (ship), 268, 269
Granada, Miss., 277
Grant, General U. S., 174, 238, 239, 260, 274, 348
Green Mountain Boys, 162
Greenpoint, N.Y., 55, 74
Greenwood, Miss., 273
Gregg, Major W. M., 178
Gregory, Captain Francis H., 65
Groveton, Va., 355, 356, 360, 388
Gulf of Mexico, 255
Gurney, Henry, 276

Halleck, Major General Henry W. "Old Brains," 348, 349, 350, 354, 358–59, 361
Hamlin, Brigadier General Cyrus, 240
Hamlin, Hannibal, 240
Hampton Legion, 157
Hampton Roads, naval battle at, 49, 50, 53–54, 55, 57, 65, 66, 68, 79
Handy, Commander Robert, 258
Harpers Ferry, Va., 322, 332–34, 340, 360; destruction in 1862, 334; John Brown's attack on, 340; United States Arsenal at, 333
Harper's Weekly, 105, 187
Harrison, Captain Napoleon B., 282

Harrisonburg, Va., 327, 328, 334
Harrison's Landing, 119, 121, 122–23, 172, 348, 392
Hartford (flagship), 268–69, 284–86, 311, 313; gun deck of, 286; men and officers of, 285
Hassler, Warren W., Jr., 447
Hatch, Brigadier General John P., 343
Haupt, Brigadier General Herman, 401, 405, 406, 415, 416, 417, 420, 421, 432, 442
Hawkins, General John P., 195
Hayes, Colonel Rutherford B., 216
Hazel River, 367
Head of the Passes, 264, 266, 268; naval battle at, 257–58
Hecksher, Lieutenant John G., 236
Heintzelman, Brigadier General Samuel P., 17, 117, 143; at Second Bull Run, 351, 353, 354, 359, 388
Henry Hill, 381
Henry House Hill, 360
Hesseltine, Colonel Francis, 281
Hesseltine, Mrs. Francis, 281
Hiawassee bridge, 410
Hill, Major General Ambrose Powell, 119, 120, 122, 159; at Second Bull Run, 349, 350, 358, 359, 383
Hill, Major General Daniel Harvey, 11, 37, 48
Hilton Head, S.C., 86, 99–111, 196, 239; General Hunter's headquarters, 99; guns and accoutrements, 99; hospital, 101; men in their camps (New Hampshire boys), 103–7; ordnance storeyard, 101; Seabrook plantation, 107–10; signal station, 101; wharf, 100
Hippisley, H. M., 28
Hoffman, Colonel Henry, 178
Hollins, Commodore George N., 257–58, 259, 260–61, 267
Hood, John B. (commander), 390
Hooker, General Joseph "Fighting Joe," 121, 146, 354, 358, 388
Horace Beals (mortar schooner), 283
Houghton, G. W., 32, 33, 130, 156, 159, 176, 216, 404
Howard, Brigadier General Oliver O., 144
Howe Turn bridge, 429–31
Huger, Benjamin (commander), 119, 122
Humphreys, Brigadier General Andrew A., 156
Hunt, Colonel Henry J., 169
Hunter, Major General David, 99
Hunter, Commander James M., 274–75
Huntsville (ironclad), 61

Imboden, Brigadier General John D., 412
Indianapolis, Ind., 409
Indianola (ironclad), 53–54, 85
Ingalls, Bandmaster G. W., 106, 108
Intrepid (balloon), 140
Iron Brigade, 357
Ironclads, 49–85; armor-clads, 59–60; at Cairo, Ill., 57; *Casco* class, 57, 65, 77; double-ender, 61–62; double-turreted monitors, 55–56, 66, 73; function of, 62; "monitor fever" (in the North), 54–55; monitor type, 54, 55–59, 62, 63, 64, 65–78; "Pook turtles" (or "city class"), 51, 56, 57; single-turret monitors, 57; South's shipbuilding program, 49–50, 59–62; three-turreted, 79; torpedo boat, semi-submerged, 85; Union's shipbuilding program, 50–59. *See also* Naval operations; names of ironclads.
Island No. 10, 55, 260, 262–63, 277; cannons mounted on rafts and floated into position, 275; fall of, 263, 266, 274
Itasca (gunboat), 268
Ivy (ship), 258

Jackson, Lieutenant Colonel J. H., 103
Jackson, Captain T. M., 103
Jackson, Colonel Thomas J. "Stonewall," 13, 118, 119, 120, 121, 122, 188, 324, 407; at Front Royal, 327, 331, 332, 334, 338; Kernstown battle, 324, 325, 326, 327, 331, 333, 335, 336, 337; mania for secrecy, 329; Port Republic battle, 327, 331, 334, 337, 346; sacking of Manassas, 352–53, 370; Second Bull Run, 349–60, 362, 388; Valley Campaign, 322–47, 358
Jackson Barracks (Baton Rouge, La.), 308, 318
Jackson (ironclad), 61, 82, 258
Jacksonville, Fla., 86
James, Post Adjutant Martin, 108
James River, 11, 16, 54, 55, 114, 115, 119, 121, 172, 322, 348, 350, 418; ironclads in, 73, 77, 83, 84, 115–16; *Virginia* defense of, 50, 53
Jason (monitor-type vessel), 55
Jenkins, Colonel Micah, 393
John (slave), 226
Johnson, Dr. John A., 96
Johnson, Sergeant R. A., 167
Johnson, Lieutenant Colonel Thomas C., 167
Johnson, Lieutenant William H., 167
Johnston, General Albert Sidney, 265
Johnston, Brigadier General Joseph E., 389, 403; army pullback (from Manassas to Fredericksburg), 12; evacuation of Yorktown, 113, 115; response to McClellan's Peninsula campaign, 112–113, 114, 117; Williamsburg retreat, 18–19; winter quarters (1862), 183; withdrawal strategy, 115; wounded, 117, 137, 149; Yorktown campaign, 12, 17, 18–19, 20, 21
Joinville, Prince de, 17, 23, 25; servants of, 196
Jones, Major General David R. "Neighbor," 378
Jonesboro, Ga., 186

Kanawha Valley, 117
Katahdin (gunboat), 277
Kautz, Captain August V., 170
Kearny, Brigadier General Philip, 121, 147, 395; at Second Bull Run, 353, 358, 360–61, 396
Kemper, Brigadier General James L., 163
Kennebec (gunboat), 268
Kennon, Commander Beverly, 269
Keokuk (ironclad), 59
Kernstown, Battle of, 324, 325, 326, 327, 331, 333, 335, 336, 337
Kernstown, Va., 325, 333
Keyes, Major General Erasmus D., 117, 164
Kickapoo (monitor), 58
Kilburn Brothers, 79
King, Chief Engineer James W., 65
King, Rufus (commander), 356
Kingston, Ga., Union ironclad at, 63
Knoxville, Tenn., 173, 408
Krzyzanowski, Colonel Wladimir "Kriz," 345

Lady of Lyons (play), 246
Lafayette (ironclad), 51–52, 59, 60
Lake Borgne, 281
Lake Pontchartrain, 281
Land mine "torpedoes," 19–20, 48
League Island, Pa., 83
Lee, General Robert E., 17, 18, 62, 115, 117, 130, 149, 150, 154, 155, 156, 158, 161, 163, 166, 167, 169, 172, 184, 188, 407, 408; as Davis's military advisor, 117; defense of Richmond, 117–19, 123; called "Granny Lee" or "King of Spades," 117; on Jackson's Valley successes, 337; Second Bull Run, 348–52, 355–62, 367, 393; Seven Day Battles, 119–22, 348
Lee, Commander S. P., 271, 292
Lee, Captain Sidney Smith, 150
Leesburg, Va., 332
Lee's Mill, Battle of, 16, 32
Lehigh (monitor-type vessel), 55
Leslie's (illustrated weekly), 187
Lexington (gunboat), 260, 272
Lincoln, Abraham, 11, 12, 16, 112, 115, 122, 277, 349, 362, 423, 440; decision for a naval force, 49;

General War Order Number One, 112; railroad bill, 405; strained relations with McClellan, 13, 17, 112, 113, 348; Valley plan, 332
Lindsey, David, 447–48
Little Rebel (ship), 295
Longstreet, Major General James, 115, 117, 119, 122, 123, 194, 408; at Second Bull Run, 350, 354, 355, 356, 357, 358, 359, 360, 361, 390
Lookout Mountain, 428
Louisiana, 406; secession of, 255
Louisiana (ironclad), 49, 50, 60, 258, 265, 266–67, 269–70, 273; destruction of, 50
Louisiana State House, 306, 316
Louisiana State Penitentiary, 306
Louisiana Zouaves, 168
Louisville, Ky., 409
Louisville & Nashville Railroad, 411
Louisville (ironclad), 51, 294
Lovell, Major General Mansfield, 256–57, 258, 265–66, 268, 270
Lowe, Professor Thaddeus S., 140–42
Lucas Bend, Mo., 260
Luray, Va., 331
Luray Valley, 327, 334
Lytle, A. D., 284, 303, 306, 312, 315

McAllister (photographer), 332
McCallum, General Daniel C., 405, 409
McClellan (bulldog), 196
McClellan, Major General George B. "Little Mac," 11–20; Crimean War, 11, 17; demoted, 13; dubbed "Young Napoleon," 112, 123; Fairfield Court House headquarters, 14; front line reconnaissances, 17; Lee's Mill headquarters, 32; Mexican War, 11; on Mississippi naval operations, 255; Peninsula campaign ("on to Richmond"), 112–23, 130, 148, 150, 151, 156, 161, 163, 164, 169, 172, 322–23, 348; Second Bull Run, 348, 350, 351, 352, 370, 392; siege of Yorktown, 11–20, 29, 45, 46, 48; strained relations with Lincoln, 13, 17, 112, 113, 348; Valley Campaign and, 322–23, 325, 326, 332, 344; "victory" over Magruder, 46; White House headquarters (on the Pamunkey), 129
McClellan, Mrs. George B., 118
McDowell, Battle of, 328
McDowell, Major General Irvin, 12, 13, 17, 115, 401; at Arlington House, 18; at Second Bull Run, 348, 349, 353, 354, 355, 356, 357, 358, 359, 366, 380, 381, 382
McDowell, Va., 328
McKay, Dr. David, 191
McLaws, Brigadier General Lafayette, 48
McPherson, W. D., 305
McPherson & Oliver, 246, 287, 305, 306, 307, 308, 313, 315, 445
McRae (ship), 258, 259, 267, 268, 269
Magruder, Major General John Bankhead "Prince John," 11, 13, 14–16, 113, 119, 122, 161; at "Cornwallis' Cave," 47; defenses and fortifications (at Yorktown), 15–16, 18, 20, 30, 31, 36, 38, 41, 42; Gloucester Point defenses, 38, 42; headquarters (June 1862), 34; at Lee's Mill, 32; reputation of, 14–15; Yorktown campaign, 12, 15–16, 18, 21, 34, 40, 45, 46, 48
Mahan, Admiral Alfred T., 258
Mahone, Brigadier General William "Scrappy Billy," 393
Mahopac (monitor vessel), 56–57
Mallory, Stephen R., 49, 62, 267, 277; ironclad strategy of, 49–50
Malvern Hill, Battle of, 122–23, 166–72
Manassas, Va., 112, 332; Confederate winter quarters (1862), 183; sacking of, 352–53, 370
Manassas Gap Railroad, 331
Manassas (ironclad), 257–58, 259, 268, 269
Manassas Junction, 12, 352–53, 354, 356, 370–74, 415
Manassas–Sudley road, 358
Manayunk (ironclad), 56–57, 65
Manhattan (monitor vessel), 56–57
Marcy, Brigadier General Randolph B., 15
Martindale, Brigadier General John H., 172
Martinsburg, Va., 327, 330; railroad shops, 413
Maryland, 174
Mason, Will, 185
Mason, William, 433
Masons (fraternal order), 196, 246
Massanutten Gap, 331
Massanutten Mountain, 327, 334, 342
Meade, Brigadier General George G., 163
Mechanicsville, Battle of, 119–20, 153, 158; casualties, 154
Mechanicsville, Va., 119, 153
Mechanicsville road, 155
Memphis, Tenn., 49, 55, 59, 263, 271; Confederate flotilla at, 272–73; Union naval operations, 55, 272–73, 294–300; viewed from the levee, 298
Memphis & Charleston Railroad, 400
Memphis *Appeal,* 187
Memphis Navy Yard, 299
Merchant of Venice, The (Shakespeare), 195
Meredith, Roy, 420, 421, 422, 439
Merrick & Sons, 54
Merrimack, see Virginia (ironclad)
Mexican War, 11, 12, 14, 264, 286
Miantonomoh (ironclad), 55–56, 73, 74
Michel, Lieutenant General Sir John, 27
Middletown, Va., 331
Milledgeville (ironclad), 61
Miller, S. R., 245
Milroy, Brigadier General Robert H., 327–28, 337
Milwaukee (ironclad), 58, 78
Miner's Hill, Va., winter tents at, 174
Mississippi, 406, 407
Mississippi (ironclad), 49–50, 258, 265, 267, 269, 270, 273
Mississippi River, 9, 399, 405; blockade, 255, 256; Confederate River Defense Fleet, 265, 268, 271, 294; ironclads, 50, 51, 53, 62, 63, 78; "Pope's Run" incident, 258, 260; Union conquest of, 255–320
Mississippi (side-wheeler), 286
Mississippi Sound, 260
Mississippi Squadron, 53
Missouri, 260
Missouri (ironclad), 61
Missouri (paddle-wheeler), 60
Mitchell, Commander, 270
Mobile, Ala., 62, 408
Mobile Bay, Ala., 58, 78, 271
Mobile Bay, Battle of, 57
Mobjack Bay, 12
Modoc (light-draft monitor), 77
Mohawk & Hudson Railroad, 399
Monadnock (double-turreted monitor), 55, 56
Monitor (ironclad), 11, 49, 51, 55, 115; design and construction of, 52, 54; Hampton Roads engagement, 49, 50, 53–54, 55, 57, 65, 66, 68; impact on public opinion (battle with *Virginia*), 54
Monitor-type ironclads, 54, 55–59, 62, 63, 64, 65–78; advantage of, 58; disadvantages of, 58–59. *See also* Ironclads; Naval operations; names of monitors.
Monroe, Mayor John, 270
Montauk (ironclad), 55, 74
Montgomery, Ala., 408
Montgomery, Captain James, 271, 273
Mooney, Father Thomas H., 222
Moore, H. P., 239; background of, 86; photographs of South Carolina, 100–7
Moore, Thomas O., 255, 256, 267
Morell, Brigadier General George, 154
Morganza, La., Federal soldiers encamped at, 321
Morris, Lieutenant M. W., 246
Morris Island, S.C., 207

Mosby, Lieutenant John Singleton, 151, 152
Moulton, Dr. and Mrs. A. A., 104
Mound City, Ill.: naval stations at, 261; wartime activity in, 262, 263
Mound City (ironclad), 51, 57
Muben, A. P., 217
Munford, Colonel Thomas T., 346
Munroe, Lieutenant George T., 27
Murray, E. C., 50
Muscogee (ironclad), 61
Myer, A. J. (commander), 382
"My Faith Looks Up to Thee" (hymn), 188–89
Mystic, Conn., 54

Naglee, Brigadier General Henry M., 148
Nahant (monitor-type vessel), 55; undergoing repairs at Hilton Head, S.C., 72
Nantucket (monitor-type vessel), 55
Nashville, Tenn., 409; Chattanooga depot, 414, 438
Nashville (hospital boat), 266
Nashville (ironclad), 60, 61
Natchez, Miss., 271, 276, 291
Natchez (wharf boat), 314
Naval operations: blockade runners, 107, 111; blockades, 54, 55, 62; ironclads, 49–85; James River, 73, 77, 83, 84, 115–16; Mississippi River, 50, 51, 53, 62, 63, 78, 255–321; Peninsula campaign, 114, 115–16; river ironclads (in the West), 50–54, 55; South's shipbuilding program, 49–50, 59–62; Union's shipbuilding program, 50–59; U.S. appropriations (1861), 50–51; in the West, 53, 57–58, 78; Yorktown siege, 11, 12. *See also* names of battles; officers; ships.
Navy Department (Confederate), 273
Navy Department (United States), 54, 260
Neill, Lieutenant J. B., 177
Nelson Church, naval battery near (in Yorktown), 38
Neosho (ironclad), 57–58, 78
Neuse (ironclad), 60–61
Neville, Colonel, 23
New Ironsides (ironclad), 51, 54, 59
New Madrid, Mo., 263; siege of, 260, 261
New Market, Va., 327
New Orleans, La., 49, 59, 255–58, 264–65, 270, 288–91; Canal Street, 288, 290; Chartres Street (French Quarter), 289; City Hall, 289; Confederate defense of, 255–57, 258, 265–67, 268, 287; Federal occupation of, 270–71; Jackson Square, 288; martial law, 265
New Orleans *Commercial Bulletin,* 264–65
New Orleans Confederate Guards, camp of, 175
New Orleans *Picayune,* 264
New Orleans Washington Artillery, 194
Newton, Brigadier General John, 118
New York Central Railroad, 399
New York Excelsior Brigade, 201
New York *Herald,* 187, 366
New York *Times,* 187
New York *Tribune,* 187
Nichols, Brigadier General Francis T., 341
19th Georgia, 167
IX Corps, 222
9th Massachusetts Infantry, 222
9th Mississippi, 229
9th New York Regiment, 192, 195
95th Illinois Infantry, 233
93rd New York, 210
Norfolk, Va., 11, 50, 61; Confederate evacuation of, 113, 115; Federal capture of, 50
Norfolk Navy Yard, 81; Confederate destruction of, 113
North Atlantic Blockading Squadron, 50, 54, 57, 79
North Carolina (ironclad), 61
Northrop, Commissary-General Lucius B., 173

Octagon House (Arlington, Va.), 349
Ohio River, 409
"Oh Lord God One Friday" (song), 196
Old Abe (mascot), 247
Old Point Comfort, 11
O'Leary, Terence P., 251
Oliver (photographer), 305
153rd New York, 177
Oneida (gunboat), 271, 275
Oneonta (monitor vessel), 56–57
"On Jordan's Stormy Banks I Stand" (hymn), 189
Onondaga (double-turreted monitor), 55; in the James River, 73
Opelousas *Courier,* 187
Orange & Alexandria Railroad, 349, 350, 351, 352, 354, 375, 380, 440; blockhouses (frontier-style forts), 408; Culpeper's railroad depot, 351; offices of, 436; terminus of, 435; at Union Mills, 403
Orléans, Louis Philippe Albert d', *see* Paris, Comte de
Orléans, Robert Philippe Louis d', *see* Chartres, Duc de
Osage (ironclad), 57–58, 78
O'Sullivan, Timothy, 14, 113, 355, 365, 368, 374, 382; photography wagon of, 350
Otter Island, signal station at, 102
Ozark (ironclad), 57–58, 62, 65

Paine, Brigadier General Halbert E., 301
Palmetto State (ironclad), 61, 80
Pamunkey River, 12, 114, 116, 119, 121, 124, 131; panorama of camps on, 126
Paris, Comte de (Louis Philippe Albert d'Orléans), 17, 23, 24
Parrotts (siege mortars), 18, 55, 285
Passaic (monitor-type vessel), 55
Patapsco (monitor-type vessel), 55
Patrick, Brigadier General Marsena R., 239
Paulding, Admiral Hiram, 64
Peck, Daniel, 176
Pemberton, Major General John C., 189
Pender, Brigadier General William Dorsey, 159
Pendleton, Brigadier General William N., 167
Peninsula campaign, 112–72, 322–23; balloon observation, 140–42; casualties, 121, 123, 138, 154, 161; conclusion of, 123; at Cumberland Landing, 116, 120, 121, 122, 124; at Eltham's Landing, 19, 48, 115; Federal strategy, 112–15; Gaines's Mill battle, 121, 123, 155–61; at Harrison's Landing, 119, 121, 122–23, 172, 348, 392; intelligence operations, 117, 134; Malvern Hill battle, 122–23, 166–72; Mechanicsville battle, 119–20, 153, 154, 158; naval operations, 114, 115–16; panorama of an army on campaign, 128–29; railroads, 131, 160; at Savage Station, 122, 160–62; Seven Days Battles, 119–23, 348; Seven Pines (Fair Oaks) battle, 117, 122, 135–48, 159; siege of Yorktown, 11–48, 115; Stuart's "ride around McClellan," 118–19, 150; weather conditions, 115, 116–17; White Oak Swamp battle, 122, 163–64, 165; Williamsburg battle, 115
Pennsylvania Railroad, 399
Pensacola, Fla., 229, 255; navy yard at, 168
Perote Guards, 229
Perry, Commodore Matthew C., 286
Petersburg, Va., 20, 221, 226, 245, 348, 416, 443; "Fruit & Oyster House," 214; hanging near (1864), 252; railroad battery near, 442
Phelps, Brigadier General John W., 260
Phelps, Captain Ledyard, 276
Philadelphia, Pa., 54
Philadelphia *Inquirer,* 187
Philadelphia Navy Yard, 283
Pickens, Francis, 149
Pickens (ship), 258
Pinkerton, Allan, 117, 134

Pittsburg (ironclad), 51
Pittsburg Landing, 263
Pittsburg (ship), 263, 278
Plantations, 107–10
Plum Run Bend, 271; naval battle at, 293, 294
Plymouth, N.C., 81
Pocahontas (ship), 109
Pook, Samuel M., 51
Pope, Captain John, 258
Pope, Major General John, 260, 262, 263, 274, 278, 395; Second Bull Run, 348, 350–59, 361, 362, 366, 367, 370, 371, 372, 387, 392
"Pope's Run" incident, 258, 260
Porter, Admiral David Dixon, 54, 61, 63, 257, 264, 267, 269–70, 271, 282, 312
Porter, Major General Fitz John, 16, 117, 119, 121, 122, 151, 153, 154, 155, 161; at Second Bull Run, 351, 354, 358, 359–60, 392
Porter, John, 59, 80
Porter, Commander William "Dirty Bill," 51, 53, 59, 60, 302
Port Hudson, La., 173, 240, 270, 273, 277, 286, 321, 445
"Portici" house, 389
Port Republic, Battle of, 327, 331, 334, 337, 346
Port Republic, Va., 327, 334, 337, 347
Portsmouth (warship), 311
Potomac Creek, train bridge over, 423
Potomac River, 322, 324, 332, 348, 349, 350, 362; car barges, 441
Preble (vessel), 258
Prince, L. I., 307
Pulaski, Tenn., 427
Puritan (ironclad), 57, 74

Quaker guns, 398
Quarles House (near Fair Oaks), 135, 147
Queen of the West (ironclad), 274–75, 276
Quintard, George W., 55

Railroad Bureau (Confederate States of America), 406
Railroads, 399–445; Atlanta campaign, 409–10; "beanpole" bridges, 423, 428; blockhouses, 408, 409, 410; boxcars, 401, 403, 441; bridges and, 410, 411, 421–31, 441; canal junctions, 414; at Chickamauga, 408–9; conductors and engineers, 432; "conductor's car," 444; engines, 433; improvised rail splices, 442; liaison between photographers and, 410; locomotives, 401, 410, 413, 419; military photographers, 416; number of miles, 402; Peninsula campaign, 131, 160; pontoon boats, 415; Presidential car, 440; rails, 401–2, 443; Second Bull Run and, 349, 350, 351, 352, 354, 355, 376, 380; "shad belly" bridges, 421–22, 426; strategic uses of, 407–10; track gauges, 400–1; trans-Appalachian routes, 399–400; in Valley Campaign, 327, 331; Yorktown siege, 12, 20. *See also* names of railroads.
Rains, Brigadier General Gabriel J., 19, 20, 48
Raleigh & Gaston Railroad, 400
Raleigh (ship), 61
Randolph, George Wythe, 115, 149
Rapidan River, 349, 350
Rappahannock River, 12, 113, 351, 352, 353, 354, 355, 367; North Fork bridge, 366
Rappahannock Station, Va., skirmish at, 369
Rawlins, Brigadier General John A., 238
Red River, 78
Red Rover (barracks ship), 278
Reekie, James, 153, 155, 160, 224
Relay House, Md., Baltimore & Ohio at, 402
Reno, Major General Jesse, 350, 354, 358, 360, 361
Republican party, 324
Revolutionary War, 11, 15, 20
Reynolds, John (commander), 354
Richardson, Lieutenant Henry H., 390
Richardson, Major General Israel B., 238
Richardson, Lieutenant J. F., 297
Richmond, Fredericksburg & Potomac Railroad, 399
Richmond, Va., 50, 61, 173, 197, 256, 257, 322, 332, 337, 348, 349, 350, 361, 362, 418, 419; McClellan's "on to Richmond" campaign, 112–72; Yorktown siege, 11–20
Richmond & Yorktown River Railroad, 12, 116, 160; destroyed bridge of, 131
Richmond Howitzers, 195
Richmond (ironclad), 258, 259, 287, 291, 303, 310
Ricketts, Brigadier General James B., 354, 355, 357
Riddle, A. J., 82
River Defense Fleet (Confederate States of America), 265, 268, 271, 294
Roanoke (three-turreted monitor), 59, 79
Robertson, Colonel Beverly, 343
Robertson, Brigadier General Felix, 394
Robertson, Colonel Jerome, 394
Robinson House (near battlefield at Cedar Mountain), 359
"Rock of Ages" (hymn), 189
Rodgers, Captain John, 260
Rodman guns, 111
"Rogue's March, The," 200
Rosecrans, Major General William S., 190, 408–9
Royal Army, 23, 28
Royal Canadian Rifles, 27
Royal Navy, 54
Russell, Major A. J., 375, 403, 416, 417, 418, 420, 421, 423, 424–25, 432, 434, 435–36, 440

St. Helena Island, signal station at, 102
St. John, Chief Engineer Isaac M., 31, 36, 37
St. Louis Cathedral (New Orleans), 288
St. Louis (ironclad), 51, 57, 260, 265, 273
St. Peter's Church (near White House on the Pamunkey), 132, 133
Salem, N.C., 242
Salem Village, Va., 352
Sallie Johnson (ship), 312
Salm-Salm, Prince Felix, 19
Saltville, Va., 394
Saltwater condenser (Bay Point, S.C.), 98
San Francisco, Calif., 66, 71
Sangamon (monitor-type vessel), 55
Sauerbier, George M., 165
Saugus (monitor vessel), 56–57
Savage Station, Va., 122, 160–62
Savannah, Ga., 55, 62
Savannah (ironclad), 61
Saxton, General Rufus, 89
Sayer's Oyster House (Petersburg, Va.), 215
Schenck, Brigadier General Robert C., 387
Scott, Thomas, 404, 409
Scott, Lieutenant General Winfield, 112, 116, 255, 395
Seabrook, John E., 107–10
Second Manassas, *see* Bull Run, Second Battle of (1862)
2nd Maryland Cavalry, 412
2nd Massachusetts, 331
2nd United States Artillery, 139
2nd United States Sharpshooters, 384
2nd Virginia, 346
2nd Wisconsin Regiment, 196
Sedgwick, Major General John, 163, 237
Semmes, Commander Raphael, 255
Sergeant, Captain William, 236
Sevastopol, siege of (Crimean War), 17
Seven Days Battles, 119–23, 348
Seven Pines, Battle of, 117, 122, 135–48, 159; casualties, 138; house

used as a hospital, 145, 146, 147; Union Fort Sumner near, 138
17th New York ("Westchester Chasseurs"), 165
7th New York, 215
73rd Ohio Infantry, 391
Shenandoah River, 341
Shenandoah Valley, 13, 18, 118, 354, 407; geography, 326–27; invasion of, 322–47; location of, 322. *See also* Valley Campaign.
Sherman, Brigadier General Thomas W., 239
Sherman, General William T., 391, 409–10
Shields, Brigadier General James, 325–26, 329, 331, 332, 333, 334, 337
Shiloh, Battle of, 109, 263, 266
Ship Island, 260, 264, 265
Ship Point, 14
Sigel, Major General Franz, 353, 358, 360, 368, 387, 388
Simmonds, J. A., 391
Sims, Lieutenant Colonel Frederick W., 406–7, 408
16th New York, 162
16th United States Infantry, 210
6th United States Cavalry, 170
6th Vermont, 162
64th New York, 135
69th New York, 222
Skinner, H., 228
Slaughter, Reverend, 361
Slocomb, Captain C. H., 194
Slocum, Major General Henry W., 118, 395
Smeed, E. C. (officer), 410
Smith, Major General Gustavus W., 48, 115, 137
Smith, Brigadier General Morgan L., 287
Smith, Brigadier General William "Baldy," 174
Smith, Brigadier General William F., 33
South Atlantic Blockading Squadron, 97
South Carolina, 117; Cooley's and Moore's photographs of, 87–107; secession of, 324. *See also* names of cities and towns.
South Carolina Railroad, 402
Southern Field and Fireside (magazine), 188
Southern Illustrated News, 187
Southwest Pass, 258
Spring, Parker, 141
Stahel, Brigadier General Julius, 19
Stanton, Edwin M., 12, 16, 272, 401, 405
States' rights, doctrine of, 11
Staunton, Va., 326, 327, 328
Steele, Major General Frederick, 244
Steuart, Brigadier General George H. "Maryland Steuart," 345
Stevens, Lieutenant Henry, 277
Stevens, Brigadier General Isaac I., 396
Still, William N., 447
Stimers, Chief Engineer Alban, 65, 77
Stokes, Colonel Mumford S., 154
Stone Bridge, 356, 360, 361; ruins of, 379
Stone House, 357, 358; hospital use of, 386
Stoneman, Brigadier General George, 148, 237
Stonewall Brigade, 349–50
Stonewall (ironclad ram), 74
Strasburg, Va., 327, 328, 331, 334
Stuart, Brigadier General James Ewell Brown "Jeb," 118–19, 121, 150, 151, 188; "ride around McClellan," 118–19, 150
Sudley Springs, 355, 356
Sumner, Brigadier General Edwin V., 117, 132, 163, 240
Sumter (raider), 255, 277
Sutlers (government-approved vendors), 212–13, 214
"Sweet Hour of Prayer" (hymn), 188
Swift Run Gap, Va., 327, 328, 329, 337

Taliaferro, Brigadier General William B., 340, 357, 377, 394
Tanner, Robert G., 447
Tecumseh (monitor vessel), 56–57
Tennessee, 260, 263, 432
Tennessee (ironclad), 49–50, 61, 84, 272, 273
Tennessee River, 409; bridge built over, 428, 429–31
Tennessee Valley, 409
10th Alabama Regiment, 197
10th Maine Infantry, 364
10th New York Infantry, 390, 394
Terrible Catastrophe on the North Atlantic R.R., A (drama), 195
Terry, Lieutenant Edward, 291
Texas (ironclad), 61
"There Is a Fountain Filled with Blood" (hymn), 189
III Corps, 351
3rd New Hampshire, 86, 103, 104, 105, 109; casualties, 110
13th Massachusetts, 218, 329
35th Georgia, 154
Thomas, Colonel Edward L., 154
Thomas, Emory M., 447
Thompson, Commander M. Jeff, 295, 297
Thoroughfare Gap, 352, 354, 355–56, 357, 358, 378
Thourat, Lieutenant Colonel Louis, 171
Tippecanoe (ironclad), 56–57, 65
Tiptonville, Mo., 260
Tonawanda (ironclad), 56, 73
Tramp Brigade, 385
Tredegar Iron Works, 50, 265
Trobriand, Colonel Philippe Régis Denis de Keredern de, 164, 171
Tupelo, Miss., 407
Tuscaloosa (ironclad), 61
Tuscarora (ship), 258
Tuscumbia (ironclad), 53–54
12th United States Infantry, 236
28th Pennsylvania, 332
25th Iowa Infantry, 248
21st Massachusetts, 390
24th Massachusetts Regiment, 195
22nd North Carolina, 157
27th Virginia, 333
26th New Jersey Regiment, 194
26th North Carolina Infantry, 241, 242
23rd Ohio Infantry, 216
Twiggs, General David E., 255–56
230th New York, 178
Tyler, General Robert O., 230
Tyler (gunboat), 260, 265, 271, 274, 275, 312

Union Mills, Va., 380; Orange & Alexandria at, 403; protection of railroads, 404
Union Pacific Railroad, 254
United States Marines, 97
United States Military Prison yard (Chattanooga, Tenn.), 250
United States Military Railroads, 401, 415; organization of, 405, 409–10
United States Sharpshooters, 30
Urbana, Va., 12, 113

Valley Army, 324–37; reorganization of, 327
Valley Campaign, 322–47, 358; beginning of, 324; casualties, 326, 332, 334, 337; Cross Keys battle, 334–35, 344, 345, 346; Federal flight, 332; Front Royal battle, 327, 331, 332, 334, 338; Kernstown battle, 324, 325, 326, 327, 331, 333, 335, 336, 337; Lee (Robert E.) on, 337; McDowell battle, 328; Port Republic battle, 327, 331, 334, 337, 346; prisoners-of-war, 331, 332; railroads, 327, 331; Winchester battle, 324–25, 331–32, 333, 334, 338, 345
Valley Pike, 326–27, 334
Van Dorn, Major General Earl, 274, 275, 276, 277, 300, 301
Van Dorn (ship), 273
Vannerson & Jones, 323
Van Vliet, Brigadier General Stewart, 15, 23, 114, 119
Varuna (ship), 269
Vermont (ship-of-the-line), 79
Vicksburg, Miss., 50, 85, 173; hospital ships, 267; Union naval

operations and, 51, 270, 272, 273, 274, 275–77, 291, 292, 300–1, 310, 321
Vicksburg, siege of, 51, 85, 189, 233
Vicksburg *Citizen,* 187
Villepigue, Brigadier General John B., 295
Vincennes (ship), 258
Virginia, 9, 402, 408–9, 420, 432; Peninsula campaign, 112–72, 322–23; Yorktown siege, 11–20. *See also* names of battles; cities; towns.
Virginia Central Railroad, 327, 349, 407
Virginia (ironclad), 11, 49, 59, 79, 84; conversion of, 50; defense of James River, 50, 53; destroyed by its crew, 50, 115; Hampton Roads engagement, 49, 50, 53–54, 79; impact on public opinion (battle with *Monitor*), 54; length and casemate, 50
Virginia Military Institute, 324
Virginia Militia, 340, 394
Virginia II (ironclad), 61

Wadley, William M., 405–6, 407
Walke, Commander Henry, 262–63, 277, 278
Walker, Reuben L. (commander), 385
Wallace, Colonel William A., 378
War of 1812, 264
Warrenton, Va., 352
Warrenton Junction, 354
Warrenton pike, 356, 357, 358, 360, 386
Warrenton Road, 381
Warrick, Thomas, 201
Warwick River, 15, 16, 19
Washington, D.C., 11, 12, 13; McDowell's protection of, 18
Washington, George, 11, 36, 46, 132; soldier birthday celebrations, 253
Washington Light Infantry of Charleston, 243
Washington Navy Yard, 79
Water Battery, 39, 40; Rodman guns in, 41
Waterwitch (ship), 258
Watkins, C. E., 66
Watkins, Sam, 197
Weehawken (monitor-type vessel), 55
Weisiger, Brigadier General David A., 394
Weitzel, Brigadier General Godfrey, 291
Welles, Gideon, 50, 59, 65, 264
West, war in the: Mississippi River and, 50, 51, 53, 62, 63, 78, 255–321; river ironclads, 50–54, 55. *See also* New Orleans; Vicksburg; names of battles and ironclads.
Westchester Chasseurs (17th New York), 165
West Coast Blockading Squadron, 58
Western & Atlantic Railroad, 399
Westover (plantation estate), 172
West Point, Va., 12, 19, 115
West Virginia, 216, 409
Wheeler, G. N. (cook), 104
White House Landing: army at, 130; contraband blacks at, 133
White House (on the Pamunkey), 129, 132
White Oak Swamp, Battle of, 122, 163–64, 165
Whiting, W. H. C. (commander), 407
Whittle, W. C. (commander), 267
Wiley, Bell I., 447
Willcox, Brigadier General Orlando B., 226
Williams, C. P. (mortar schooner), 282
Williams, Brigadier General Alpheus S., 326, 338
Williams, Brigadier General Thomas, 271–72, 276, 291, 301, 304, 309
Williamsburg, Battle of, 115
Williamsburg, Va., 12, 15, 19
Williamsport, Md., 218, 328, 329; surgeons in, 330
Wilmington, N.C., 61, 62
Wilmington & Weldon Railroad, 404
Winchester, Battle of, 324–25, 331–32, 333, 334, 338, 345
Winchester, Va., 322, 323, 325, 327, 331; Taylor's Hotel, 339
Winder, Brigadier General Charles S., 362
Winnebago (monitor ironclad), 58, 65
Winona (gunboat), 268, 284, 310
Winslow, Lieutenant John A., 299
Women: in the army, 233; in camp, 231–32
Wood, R. C. (hospital ship), 267
Wood & Gibson, 120
Woodbury, David B., 135, 333
Wool, Major General John E., 11, 12
Wright, W. W. (officer), 410
Wyandotte (monitor vessel), 56–57
Wynn's Mill, 16

"Yankee Doodle," 200
Yazoo City, 274
Yazoo River, 273, 274, 276
York River, 11, 15, 16, 18, 19, 41, 114, 116; parapet overlooking, 40
Yorktown, siege of (1781), 36, 46
Yorktown, siege of (1862), 11–48, 115; defenses and fortifications, 15–16, 18, 19, 20, 30, 31, 35, 36, 37, 38, 39, 41, 42, 43, 44, 45; earthworks, 37, 43, 44; at Eltham's Landing, 19, 48; engineers, 29, 31; European observers and volunteers, 17, 21, 23, 24, 25, 26; Federal capture, 19–20, 24; front line of the works, 36; Gloucester Point defenses, 14, 38; Johnston's retreat (May 4), 18–19; land mine "torpedoes," 19–20, 48; Lee's Mill attack (April 16), 16, 32; naval operations, 11, 12; observation balloon at, 16; prisoners-of-war, 20; railroad operation, 12, 20; ravine behind the defenses, 35; sally port into the defenses, 35; shipping the siege train, 20; Union shipping delays, 13
Yorktown, Va., 113; baseball game, 191–92

Zouave Dramatic Club (9th New York Regiment), 195
Zouaves, 168, 195, 360, 384

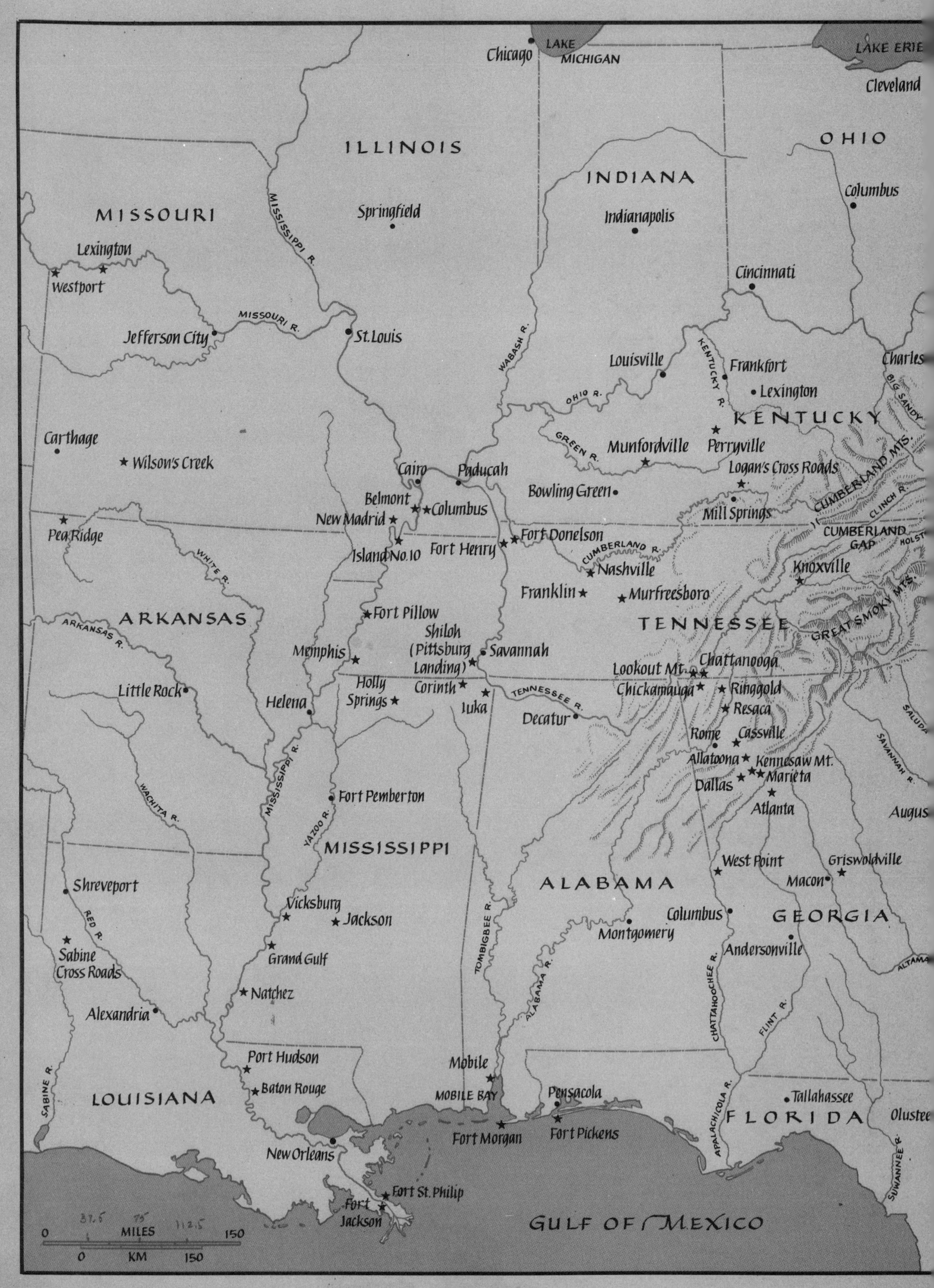

Chicago
LAKE MICHIGAN
LAKE ERIE
Cleveland
OHIO
ILLINOIS
INDIANA
MISSOURI
Columbus
Springfield
Indianapolis
MISSISSIPPI R.
Lexington
Westport
Cincinnati
MISSOURI R.
Jefferson City
St. Louis
WABASH R.
Louisville
KENTUCKY R.
Frankfort
Charles
Lexington
BIG SANDY
OHIO R.
KENTUCKY
Carthage
GREEN R.
Munfordville
Perryville
Wilson's Creek
Logan's Cross Roads
CUMBERLAND MTS.
Cairo
Paducah
Bowling Green
Belmont
Columbus
Mill Springs
CLINCH R.
New Madrid
Pea Ridge
Fort Donelson
CUMBERLAND GAP
WHITE R.
Island No. 10
Fort Henry
CUMBERLAND R.
Nashville
Knoxville
Franklin
Murfreesboro
GREAT SMOKY MTS.
Fort Pillow
ARKANSAS
ARKANSAS R.
TENNESSEE
Shiloh (Pittsburg Landing)
Savannah
Memphis
Lookout Mt.
Chattanooga
Little Rock
Holly Springs
Corinth
Chickamauga
Ringgold
Helena
Iuka
TENNESSEE R.
Resaca
Decatur
Rome
Cassville
SALUDA
Allatoona
Kennesaw Mt.
SAVANNAH R.
WACHITA R.
MISSISSIPPI R.
Dallas
Marietta
Fort Pemberton
Atlanta
YAZOO R.
August
MISSISSIPPI
West Point
Griswoldville
Shreveport
ALABAMA
Macon
Vicksburg
Jackson
Columbus
GEORGIA
RED R.
Montgomery
Grand Gulf
TOMBIGBEE R.
Andersonville
Sabine Cross Roads
ALABAMA R.
CHATTAHOOCHEE R.
Natchez
Alexandria
FLINT R.
Port Hudson
Mobile
SABINE R.
Baton Rouge
MOBILE BAY
Pensacola
Tallahassee
LOUISIANA
APALACHICOLA R.
FLORIDA
Olustee
Fort Morgan
Fort Pickens
New Orleans
SUWANNEE R.
Fort St. Philip
Fort Jackson
GULF OF MEXICO
0
MILES
150
0
KM
150